THE UNITED NATIONS:

THE NEXT TWENTY-FIVE YEARS

Twentieth Report of the

COMMISSION TO STUDY THE ORGANIZATION OF PEACE

Louis B. Sohn, *Chairman*

1 9 7 0

OCEANA PUBLICATIONS, INC.
Dobbs Ferry, New York

COMMISSION TO STUDY THE ORGANIZATION OF PEACE

Honorary Chairman
ARTHUR N. HOLCOMBE

Chairman
LOUIS B. SOHN

Executive Director
CLARK M. EICHELBERGER

Executive Committee
LUTHER H. EVANS, *Chairman*

CLARENCE A. BERDAHL — RAYMOND D. NASHER

BENJAMIN V. COHEN — LESLIE PAFFRATH

NORMAN COUSINS — WILLIAM R. ROALFE

VERNON L. FERWERDA — RICHARD N. SWIFT

FRANK P. GRAHAM — URBAN G. WHITAKER, JR.

GERARD J. MANGONE — RICHARD R. WOOD

QUINCY WRIGHT

Drafting Committee for Twentieth Report

(In addition to Officers and Executive Committee)

JOHN CAREY — ERNST B. HAAS

CARL Q. CHRISTOL — MARION H. McVITTY

ROGER FISHER — HOWARD TAUBENFELD

v

FOREWORD

During the first seven decades of the Twentieth Century mankind has passed from the automobile age through the air age to the space age. Fifty years ago the League of Nations was established, and the United Nations is approaching its twenty-fifth anniversary. This Commission is thirty years old, and this is its twentieth report.

This seems to be an appropriate time for stocktaking and for braving the future. Most persons born today will spend the larger part of their life in the Twenty-First Century. Those who are in college today will be at the peak of their influence when the new century arrives.

What role can the United Nations play in the coming century? What can be accomplished in the next twenty-five years to bring peace and justice and freedom to all mankind? It is the purpose of this report to provide some guidance for those in search of a better world, for the decision-makers during the next twenty-five years and for those who will conduct the affairs of mankind in the next century. This is an ambitious goal, but not an impossible dream. Progressive steps can be taken in the next twenty-five years which can bring us close to that goal. This report discusses more than a hundred such steps. During the next five years some twenty steps may easily be taken in various areas. The next twenty will require more time, but if they are also taken, a momentum may be gathered which will enable us to face the most difficult final steps. The first astronauts reached the moon as a result of many small steps taken by many people; millions of bits of machinery had to be invented and manufactured in order to provide them with the smoothly operating vehicles which got them there. World peace can be achieved by a similar cumulative effort. This report, drawing on the work of many people in many countries, hopes to provide a beginning for such an effort, the first blueprint which may stimulate others to come with an even better one. In the life of mankind twenty-five years is less than a second is in the life of an individual, but the next twenty-five years may be crucial to the future of humanity and of the small world it inhabits. The problems to be tackled are hard but they can be solved.

Louis B. Sohn

Cambridge, Mass.
December 1969

ACKNOWLEDGMENTS

This report was prepared by the Chairman of the Commission, with the assistance of the Executive Director and the Chairman of the Executive Committee. The scope of the report was agreed upon at a special meeting of the Commission held at Wingspread, Racine, Wisconsin, under the auspices of the Johnson Foundation. Four drafts of the report were revised extensively at the meetings of the Drafting Committee held on June 4, 1969 and September 19, 1969, and at the meetings of the full Commission held on June 21, 1969 and on September 20, 1969.

The Drafting Committee consisted of the members of the Executive Committee and the authors of the background papers which are annexed to this report.

In addition, a separately published paper by the late James P. Warburg, entitled "Wanted: A New American Approach to Peace," provided important ideas for several sections of the Commission's report. His passing was a grievous loss to the Commission.

The Chairman of the Commission is especially grateful to the Center for International Studies of New York University which made it possible for him to spend a year in New York and to devote a considerable amount of time to the preparation of this report.

The Commission wishes to acknowledge the assistance it received to meet the expenses connected with this report from the Johnson Foundation, the IOS Foundation, the Blaustein Foundation, the United Auto Workers (UAW), and from its members, friends and associates.

TABLE OF CONTENTS

TWENTIETH REPORT
OF THE
COMMISSION

THE UNITED NATIONS: THE NEXT TWENTY-FIVE YEARS

I. INTRODUCTION

1. The First Twenty-Five Years of the United Nations

The last fifty years have seen basic changes in the legal and constitutional framework of the world community and in the structure of international relations. Before World War I the system for limiting international conflict and avoiding war consisted mainly of certain generally accepted principles of international law, supported by certain understandings as to spheres of influence and by alliances to maintain balances of power, as a means for discouraging any nation from dominating the world. A complex network of diplomatic missions served as a means for settling disputes by negotiation and mediation. A few international unions were established, codification conferences were held at The Hague, and arbitration procedure and machinery were developed.

World War I made it clear to many thinkers and statesmen that the system had glaring deficiencies, that it was based on certain wrong premises, and that an effort should be made to improve the system. What resulted at the end of the war was the League of Nations. The basic concept of the League was that its members should be protected by collective action from aggression. A court was provided to settle certain kinds of disputes and an effort made to limit armaments. The peace treaties adopted at the same time, though widely criticized, recognized certain demands of justice based on principles of self-determination of peoples and the protection of the right of minorities within States.

In the twenty years of the League's activity, 1920 to 1939, events did not fulfill expectations. The United States did not join the League, other big powers did not participate on a continuing basis, the support its members gave to the League was halting and reluctant, and certain States dissatisfied with the post-war arrangements were deter-

1

mined to destroy it. It was clear by the outbreak of World War II that a new beginning was called for, and before war's end the purpose of making a new beginning was actually realized in the Charter of the United Nations.

The Charter stands in time half-way between the creation of the League and today. The Charter and the United Nations will be twenty-five years old in 1970. As we enter the second quarter century of the United Nations, it seems appropriate to consider what our goals in relation to its improvement should be and how we may reasonably proceed with the task.

We cannot do this by imagining the world as it was in 1945. We must take into account the many ways in which the world and man have changed. The Second World War was truly worldwide; the desire for peace became thus also universal. The war also brought many peoples for the first time into contact with modern civilization, and the balance of power between Europe and the rest of the world was considerably changed. The war was followed by the most profound scientific and human revolutions of a global nature in man's history.

As President Nixon pointed out in his speech to the General Assembly on 18 September 1969:

"We have entered a new age, different not only in degree but in kind from any that has ever gone before.

"For the first time ever, we have truly become a single world community.

"For the first time ever, we have seen the staggering fury of the power of the universe unleashed, and we know that we hold that power in a very precarious balance.

"For the first time ever, technological advance has brought within reach what once was only a poignant dream for hundreds of millions: freedom from hunger and freedom from want . . .

"For the first time ever, we have seen changes in a single lifetime—in our lifetime—that dwarf the achievements of centuries before; and those changes continue to accelerate . . .

"In this new age of 'firsts', even the goal of a just and lasting peace is a 'first' we can dare to strive for. We must achieve it. And I believe we can achieve it."

Some of the scientific changes of the last twenty-five years were accelerated by the war; others would have occurred anyway, for it is estimated that of all the scientists the world has ever known, ninety per cent are alive today. The forces of science and technology were unleashed in both negative and positive directions, creating in man both a new sense of insecurity and terror and a renewed hope that a better life is within his reach.

First of all, atomic energy has been brought to mankind, with all of its potential for good and evil. Though a nuclear war between the two superpowers could destroy mankind, other nations have had too small a share in the decisions of the nuclear giants which could release these forces of destruction. The survival of mankind has depended during the past two decades on an unstable system of mutual deterrence and a precarious balance of terror.

Secondly, there have been other advances in science, technology and medicine which have changed the relations of nations. Some of these relate to communications, including transportation, others to the creation of new materials which change the economic relations between advanced and less developed countries, others to the modification and pollution of the human environment, and still others to the rate of population growth and its attendant dangers. The astronauts of the Soviet Union and the United States have invaded the frontiers of outer space and have begun to explore the celestial bodies. Another frontier beckons as technology has finally made accessible the riches on the ocean floor. Travellers will soon circle the globe at speeds faster than sound. National frontiers stop neither people nor problems.

Thirdly, men's attitudes have changed in a number of ways: (1) there is greater demand for self-determination, both political and economic; (2) the demands for more equality and wealth, and for an opportunity to improve the economic, educational and social status of various groups are insistent over most parts of the globe, including both developed and developing nations, no matter what has to give way to satisfy them; (3) science and education are seen by the disadvantaged nations as important avenues to such an objective, as are the easy and plentiful transfer of capital, the improvement of the terms of trade, and the acceptance of less strict rules with respect to the payment of compensation for nationalized assets.

One may truly say that much of the world has been aroused from the lethargy of ages. Of the forty-five per cent of mankind which was in colonial status in 1945, all but three per cent of mankind achieved independence by 1970. The colonial powers no longer had either the strength or the will to maintain their empires. The Charter of the United Nations held out hope of self-government for the colonial areas and the United Nations helped most of them achieve independence. It is to be noted that a few colonial problems remain, particularly in southern Africa; one of them, the former mandated territory of South West Africa (Namibia), is of special interest to the UN. That the end of colonialism was not foreseen in the United Nations in the late 1940s and early 1950s is shown by the fact that the headquarters buildings were planned and built in anticipation of a membership of 70 States; that number had almost doubled, however, by 1970, as more than fifty new States had been established in the former colonial areas. They found in the United Nations a forum in which they could assert their independent points of view and ventilate their grievances. For some of them the United Nations provides the main means of diplomatic contact with the rest of the world.

It seems clear that the emergence from technological and political backwardness of much of the world has stimulated efforts by certain ideological groupings of States to bring the new States to their respective sides, with resulting exacerbation in the relations of these groupings. The United Nations has been buffeted about and sometimes ignored in this competition, and has fallen short from the ambitious goals of the Charter. Nevertheless, the existence of the United Nations has contributed significantly to the maintenance of the peace, however uneasy and precarious it may have been and still is. In many cases small conflicts have been kept from growing into larger ones, and the pressures exerted by the majority of small powers in the United Nations have blunted the attempts of several larger powers to have their way. The United Nations made available meeting places in the Security Council, the General Assembly and other bodies, where "parliamentary diplomacy" could be practiced. Time and time again statesmen have met at the United Nations to deal with what seemed an almost hopeless problem, and frequently worked out tentative or even long-lasting adjustments of conflicting claims. Whether a third world war would have come without the United Nations we cannot know for certain, but we believe that it would have been more likely.

But "peace and security" involve more than an absence of armed conflict. They require a general sense of contentment that can be realized only by satisfying many of the aspirations of men in all countries. Thus the work of the United Nations and its family of agencies to eliminate poverty, ignorance, intolerance, violations of human rights, etc., is of enormous importance. While peace is uneasy, much is being done to firm up the foundations of a more stable peace.

Even in the field of world law there have been important developments. The General Assembly adopted in 1948 the Universal Declaration of Human Rights which has become widely accepted as having more binding effect than a mere statement of aspiration. It was followed by the Declaration on the Granting of Independence to Colonial Countries and Peoples and the Declaration on the Elimination of Racial Discrimination, which have more influence than the absence of enforcement provisions might imply. The International Atomic Energy Agency is developing standards to safeguard the peaceful uses of atomic energy. Several specialized agencies are developing regulations relating to health, aviation, communications, trade, and other fields of common interest to all.

Possibly the most dramatic extension of world law has been in the frontier of outer space. In 1961 the United Nations

General Assembly proclaimed that the law of the Charter and international law would apply to outer space and that the celestial bodies were not subject to appropriation by any State. A later resolution banned the installing or stationing of nuclear weapons or other weapons of mass destruction on the celestial bodies or placing them in orbit around the earth. These principles have been incorporated in a treaty, which has been ratified by 47 nations, including the Soviet Union, the United Kingdom and the United States.

A Committee of the General Assembly is attempting to apply similar principles to the deep seabed to ensure that no part of it will be annexed by any State; that weapons of mass destruction will not be implanted in it; and that it will be developed for the common good of mankind.

What of the future? The many accomplishments of the United Nations in the past twenty-five years cannot obscure the fact that there is a widespread consensus that it has not fulfilled all of the legitimate expectations of 1945. It has not been able to check the race in armaments, especially in nuclear weapons and the means to deliver them rapidly over vast distances. It has not settled major international disputes in the Middle East, Kashmir, Berlin, Korea, Vietnam and other areas. There is also deep disquiet as to its capacity to guide the advanced nations toward the necessary adjustments in the international system which they built for themselves in the last three hundred years to the needs of international peace and security and the revolutionary demands of the developing countries and of the younger generation. There are strong forces ready to defend the status quo and vested interests, including unfair economic advantages. While there is danger, and even much evidence that various contestants will try to settle problems by brute force, by revolution and counter-revolution, and by civil and international wars, it is to be hoped that better methods will prevail and catastrophe be avoided. It seems clear that the price of peace will be the acceptance of dynamic change on all levels of society, domestic and international. By the end of the next twenty-five years, if the world survives the many crises it now experiences and the new ones likely to arise, the international system will probably have to change considerably from the present system. It may have to change in directions which we can only dimly imagine at present. But mankind should be deeply concerned with the task of trying to create a more effective system. The Commission to Study the Organization of Peace intends to help in making mankind aware of this task and of ways for coping with it.

Secretary-General U Thant said on 9 May 1969 ". . . I can only conclude from the information that is available to me as Secretary-General that the Members of the United Nations have perhaps ten years left in which to subordinate their ancient quarrels and launch a global partnership to curb the arms race, to improve the human environment, to defuse the population explosion, and to supply the required momentum to world development efforts.

"If such a global partnership is not forged within the next decade, then I very much fear that the problems I have mentioned will have reached such staggering proportions that they will be beyond our capacity to control."

The challenge is political, economic and moral. War threatens in various areas of the world where armistice agreements have worn thin. Despite the more than twenty years of disarmament negotiations, the conclusion of a few arms control agreements such as the limited test ban treaty, and the persistent efforts of the Twenty-Six-Nation Conference of the Committee on Disarmament at Geneva, and of its predecessors, the race in both nuclear and conventional armaments continues and the arms budgets of the world are at their highest point—approximately one hundred and eighty billion dollars a year. Many small nations spend a large portion of their budgets on armaments, diverting crucial sums from economic development and other important objectives. Notwithstanding the work of the United Nations, its specialized agencies and other international and regional organizations, the income gap between the rich and the poor nations continues to widen.

The fundamental obstacle to success of the United Nations from the beginning has been the fact that the governments of the world have not developed a strong enough allegiance to the Charter of the United Nations. Too few countries, and none of the great powers, have taken the United Nations sufficiently into account in formulating and executing their foreign policies. Five powers were given permanent seats on the Security Council and a veto on certain kinds of action, because it was felt that the peace of the world would depend upon their unity. This unity has not been maintained by them. Without pretending to apportion all the blame for this, we dare say that all of them share in it. Frequently one or more of them have substituted unilateral action and alliances for collective action under the Charter, or for determination by the Court. They have also sometimes brought issues to the United Nations when it was too late for it to solve them successfully. They have often supplied arms to small States and sometimes have encouraged them in making unreasonable or even belligerent demands. Their aspiration in some cases seems to be to achieve short-run national objectives rather than permanent peace on just principles. And many of the new States that entered the United Nations with such high idealistic purposes have frequently concentrated their attention on a few political objectives, trying to get the most for their countries. They have sometimes refused to see the larger moral obligations of the Charter or to realize that the obligations of the Charter, especially with respect to human rights, apply to them as well as to others.

Nations sometimes justify their unilateral action by alleging that the United Nations is not strong enough to assure their security or to solve their problems. Since such unilateral action seldom has proved successful, the only other viable alternative seems to the Commission to be the improvement of the capacity of the United Nations to realize the goals set forth in the Charter.

It will not come as a surprise to those who have followed the previous work of the Commission to Study the Organization of Peace that it believes that the international community in the not too distant future will develop to the point that the United Nations will actually be able to maintain "international peace and security, and justice" and to ensure to all "better standards of life in larger freedom," as was promised in the United Nations Charter.

The Commission presented this point of view as early as its First Report in 1940 when it stated:

> Peace under modern conditions cannot be a static condition of life achieved by the renunciation of war, nor a mere pious desire to live at peace. Peace must be a dynamic and continuous process for the achievement of freedom, justice, progress and security on a world-wide scale. Many problems can never be finally solved. They recur in different forms as eternally as life itself. The processes of peace, however, should make possible ways of meeting these emerging problems on a plane higher than mass physical combat.

> Peace requires the substitution for war, which becomes ever more destructive, of international processes which while protecting national ways of life against external violence will facilitate adaptation to new conditions and will promote creative changes in the general interest. Peace involves whatever international organization is necessary under conditions of the times to protect the interests and promote the progress of mankind. The world has so shrunk that the loose political organization of the past which rested on balance of power, on neutrality and isolation, is no longer adequate.

The Commission listed at that time the following five goals:

> (a) Nations must renounce the claim to be the final judge in their controversies with other nations and must submit to the jurisdiction of international tribunals. The basis of peace is justice; and justice is not the asserted claim of any one party, but must be determined by the judgment of the community.

> (b) Nations must renounce the use of force for their own purposes in relations with other nations, except in self-defense. The justification for self-defense must always be subject to review by an international court or other competent body.

(c) The right of nations to maintain aggressive armaments must be sacrificed in consideration for an assurance of the security of all, through regional and worldwide forces subject to international law and adequate to prevent illegal resorts to international violence.

(d) Nations must accept certain human and cultural rights in their constitutions and in international covenants. The destruction of civil liberties anywhere creates danger of war. The peace is not secure if any large and efficient population is permanently subject to a control which can create a fanatical national sentiment impervious to external opinion.

(e) Nations must recognize that their right to regulate economic activities is not unlimited. The world has become an economic unit; all nations must have access to its raw materials and its manufactured articles. The effort to divide the resources of the world into sixty economic compartments is one of the causes of war. The economic problem arising from this effort has increased in gravity with the scientific and industrial progress of the modern world.

These principles were incorporated in the Charter of the United Nations, but they have not been fully implemented. The United Nations still lacks sufficient powers: (1) to develop and enforce world law; (2) to ensure that all disputes are settled peacefully; (3) to solve interconnected problems of disarmament and international security; (4) to promote a more effective economic growth in the developing areas of the world and a more rational international economic system; (5) to protect human rights; (6) to promote the right of peoples to self-determination; and (7) to establish new international regimes in areas requiring adequate international control. Proper exercise of these substantive powers requires: (8) further broadening of the United Nations membership toward universality; (9) the strengthening of the United Nations decision-making capacity; (10) the assurance of more adequate financing; and (11) the mobilization of popular support for the United Nations through a world communication system and better education toward world understanding. The powers to be given to the United Nations would thus be exercised on a universal basis and in a manner quite different from the present practice.

Should anyone contend that new limitations on national sovereignty might result from the strengthening of the United Nations and its peacekeeping and peacemaking machinery, one could point out that these limitations would be clearly less dangerous than the attempts to adhere to old, outworn paths of power politics and unlimited sovereignty which lead directly to a nuclear holocaust. The United Nations Charter already contains a proper beginning, and over the last twenty-five years the United Nations has taken many steps in the right direction. But all these processes need to be greatly speeded up, and to do that will require a renewal of the faith which accompanied the birth of the United Nations, and a real dedication of both the peoples and governments of all Members to a new spirit of effective cooperation.

2. Proposal for a Draft Declaration

As a first step in that direction, all the Members of the United Nations might wish to make, through the General Assembly, a declaration stating their determination to achieve certain specific goals with respect to the strengthening of the United Nations through various progressive steps. Such a declaration, which the Commission suggests be adopted on 24 October 1970, the twenty-fifth anniversary of the coming into force of the Charter of the United Nations, might, for instance, be worded as follows:

"DRAFT DECLARATION

"The peoples of the United Nations, through the representatives of their Governments assembled in the City of New York on 24 October 1970, the twenty-fifth anniversary of the coming into force of the Charter of the United Nations,

"Having resolved to rededicate themselves to the great goals stated in the preamble and Article 1 of the Charter, and to give higher priority than in the past to using the United Nations machinery for maintaining peace,

"Solemnly declare that, in order to achieve these goals over the next twenty-five years, they will take the necessary steps:

"1. To accelerate the development of a body of world law, applicable not only to all States but also to individuals, and to develop new methods of international legislation to ensure that international law can cope with the rapid growth in the number of States and the increasing complexity of relations among them;

"2. To strengthen various methods for the just and peaceful settlement of all international disputes in order to provide an effective substitute for the use or threat of force;

"3. To make the United Nations strong enough so that all States will feel secure, and the States of the world disarmed enough so that no State would be able to challenge the authority of the United Nations to maintain international peace and security;

"4. To assist individuals everywhere in achieving higher standards of living, to increase world economic cooperation and social and cultural progress, and to make the terms of international trade more equitable and thus advance worldwide economic development;

"5. To ensure universal respect for, and observance of, human rights and fundamental freedoms throughout the world;

"6. To remove the remaining vestiges of colonialism and to assure the right of political and economic self-determination to all non-self-governing peoples;

"7. To establish under the auspices of the United Nations new procedures, regimes or institutions whenever new circumstances or new developments in science and technology indicate the need for international regulation of new areas in the interest of all mankind, thus avoiding potential conflicts and undue domination by the technologically more powerful or geographically more fortunate States;

"8. To increase the effectiveness of the United Nations by making its membership more nearly universal;

"9. To ensure that the decisions of the United Nations are made expeditiously and authoritatively;

"10. To provide the United Nations with financial resources adequate for the many tasks which the increasing interdependence of nations continuously imposes upon it; and

"11. To assist the United Nations in developing a world point of view among all peoples through independent worldwide communications facilities and other educational and informational means."

The subsequent sections of this report are built around this statement of goals. Each section contains a general background comment, and also lists various concrete steps by which a particular goal might be reached. These steps are merely illustrations and are not always listed in an order of priority or of feasibility. While the steps to be taken in various areas are not necessarily parallel, progress in one area would in many cases make it easier to take steps in other areas. In particular, the sooner structural changes (Section 9, below) are made, the more practicable it would be to endow the United Nations with new powers. The suggestions embodied in the report are by necessity general in character. A number of more detailed proposals may be found in the papers which will accompany this report in a later edition. It may be noted that the report is mainly concerned with the United Nations itself; many of the proposed steps would, however, require implementation through, or with the cooperation of, various agencies in the United Nations family and other international organizations, both universal and regional.

II.   THE GOALS AND THE STEPS

1.   Development of World Law and International Law

The Goal: To accelerate the development of a body of world law, applicable not only to all States but also to individuals, and to develop new methods of international legislation to ensure that international law can cope with the rapid growth in the number of States and the increasing complexity of relations among them.

Comment: The Charter of the United Nations is the first instrument of world law.   Even the Covenant of the League of Nations was considered by many as merely another treaty, applicable to a small group of countries and leaving other international agreements intact.   But the Charter prevails over any inconsistent international agreement (Article 103), and in matters relating to the maintenance of international peace and security applies not only to Member States but even in some cases to non-members (Article 2, paragraph 6).   Similarly, the Charter protects all States, whether Members or not, against attack and against interference in their domestic affairs (Article 2, paragraphs 4 and 7).   The Charter is truly universal in its scope and application and is thus the cornerstone of world law.

Additional principles of world law are contained in various resolutions and declarations adopted on behalf of the world community by the General Assembly either unanimously or with a few minor dissents.   (See also Section 5 below, relating to human rights.)   More principles are in preparation, though the Special Committee on Principles of International Law Concerning Friendly Relations and Cooperation Among States has encountered some difficulties in its work.   Little progress has been made also with respect to defining aggression and various crimes against mankind.   New ways must be found to achieve better results.

While international law is primarily a law among States, world law applies also to individuals.   Individuals should be able to invoke it in domestic and international courts for their protection, and they should be punished in appropriate cases for its violations.

World law has now become in a sense the constitutional law of the world community, but other areas of law similar to those developed in domestic law are covered by various branches of international law. Domestic administrative law finds its counterpart in the law of international organizations, many of which have administrative functions. There are more than two hundred international organizations, both global and regional, and international administrative law has been developing at a rapid pace. Other areas of international law are not far behind. Both treaty and customary law have been growing in an accelerating fashion. Dynamic changes have appeared in many fields, and new methods are needed to prevent conflict and confusion and to direct future developments into more regular channels.

One useful device might be to empower the United Nations and other international organizations, within their respective spheres of activity, to dispense with the need to have new international rules ratified before they bind a particular State. States have already agreed that the regulations on international air navigation adopted by the International Civil Aviation Organization and the sanitary regulations adopted by the World Health Organization should come into effect on a specified date when approved by an appropriate majority. States which do not want to apply them, in whole or in part, must notify the Organization concerned of that fact before the date of their entry into force. If they remain silent, and most of them do, the regulations become binding upon them without any further action by them. The cumbersome procedure of ratification and the accompanying delays can thus be avoided.

Once a treaty is ratified or a regulation becomes binding, States should be obliged to report to an international organization on the steps taken to incorporate the rules into their domestic law and on the problems which may have arisen with respect to their interpretation or enforcement. The International Labor Organization has developed effective procedures in this area, and they exist also in a few other international organizations. The United Nations and other international agencies could usefully copy these procedures.

Progressively the United Nations should be endowed with a legislative capacity. It should have power: to adopt generally binding declarations developing rules of world law implementing the Charter; to adopt regulations binding on all States which do not specifically reject them; to enact a code of offenses against the peace and security of mankind (similar to the one prepared by the International Law Commission in 1954); and to establish procedures for prosecuting individuals accused of gross violations of the Charter or of other important provisions of world law or international law. Later, when the authority of the United Nations has been firmly established in the field of peace and security and adequate changes have been made in the structure of the United Nations, further legislative powers in other clearly defined and properly limited fields should be conferred on the United Nations.

Recommendations: The Commission proposes that the new status of world law as the supreme law of the world community should be properly recognized, and appropriate measures be taken to develop both world law and international law. In particular it suggests the following steps:

a. *With respect to world law:*

Step 1: The Special Committee on Principles of International Law Concerning Friendly Relations and Cooperation Among States should be transformed into a permanent World Law Commission, for developing rules of world law which are needed to implement the provisions of the United Nations Charter. Its scope should be increased, its working methods should be improved and its composition and the qualifications for membership in it should be reviewed.

Step 2: The General Assembly should proclaim that it has the power to adopt declarations developing rules of world law which are needed to implement the provisions of the Charter, after they have been prepared by the World Law Commission. Such declarations would become binding on all

States when adopted by a unanimous vote, or at least by a majority of four-fifths including the permanent members of the Security Council.

Step 3: The General Assembly should adopt a declaration reminding Members that the Charter of the United Nations prevails not only over other international agreements (Article 103 of the Charter) but also over conflicting provisions of national constitutions and laws, and that they should change their constitutions and laws accordingly.

Step 4: Through a declaration of the General Assembly world law should be made binding not only on all States, but in appropriate cases also on all self-governing communities, international organizations, public and private associations, and individuals.

Step 5: Procedures should be established for ensuring to everyone equal protection of world law. In particular, the International Court of Justice should be given jurisdiction to determine whether a gross violation of world law has occurred and in appropriate cases to issue "cease and desist orders", to be directed to States which commit gross violations of the Charter or of other basic provisions of world law, asking them to take specified action to comply with their obligations. In case of non-compliance, the United Nations would take the necessary action to enforce the decision of the Court.

Step 6: The United Nations should establish tribunals and procedures for prosecuting any person accused of gross violations of the Charter. The drafts of the Code of Offenses against the Peace and Security of Mankind and of the Statute for an International Criminal Court, which have been prepared by United Nations committees, should be completed and put into force.

Step 7: These procedures should be later extended to other important violations of international law or world law.

Step 8: Finally, after appropriate changes have been made in the structure of the United Nations (see Section 9, below), the United Nations legislative capacity should be further broadened with respect to specified topics, subject to proper safeguards.

b.   *With respect to international law:*

Step 9:   The International Law Commission of the United Nations should be sufficiently strengthened to enable it to speed up the process of codifying and developing general international law.

Step 10:   The United Nations, and all specialized agencies which do not at present possess such powers, should be authorized to adopt, in a manner similar to that already granted to the International Civil Aviation Organization and the World Health Organization, regulations which would become binding on all Member States which have not rejected them within a specified period.

Step 11:   The United Nations and all specialized agencies should be granted the power now possessed by the International Labor Organization and some other organizations to monitor the ratification, interpretation and enforcement of international conventions adopted under the auspices of the international organization concerned, and to take such action as may be necessary to ensure compliance.

2. Peaceful Settlement of Disputes, Peacemaking, and Peaceful Change

The Goal: To strengthen various methods for the just and peaceful settlement of all international disputes in order to provide an effective substitute for the use or threat of force.

Comment: International disputes can be divided into two groups: legal disputes in which the parties are in conflict as to their respective rights under the existing rules of international law; and political disputes in which at least one of the parties demands that a rule of law or a legal situation be changed. If a claim in the second category is not satisfied through peaceful change, the situation may deteriorate to the point that a threat to the peace may result.

While the United Nations has often succeeded in stopping hostilities caused by a political dispute, it has been less successful in securing a settlement of the dispute itself. Even in legal disputes, where the International Court of Justice is available for their adjudication, States now hesitate to submit a dispute to its final decision.

There is a close connection between the Charter provisions relating to the peaceful settlement of disputes and those relating to the maintenance of international peace and security. As long as there is no general acceptance of effective means for settling disputes between nations in a peaceful manner, nations will hesitate to renounce the use of force for achieving what they consider as their legitimate aspirations. Only the establishment of international tribunals, conciliation and investigation commissions and other institutions, granted broad jurisdiction to deal with all kinds of disputes, can encourage nations to rely less on their power to achieve important national objectives. Use of such power, including use or threat of force, cannot be effectively proscribed when no adequate substitute for it is available.

The other side of this dilemma is also apparent. If the nations should concentrate first on creating international institutions for settling disputes and on endowing them with ever-increasing powers, it would become important to ensure that their judgments were properly enforced. For this purpose, an international force would be required, and such a force could function effectively only in a world in which national armaments had been cut down considerably.

There is also a strong link between international tribunals and world law. Nations are reluctant to submit international disputes to the International Court of Justice if they do not know what rules, principles and standards the Court will apply. On the other hand, if nations do not submit cases to the Court, it cannot contribute effectively to the clarification of legal principles. This vicious circle must be broken if satisfactory progress is to be obtained in these twin areas of adjudication and law-making.

Similarly, effective functioning of an international force would depend on formulating clear rules of international law to govern the force. If the force is authorized to come to the aid of a nation against which aggression has been committed, a careful definition of "aggression" will be needed. Otherwise, there would be constant danger that the force would not act when it should assist a nation, or would take unauthorized steps in a situation not actually involving aggression. At the same time, there must be strong international courts to which quick recourse could be had should the international force abuse its authority, and these courts would function much better if they had a clear set of rules to apply.

Recommendations: The Commission believes that the peaceful settlement of disputes is an important element in the structure of peacemaking, and that the powers of the International Court of Justice and the United Nations in this area need to be strengthened considerably. It suggests, therefore, that the following steps be taken:

a. *With respect to legal disputes:*

Step 12: All States should accept the jurisdiction of the International Court of Justice to decide all disputes relating to the interpretation and application of international treaties.

Step 13: All States should accept the jurisdiction of the

International Court of Justice to decide disputes relating to various categories of rules of international customary law, category by category or as a whole.

Step 14: All States should accept the jurisdiction of the International Court of Justice with respect to legal disputes or legal issues in other disputes which have been referred to it by a party to the dispute, in pursuance of a request by the General Assembly or the Security Council of the United Nations.

Step 15: In the next stage, all States should accept the jurisdiction of the International Court of Justice, under the optional clause in its Statute, with respect to all legal disputes, without any exception or reservation.

Step 16: The Statute of the International Court of Justice should be revised to permit the United Nations to bring a case before the Court against any State which voluntarily accepts a jurisdictional clause to that effect, and in turn to permit any State to sue the United Nations in specified cases. Subsequently this right to sue States should be extended to all intergovernmental organizations, global and regional; and should be balanced by also granting to all States the right to sue these organizations.

Step 17: All intergovernmental organizations, global and regional, should be authorized to request advisory opinions of the International Court of Justice on legal questions arising within the scope of their activities.

b. *With respect to political disputes and peaceful change*:

Step 18: The mediation and conciliation machinery of the United Nations should be strengthened, and a permanent conciliation commission should be established.

Step 19: A permanent subsidiary organ of the United Nations should be established, composed of independent experts, to examine the facts, to make the necessary investigations on the spot, and to present recommendations to the General Assembly or the Security Council on the adjustment of political disputes and questions of peaceful change referred to it by the General Assembly or the Security Council.

Step 20:   If this subsidiary organ should prove successful, it might later be transformed into a permanent international equity tribunal.   Steps should then be taken to enable States to accept the binding character of decisions of the General Assembly or the Security Council endorsing the recommendations of that tribunal.

Step 21:   Finally, all States might accept the jurisdiction of the equity tribunal to make directly binding decisions concerning various categories of political disputes involving demands to change legal rights or situations.

3. Disarmament and the Maintenance of International Peace and Security

The Goal: To make the United Nations strong enough so that all States will feel secure, and the States of the world disarmed enough so that no State would be able to challenge the authority of the United Nations to maintain international peace and security.

Comment: The basic object of the United Nations is to save mankind from the scourge of war, and the Charter contains elaborate provisions for the maintenance of international peace and security. But the disagreements among the permanent members of the Security Council have prevented the actual establishment of the machinery for the collective measures envisaged in Chapter VII of the Charter. While the framers of the Charter included in it only a few general provisions concerning disarmament, the atomic bombs dropped at the end of World War II caused a shift in priorities and led to a concerted effort to control nuclear armaments. This resulted in further neglect of the provisions for making military forces available to the United Nations in accordance with Article 43 of the Charter.

The bold United States proposal for putting all nuclear materials under the control of an international authority—the Baruch plan—was rejected by the Soviet Union. No heed was paid to Mr. Baruch's warning, made in his statement of 5 December 1946 to the United Nations Atomic Energy Commission, that the "stakes are greater than ever before offered mankind—peace and security. For who can doubt, if we succeed in controlling the atomic weapon, that we can go on to the control of other instruments of mass destruction? The elimination of war itself is within the range of possibility." After many false starts had led nowhere, the idea was revived that disarmament cannot be achieved without simultaneous improvement of United Nations peacekeeping and peacemaking capacities. Near the end of the Eisenhower Administration, Secretary of State Herter, on 18 February 1960, redefined the goal of disarmament negotiations as follows: "to cut national forces and armaments further and to build up international peacekeeping machinery, to the point where aggression will be deterred by international rather than national force." He pointed out also that to achieve this goal, the following objectives needed to be accepted:

> *First,* to create universally accepted rules of law which, if followed, would prevent all nations from attacking other nations. Such rules of law should be backed by a world court and by effective means of enforcement—that is, by international armed force.
>
> *Second,* to reduce national armed forces, under safeguarded and verified arrangements, to the point where no single nation or group of nations could effectively oppose this enforcement of international law by international machinery.
>
> Unless *both* these objectives are kept firmly in view, an agreement for general disarmament might lead to a world of anarchy. In the absence of effective international peacekeeping machinery, nations might violate the disarmament agreement with impunity and thus seek to gain a decisive headstart in building up their armaments. Moreover, since each state would be allowed to retain internal security forces, populous states would retain quite substantial forces which they might—in the absence of such peacekeeping machinery—use effectively against their smaller neighbors.
>
> To guard against these dangers, we should, as general disarmament is approached, work toward effective international arrangements which will maintain peace and security and promote justice according to law. We are ready now to take part in appropriate studies to this end. A useful framework and a considerable body of experience already exists in the United Nations.
>
> These studies could focus on two types of basic and needed change:
>
> *First,* the strengthening and development of international instruments to prevent national aggression in a world that has been disarmed, except for internal security forces.

Second, the strengthening and development of international machinery to insure just and peaceful settlement of disputed issues in a disarmed world.

Progress along both these basic lines will be needed if the goal of general disarmament is to be fulfilled.

This theme was followed a year later by President Kennedy, in his historic speech to the United Nations on 21 September 1961. In it, he challenged the Soviet Union to a "peace race" and presented to the world a new United States plan for general and complete disarmament under effective international control, a plan "which would create machinery to keep peace as it destroys the machines of war." After listing various disarmament steps which the United States was willing to accept, he came back to peacekeeping:

"To destroy arms, however, is not enough. We must create even as we destroy—creating worldwide law and law enforcement as we outlaw worldwide war and weapons."

He recommended, therefore, the earmarking of special peacekeeping units in national armed forces to be on call of the United Nations and the improvement of the "machinery for the peaceful settlement of disputes" and "for extending the rule of international law." He concluded this part of his speech by stating that "unless man can match his strides in weaponry and technology with equal strides in social and political development, our great strength, like that of the dinosaur, will become incapable of proper control and, like the dinosaur, vanish from the earth."

On the same day, the United States presented to the United Nations its new program for general and complete disarmament in a peaceful world, a most comprehensive document on this subject, much superior to any of its previous proposals.

The principal goal toward which we should strive was defined in this proposal in the following ringing phrase: "A free, secure, and peaceful world of independent states adhering to common standards of justice and international conduct and subjecting the use of force to the rule of law; a world where adjustment to change takes place in accordance with the principles of the United Nations; a world where there shall be a permanent state of general and complete disarmament under effective international control and where the resources of nations shall be devoted to man's material, cultural, and spiritual advance."

These unilateral United States proposals were followed closely by the McCloy-Zorin statement, released on 22 September 1961, which contained a compromise between the Soviet insistence on general and complete disarmament and United States emphasis on the link between disarmament, peacekeeping and peacemaking. The joint statement formulated this compromise in the following manner:

1. The goal of negotiations is to achieve agreement on a programme which will ensure:

(a) That disarmament is general and complete and war is no longer an instrument for settling international problems, and

(b) That such disarmament is accompanied by the establishment of reliable procedures for the peaceful settlement of disputes and effective arrangements for the maintenance of peace in accordance with the principles of the Charter of the United Nations. . . .

7. Progress in disarmament should be accompanied by measures to strengthen institutions for maintaining peace and the settlement of international disputes by peaceful means. During and after the implementation of the programme of general and complete disarmament, there should be taken, in accordance with the principles of the United Nations Charter, the necessary measures to maintain international peace and security, including the obligation of States to place at the disposal of the United Nations agreed manpower necessary for an international peace force to be equipped with agreed types of armaments. Arrangements for the use of this force should ensure that the United Nations can effectively deter or suppress any threat or use of arms in violation of the purposes and principles of the United Nations.

No statement could be more explicit. The United States

made here an unequivocal commitment to general and complete disarmament under effective control, and the Soviet Union agreed to strengthen the United Nations sufficiently to enable it to deter or suppress "any" threat or use of arms in violation of the Charter.

On 15 March 1962, the Soviet Union submitted to the Eighteen-Nation Disarmament Committee in Geneva a "draft treaty on general and complete disarmament under strict international control." This was followed on 18 April 1962 by the presentation by the United States of a "blueprint for the peace race", in the form of a detailed "outline of basic provisions of a treaty on general and complete disarmament in a peaceful world." As distinguished from the Soviet proposal which was devoted almost exclusively to disarmament, the United States draft contained not only far-reaching proposals on disarmament but also important suggestions for strengthening the peacekeeping arrangements within the framework of the United Nations.

Though the United States has retreated from this comprehensive approach in the last seven years, concentrating instead on partial arms control measures, the goal of "general and complete disarmament under strict and effective international control" has been repeated in 1968 in the Treaty on the Non-Proliferation of Nuclear Weapons. There needs to be, however, simultaneous renewal of the emphasis on the link between disarmament and other requirements for a just and secure peace. We believe it useful to explore further the implications of that link.

Neither disarmament nor an international police force nor world law nor world courts nor greater education toward world-mindedness nor even a strengthened United Nations can, if taken singly, remove all the dangers to peace. It is in the combination of these various remedies that a chance of success lies.

Reductions in armaments do not by themselves guarantee peace. In the early stages of the disarmament process nations will still have sufficient arms to wage a limited war, and such a war can easily grow into a nuclear war. Even in a completely disarmed world, a nation could use its remaining police forces for an attack or, as in ancient days, employ even primitive weapons to destroy its enemy. It should also be remembered that knowledge of the new weapons cannot be obliterated and, if a war should start, arms production would be revived, the arms race resumed and nuclear weapons brought back. It is not sufficient, therefore, to devise methods for reducing arms and for verifying effectively that nations have disarmed; parallel steps must be taken in other areas to strengthen the institutions for maintaining peace.

Not all these steps need, however, be taken simultaneously. In particular, some disarmament steps do not require immediate strengthening of the peacekeeping machinery. The two superpowers seem to have at present so many weapons of mass destruction that they should be able to destroy a large number of them without upsetting the existing balance of military deterrence. For instance, the United States and the Soviet Union could cut down their nuclear weapons and the means for delivering them by considerable percentages and still each of them would retain enough to be able to intimidate the rest of the world; at the same time, they would also have enough to stop each other from any rash action. Further reductions would depend, however, on bringing in other militarily significant States, and at some point a start will have to be made toward strengthening the peacekeeping machinery. It is difficult to determine at present when this point will be reached. There can be no doubt, however, that when the final stage of disarmament is approached nations will insist that before they dispense with the remaining national military forces, the world community must guarantee their security. Conversely, several disarmament steps could obviously be taken without prior solution of all the intricate problems of establishing and controlling the peacekeeping machinery.

It has been mentioned before that it might be possible to remove some of the present "overkill" capacity without endangering the security of either superpower; neither the United States nor the Soviet Union needs more weapons than is necessary to kill all its enemies. But one cannot expect nations to disarm completely, unless they have obtained first, sufficient guarantees against any threats to their security. It is well known that no inspection system is foolproof and that a determined aggressor can secrete a sizable number of dangerous weapons without risk of immediate detection. Those nations which have, nevertheless, been asked to abandon almost all their armaments will not consider it possible to take such a step unless disarmament is accompanied by the creation of a strong international peace force, able to cope with a sudden threat of aggression. Without a stronger United Nations, able to deal severely with an aggressor or, even better, able to stop him at the first sign of danger, a mere agreement on disarmament might become a perilous trap.

On the other hand, an international armed force established in a world armed to the teeth, would present only a limited guarantee against aggression. It could probably prevent small wars in which none of the big powers has become involved and it might be able to deal with future crises similar to those in Egypt in 1956 and in the Congo in 1960; it could police areas of potential danger and help to relieve some tensions. But it would not have sufficient strength to deal with the principal threat to peace which results from the constantly growing armaments of the big powers. Only after a considerable measure of disarmament would it be possible to rely on an international peace force as a real guarantee against war from any quarter.

Once a decision is made to establish United Nations forces, several options are available. As a minimum one might wish to supplement the present type of peacekeeping forces based on national contingents with a small permanent United Nations interposition force, a "fire-brigade" to be available for quick action while the contingents are being assembled. It is not likely that even the most devoted United Nations Members will pledge military contingents to the United Nations to be used in an unrestricted manner. Pledges will continue to be circumscribed by the requirement that each peacekeeping action, including the rules governing the activities of the force, must be approved by the government concerned before its contingents will become actually available. If a country should find certain action distasteful or certain rules unsatisfactory, its contingent would not be forthcoming.   One cannot blame any State for being so cautious, as no State can be asked to pledge its forces for unknown emergencies and to train them properly for all possible tasks, especially as many of the future crises cannot be easily anticipated.   But if there were available a small permanent United Nations force, free to go immediately wherever the United Nations directs it to go, national contingents could be easily adapted to supplement such a force in a more leisurely fashion.   Thus a two-step approach might be adopted.   In the first step, the permanent United Nations force would be sent to the trouble spot; in the second step, national contingents would temporarily take the place of the permanent force wherever it was employed before the emergency arose.   For instance, as long as there is a United Nations Force in Cyprus, its function could be normally performed not by national contingents, as at present, but by a directly-recruited volunteer United Nations force owing its allegiance to the United Nations only.   Such a force could be trained for a variety of tasks, and it could be used anywhere. Should an emergency arise, the United Nations force would be able to move immediately to the trouble spot as it would have the necessary transportation facilities and equipment. Once an agreement on the employment of the force is reached by the United Nations and the country concerned, quick action would be possible, thus avoiding the delay which in the past has often aggravated the situation and has made the task of the United Nations forces more difficult.

In order to use the new United Nations force stationed in Cyprus (or in some other place), it would be necessary to replace temporarily the units sent to the danger area with national contingents.   Thus, in the second step, national contingents would be quickly flown to Cyprus (or its future equivalent) to fulfill the duties of the United Nations force there, while the force is employed elsewhere.   As this replacement obligation can be clearly defined in advance, would be limited in scope, would permit special training and would involve practically no danger for the troops in view of the relative peacefulness of the area in which they would be stationed, it ought to be much easier for many States to accept this specific duty. It is likely that most countries would be able and willing to provide contingents for a temporary replacement duty in a specified area though they would hesitate to sign a blank check committing national units to service anywhere in the world and to unspecified future tasks which might involve grave danger to the troops.

The original United Nations interposition force need not be large, as its function would be local peacekeeping and not fighting a war against an aggressor. It would be a police force in the narrower sense of the word rather than a full-fledged military force. If the United Nations could have at least 5,000 men ready for quick action, well-trained and properly equipped, it would make an important difference in many situations where the speed of United Nations interposition is more important than the size or military strength of the force. Later such a force might be increased to 10,000 or more.

At the same time, the standby contingents made available by various States to the United Nations for peacekeeping purposes need to be strengthened on the lines suggested in the report on "Controlling Conflicts in the 1970's", prepared in April 1969 by a UNA-USA National Policy Panel. Some units might be available automatically for prompt action; for instance, for replacing the "fire-brigade" force in a stabilized situation, or to assist that force where a larger number of troops is needed. Other units might be earmarked as reserves, to be available on a few weeks' notice.

By the time we reach the later stages of disarmament, it might be possible to establish a more ambitious United Nations military force strong enough to challenge any violator of international obligations. The achievement of that goal would depend on progress toward disarmament, since no international force could dream of challenging one of the heavily-armed States of the present century. But should it prove possible to achieve disarmament of the scope envisaged by the 1962 proposals of the United States and the Soviet

Union, a strong United Nations Peace Force would become a necessity.   Such a force would have to be truly international, and would be composed not of national contingents but of well-trained volunteers.   It should be highly mobile, able to step quickly into any situation.   As far as possible, such a United Nations force should try to prevent a violation or to stop it before it became serious; it should ordinarily act to prevent a threat to peace rather than wait until an act of aggression had to be suppressed.   It should, therefore, be supplemented by a United Nations Peace Observation Corps, the members of which might be stationed throughout the world, establishing a United Nations "presence" in every country.   Such observers could keep the United Nations informed about every incipient threat to peace, and thus allow prompt action before a situation got out of hand.

Various safeguards will have to be built into the structure of the United Nations force to ensure that it will fulfill its role in an impartial and objective manner.   It will be necessary, in particular, to prevent the domination of the force by any group of nations, or by its own commanders.   Studies made in the United States, the United Kingdom, Canada and the Scandinavian countries make clear that such guarantees, though difficult and not perfect, can be devised.

Recommendations: *Taking these considerations into account, the Commission believes that parallel steps are needed with respect to disarmament and the strengthening of the capacity of the United Nations to maintain international peace and security.   Once the United Nations is sufficiently strengthened, far-reaching disarmament measures will become possible.* The following steps might, in particular, be taken in these two areas:

a.   *To increase the United Nations capacity to maintain international peace and security*:

Step 22:   An effective United Nations Peace Observation Corps should be developed, the members of which would be used to establish a United Nations "presence" in any place in the world where a danger to peace might arise.   Each State would be obliged to permit such presence, when so requested by the General Assembly, the Security Council or, in an emergency case, the Secretary-General.

Step 23: A permanent United Nations "fire-brigade" should be established. It should be composed of at least 5,000 well-trained and well-equipped volunteers who should be able to move quickly to any crisis area to prevent a breach of the peace, to assist in a cease-fire, to interpose between fighting forces, or to re-establish local law and order in case of a breakdown. Such volunteers would be exempt from national military service.

Step 24: In view of constant difficulties encountered by the United Nations in obtaining funds for a particular action to maintain or restore peace, a United Nations Reserve Fund should be established by the General Assembly to finance such activities.

Step 25: In addition to the small interposition force, a standby United Nations Peace Force of 25,000 should be established, composed of specially trained national contingents from States other than the permanent members of the Security Council. This force would be available automatically for any United Nations action to maintain or restore peace whenever a United Nations authority should decide that additional assistance is needed for the volunteer interposition force.

Step 26: Arrangements should be also made for a supplementary force of 50,000, composed of earmarked units which would be available on two to eight weeks' notice whenever the State supplying particular units agreed to their use in a specific case.

Step 27: Finally, in a substantially disarmed world, it should be possible to establish a preponderant United Nations military force, which would be individually recruited by, and would owe allegiance to the United Nations. Such a force should be strong enough to deal with any challenger, as long as it had the support of the vast majority of the States and the peoples of the world, expressed through a properly reorganized United Nations (see Section 9, below). To ensure that the

United Nations force should not be able to impose its will on the majority of the peoples of the world, appropriate safeguards would be devised.

b.   *To reduce armaments*:

Step 28:   Various agreements to diminish the arms race, which already have been signed or are under negotiation, should be completed and put into effect.   To this category belong, for instance: the Nuclear Non-Proliferation Treaty, an agreement to halt further deployment of offensive and defensive ballistic missiles, regional denuclearization agreements, an agreement on preventing an arms race on the bed of the sea, a treaty relating to underground testing, agreements on biological and chemical weapons, agreements on registering and licensing sales of conventional armaments, agreements to stop the sale of conventional armaments to States in certain regions, and agreements to stop arms races in the developing areas of the world.

Step 29:   An agreement should be concluded to stop production of nuclear weapons and of means for delivering them.

Step 30:   The United States and the Soviet Union should prepare revised drafts of their proposals for general and complete disarmament, and the non-aligned nations in the Twenty-Six-Nation Conference of the Committee on Disarmament should prepare alternative compromise proposals on the subject.

Step 31:   A United Nations authority should be established to assist in disarmament negotiations, to coordinate the supervision of the execution of existing arms control agreements and to supervise such further steps as may be later agreed upon.

Step 32:   Upon the completion of a disarmament treaty, large-scale reductions should be made in nuclear weapons and in the means for delivering them.   Simultaneously, limitations should be imposed on the production of and trade in, conventional weapons.

Step 33:   In the next stage further reductions in nuclear weapons, in means for delivering them, and in conventional weapons and armed forces should be made.

Step 34: In the third stage, final reductions should be made in armed forces and armaments to the point where each State would retain only those armed forces and armaments which would be necessary to maintain internal order and to provide, with similar forces in other States, a counterbalance against possible abuse by the United Nations forces of their strength. When sufficient confidence in the United Nations security arrangements (Subsection (a), above) had been established, such national forces would be limited to national police forces, and general and complete disarmament would come into effect.

4. Economic and Social Development

The Goal: To assist individuals everywhere in achieving higher standards of living, to increase world economic co-operation and social and cultural progress, and to make the terms of international trade more equitable and thus advance worldwide economic development.

Comment: It is clear that there can be no peace in the world as long as more than two-thirds of the world's population are underfed, underhoused and undereducated.   One cannot expect them to accept this fate forever, and if there is no hope of improving their lot peacefully, they will not forever refrain from disturbing the peace if force should appear to them to be the only way out of their present misery.   While success will depend to a large extent on the efficacy of local efforts, sufficient means will have to be provided by the world community for removing this great danger to world peace. Economic development of underdeveloped areas of the world will also be helpful to developed countries, providing new outlets for their trade and increasing the general resources of the world community available for pushing further forward the frontiers of the developed world.

While unilateral aid by various developed countries has contributed to the development of many developing areas, such aid often breeds resentment and is sometimes used to influence the policies of the receiving countries either in the United Nations or elsewhere.   On the other hand, the countries giving assistance have frequently found it difficult to impose conditions which were necessary to assure effective utilization of their aid.   It is much easier for the United Nations and its specialized agencies to require compliance with specific requests for economic and social changes such as land or tax reform.   As demand exceeds available funds, those who are reluctant to accept certain conditions, quickly find themselves at the end of the line and have to reconsider their position.

Both the developing nations and the developed nations must be adequately protected against undue United Nations interference with their respective economic and social structures. On the one hand, there is the danger that the United Nations might use its new powers in the economic sphere to impose on the developing nations some special ideas of its own about the social and political changes needed to facilitate economic growth. On the other hand, the United Nations might abuse its power to channel development funds from the developed countries to the developing ones in such a way as to cause a detrimental impact on the developed countries' own programs of internal development. Proper safeguards must be provided against both these possible, though unlikely, trends.

Money for development can be obtained more easily if there is significant progress toward disarmament, as funds currently devoted to arms are the largest potential source. Conversely, need for a large productive effort to build up the basic economic structure of many countries would make it easier to contemplate the cessation of the armament orders which constitute an important factor in industrial production today, provided that national legislatures would be willing to allot adequate funds for the purpose in view of competing domestic needs. If proper plans can be prepared for the use of the industrial capacity of highly developed nations to increase the rate of development of other nations, the fear that a sudden end of military production would cause grave problems of reconversion and economic dislocation would be greatly diminished.

Economic development must be closely interrelated with social development, and must take into account the possible social and political impact of scientific, medical and technological changes. General economic growth must be accompanied by more equitable distribution of incomes in the light of the needs of each nation and a dramatic improvement in educational and cultural facilities and in health, communication and transportation. To the extent consistent with national objectives and culture and the beliefs of conscience of the population, adequate information should be made available concerning family planning, and the United Nations should assist any country asking for help in controlling the expansion of its population whenever such expansion is detrimental to national economic and social growth. A better coordination of international and national efforts and careful planning on the international and national levels are required in order to implement these steps effectively and efficiently, and to avoid serious imbalances and dangerous countertrends. The United Nations should assist all developing countries in improving their political and administrative machinery in so far as it may be necessary to enable it to perform the tasks essential for effective economic and social development.

In some areas of the world, large river development schemes, similar to that administered by the Tennessee Valley Authority in the United States, might be established. Various plans of this kind have already been started: on the Mekong River in Southeast Asia; on the Volta, Niger and Senegal Rivers and Lake Chad in West Africa. An authority of this kind has also been proposed for the Jordan River, and explorations have been initiated with respect to the Amazon River. The United Nations should be given authority to assist in such regional development schemes, and should in general encourage projects of regional scope, transcending national boundaries. (See also Section 7, below.)

Recommendations: *The Commission believes that world peace and better world understanding depend to a large extent on a new intensive effort to speed up economic and social development throughout the world.* To achieve these goals, the following steps should be taken:

a. *With respect to economic development*:

Step 35: The approval by the United Nations of the plans for the second Development Decade should be followed by a more detailed program of action for the next twenty-five years, which should deal not only with industrialization but also with agricultural development.

Step 36: United Nations machinery for coordinating and supervising the work of the specialized agencies and of the various organs of the United Nations should be greatly strengthened. There should be better coordination both at the center and in the field.

Step 37: Economic aid and technical assistance should be made multilateral to the maximum possible extent, and the United Nations Development Program should be more adequately financed. An amount at least equal to one per cent of gross national product of the developed countries should be made available to the developing countries in the form of grants or long-term, low-rate loans to be dispensed through international institutions. In particular, the International Development Association should be endowed with sufficient capital funds to enable it to pursue its activities without dependence on recurrent appropriations.

Step 38: The role of UNCTAD in promoting the growth of trade of the developing countries and maintaining equitable terms of trade should be increased.

Step 39: Appropriate structural changes in the Economic and Social Council, GATT, UNCTAD, the international financial institutions and the United Nations Development Program should be made to enable them to implement more effectively the world development plans.

Step 40: New United Nations machinery should be established for examining the likelihood that new scientific breakthroughs will further worsen the disequilibrium between the developed and the developing world by widening the gap between them. Such machinery should seek to anticipate scientific discovery and its technological application and make recommendations for minimizing its undesired social and economic consequences as regards the speedy evolution of the developing nations.

Step 41: When appropriate changes have been made in the structure of the United Nations (see Section 9, below), the United Nations should be given adequate powers to regulate international trade to the extent needed to increase the productivity of the world economy and to maximize the export earnings of developing countries. In particular, it should have the power to hasten the elimination of inequitable barriers to international trade.

Step 42:   The International Monetary Fund should be given such additional powers as may be necessary to protect the monetary system against recurrent crises.

Step 43:   The United Nations should assist in redirecting resources from arms production to the economic development of developing countries, including a better use of the industries of developed countries for the building in the developing countries of general facilities such as roads, power plants, schools, etc., which are necessary for effective economic growth.

b.   *With respect to social development*:

Step 44:   The United Nations should provide assistance for the preparation of comprehensive national plans for social development which should provide for reasonable allocation of resources and not a mere listing of needs.

Step 45:   A United Nations Social Planning and Co-ordinating Board should be established in order to provide an effective coordination of the specialized agencies in the social field.

Step 46:   Sufficient funds (as suggested in Step 37, above) should be allocated for social development to ensure an effective improvement in educational, cultural and health facilities in the developing countries, which are needed to provide an adequate social foundation for economic growth.

Step 47:   The United Nations should have the power and the duty to assist nations in protecting their national characteristics, in so far as they are consistent with the Purposes and Principles of the United Nations Charter.   In particular, the United Nations should help nations to defend their cultural, ethical and social values and accomplishments against the improper inroads of the different values prevailing in other countries, and should assist each country in developing its national culture to the maximum possible extent.

5. Human Rights

The Goal: To ensure universal respect for, and observance of, human rights and fundamental freedoms throughout the world.

Comment: One cannot expect peace in the world as long as gross violations of human rights are committed in some countries, causing strong animosities in whole regions of the world. The United Nations must develop a better system to protect human rights throughout the world, especially in cases of racial and religious discrimination.

Over the first twenty-five years of its existence, the United Nations adopted more than a dozen special international conventions relating to specific human rights matters. Some of these are relatively narrow in scope (e.g., the Convention on consent to marriage and registration of marriage); others deal with such gross violations of human rights as genocide or slavery. The nature of each of these instruments depends on its content. The Genocide Convention, for instance, confirms that genocide is a crime under international law, enumerates the acts which are genocidal and provides for their punishment. Some of the other instruments, while designed to promote human rights, seem to be more in the realm of what is desirable rather than mandatory. Thus a State which departs from the provisions of the Convention on the nationality of married women is not likely to find itself denounced as an enemy of the human race or a violator of basic human rights.

These value judgments are, of course, not immutable. In some areas there has been an important shift in this respect. While one could argue before 1945 whether discrimination on the basis of race constituted a gross violation of human rights justifying intervention by the world community, certain types of discrimination, such as *apartheid* and similar practices, are now receiving treatment similar to genocide and are approaching the status of not merely gross violations of human rights but that of crimes against humanity. It may be expected that over the years more and more infringements of human rights will be classified at least as gross violations of human rights,

and that the United Nations will be granted increasing jurisdiction to deal with them in a more effective manner. Nineteenth century standards of permissible State behavior no
longer can prevail; new and stricter standards of a global
scope are constantly formulated.

In addition to these specific international agreements, the
United Nations adopted various general instruments designed
to implement more widely the provisions of the Charter relating to the promotion of universal respect for, and observance
of, human rights and fundamental freedoms. In 1948, the
General Assembly approved the Universal Declaration of
Human Rights, listing and defining a large group of civil,
political, economic and social rights. When the Declaration
was adopted, it was not clear what its character and role would
be. Some of its chief draftsmen considered it merely as an
inspirational document, a standard for future achievements,
but without much legal significance or any binding force. On
the other hand, several of the principal draftsmen were willing
from the beginning to endow the Declaration with a supra-
national quality and to consider it a binding instrument of a
legislative character. The latter view has prevailed, and it is
now accepted that the purpose of the Declaration was to spell
out which human rights were then in existence and thus to
provide an authoritative interpretation of the scope of the
Charter obligations. The Charter had brought human rights
within the scope of positive international law, and the Declaration as an instrument interpreting the Charter was vested with
the same mandatory legal force as the Charter itself and consequently became also a part of positive international law.

The practice of the United Nations certainly confirms this
interpretation. Despite some isolated protests against this
practice, the General Assembly has consistently invoked the
Declaration as a source of international obligations and on
several occasions has condemned a particular Member for activities which it considered to be contrary to the Principles
and Purposes of the Charter, in violation of that State's obligation as a Member of the United Nations, and in violation of
the provisions of the Declaration.

The increasing conviction that Members of the United Nations, and even all States, are bound not only by the Charter but also by the Universal Declaration of Human Rights was strongly confirmed when the General Assembly adopted unanimously two additional declarations which contained special clauses requiring all States to comply not only with these new declarations but also with the Universal Declaration.

Thus in 1960 the General Assembly unanimously proclaimed in the Declaration on the Granting of Independence to Colonial Countries and Peoples that: "All States shall observe faithfully and strictly the provisions of the Charter of the United Nations, the Universal Declaration of Human Rights and the present Declaration on the basis of equality, non-interference in the internal affairs of all States, and respect for the sovereign rights of all peoples and their territorial integrity."

Even more strongly, the Declaration on the Elimination of All Forms of Racial Discrimination, approved in 1963, provided that: "Every State shall promote respect for and observance of human rights and fundamental freedoms in accordance with the Charter of the United Nations and shall fully and faithfully observe the provisions of the present Declaration, the Universal Declaration of Human Rights and the Declaration on the Granting of Independence to Colonial Countries and Peoples."

Consequently, it was possible for the International Conference on Human Rights in 1968 to declare in the Proclamation of Teheran that the "Universal Declaration of Human Rights states a common understanding of the peoples of the world concerning the inalienable and inviolable rights of all members of the human family and constitutes an obligation for the members of the international community."

The Universal Declaration was further implemented by the two Covenants on Human Rights, dealing respectively with civil and political rights and with economic and social rights. These Covenants were long in preparation but were finally adopted by the General Assembly on 16 December 1966. For the first time there was a universal agreement not only on a list of all the basic human rights but also on the general content of each right and the most important limitations.

The Covenants differ in at least four respects from the Universal Declaration of Human Rights. In the first place, they are more universal; while the Declaration was adopted by less than fifty votes, with some important abstentions, 105 States voted for the Covenants and only a few States (such as Portugal and South Africa) absented themselves at the time of the votes, not willing to interfere with the unanimous vote of the Assembly. Secondly, the Covenants are more precise than the Declaration, providing more detailed guidelines for the conduct of Governments and more legal protection for the individuals. Thirdly, the Covenants contain various measures of implementation; though some of these remedies are optional in character, the Covenants recognize clearly the right of individuals to seek redress of their grievances on the international plane. Fourthly, while the Declaration was an early attempt, denied at the beginning, to exercise the legislative powers of the General Assembly, the Covenants constitute a mixture of the traditional and the new. They were drafted by the General Assembly and its subsidiary bodies and they were launched by the General Assembly without the benefit of a diplomatic conference; at the same time, they were not proclaimed by the General Assembly, but were made subject to ratification and will enter into force only when ratified, or acceded to, by 35 States. They thus resemble traditional international agreements binding merely those who ratify them. One could argue, however, that they also partake of the creative force of the Declaration and constitute a universal interpretation of the rules of international law on the subject of human rights which became embodied in the Charter of the United Nations and were enumerated in the Declaration. Apart from the binding force resulting from their ratification, the Covenants might thus benefit from the new legislative processes of the world community.

The Eighteenth Report of the Commission dealt thoroughly with the work of the United Nations in the field of human rights, and provides additional background for this section of the Twentieth Report. The recommendations which follow are also further documented in the previous report.

Recommendations: The Commission recommends that the powers of the United Nations in the field of human rights be further strengthened, that international legislation in this field be continued, and that additional measures be devised for enforcing this legislation by national and international means. In particular, the Commission suggests the adoption of the following steps:

a. *With respect to international legislation in the human rights field:*

Step 48: The two International Covenants on Human Rights and the Optional Protocol to the Covenant on Civil and Political Rights should be brought into force and widely ratified.

Step 49: The United Nations should complete international conventions relating to religious intolerance and freedom of information, revise conventions relating to humanitarian aspects of warfare and extend them to civil wars, and prepare conventions dealing with scientific and technological encroachments on human rights.

Step 50: Special effort should be made to achieve the widest possible ratification of international instruments on human rights, including the convention on genocide and the various conventions on discrimination.

Step 51: Special measures should be developed for the protection of national, racial and religious minorities.

Step 52: The United Nations should take vigorous action to assist all countries in dealing with problems arising from the population explosion.

Step 53: Various instruments for the prosecution and punishment of crimes against humanity should be completed.

Step 54: A comprehensive Human Rights Code should be prepared, containing a systematic presentation of all previously adopted instruments, both general and regional, with such additions as might be necessary to fill in the gaps. Such a code would provide protection to all individuals throughout the world.

b. *With respect to national measures of implementation*:

Step 55: A national committee on human rights should be established in each country. It should be composed of eminent citizens, including members of the judiciary, and it should have the duty to report annually to the national parliament and to the United Nations on the status of human rights in its country and on the progress made in enjoying and protecting them.

Step 56: Each individual should be granted the right to petition his national legislature for changes in the laws of the country, and a special legislative office should be established to consider and investigate such petitions.

Step 57: The United Nations should promote the establishment in each country of a specialized office or institution, such as an ombudsman or a procurator general, to assist individuals in vindicating their rights under the existing law, including international conventions, through investigation, consultation and, in the last resort, publicity.

Step 58: The United Nations should prepare guidelines for creating and maintaining in each country independent and impartial courts, and for securing to each individual maximum access to these courts in cases of human rights violations.

c. *With respect to international measures of implementation*:

Step 59: The United Nations should establish the office of a United Nations High Commissioner for Human Rights to consider human rights problems on a global scale on the basis of reports of national committees, to render assistance to States which request his help, to receive communications from individuals and to discuss them with the governments concerned, and to present to the United Nations an annual report both on areas in which progress has been achieved and on areas in which difficulties have been encountered.

Step 60: The United Nations Commission on Human Rights should be changed into a Human Rights Council having equal status with the Economic and Social Council, a separate Committee of the General Assembly should be established to deal with human rights questions at each session of the Assembly, and the Human Rights Division in the Secretariat of the United Nations should be developed into a Department, to be headed by an Under-Secretary.

Step 61: The United Nations should arrange for the integration of the various Human Rights Committees already established, or to be created, under various universal instruments into the structure of the United Nations, and should make arrangements for more adequate coordination of United Nations activities with those of specialized agencies and of regional organizations for the protection of human rights.

Step 62: The right to petition the United Nations in cases in which local redress has not been obtained should be granted to every individual wherever he may live, and adequate procedures should be developed for the consideration of such petitions, for conducting investigations in the State against which a complaint had been brought, and for protecting a petitioner against reprisals for bringing a petition.

Step 63: An International Court of Human Rights should be established with a jurisdiction which would be at first similar to that of the European Court of Human Rights, in which only a State or the European Commission of Human Rights can bring cases before the Court. Subsequently this jurisdiction might extend to direct complaints by individuals to the Court, which should, however, have discretion in deciding which complaints to consider.

Step 64: A World Assembly on Human Rights should be established, which would be similar in composition to the interparliamentary assemblies of several European regional organizations, would assist the General Assembly of the United Nations in dealing with human rights questions, and would provide liaison with national parliaments on human rights matters.

6.   Self-determination of Peoples and Abolition of Colonialism

The Goal: To remove the remaining vestiges of colonialism and to assure the right of political and economic self-
determination to all non-self-governing peoples.

Comment: One of the most outstanding developments in
the first twenty-five years of the United Nations was the abolition of colonialism in most areas of Asia, Africa and the
Caribbean, and the achievement of independence by some sixty
countries in those areas.   Two types of problems still remain:
those connected with the stubborn refusal of Portugal, Rhodesia
and the Republic of South Africa to comply with various recommendations of the United Nations; and those relating to small
islands and territories which find it more convenient to remain
under the protection of one of the major powers until the
United Nations devises a better solution for their special
situation.   (The latter question is discussed further in Section
8, below.)

The choice should not be merely between colonialism and
independence.   Some areas or peoples might be satisfied with
local autonomy and self-government in all fields of local concern.   Others might prefer various types of association with
the former colonial power or some other State.   There might
be also a few areas which might opt for some new form of
trusteeship, either by the United Nations itself or by the
United Nations in cooperation with one or more States.

In addition, there is the more general question, whether
the right of self-determination should be limited only to
colonial areas or might be claimed also in other areas where
certain peoples suffer under a rule which they consider alien.
Are all the old boundaries of States sacrosanct or is peaceful
change permissible also in this area?   How can the aspirations of various territorially distinct minorities be reconciled
with the need for international stability, especially in areas
which recently have achieved independence?   What can the
United Nations do, if these local tensions result in a civil war?

Finally, it is claimed that political self-determination is
not sufficient, as many countries remain under foreign economic

domination. By what means should economic self-determination be achieved? What role can the United Nations play in smoothing the path of transition in this area?

The questions with respect to self-determination which have been listed above are among the most intractable issues of world order, and the Commission may wish to devote a special study to them in the future. For the moment, only a few general recommendations can be made.

Recommendations: The Commission believes that the United Nations should make a special effort to develop more effective means for ensuring to all peoples the right of political and economic self-determination. The following preliminary steps might be taken in this area:

Step 65: The Secretary-General of the United Nations should be authorized to appoint a committee of experts to study the role which the right of self-determination should play in the post-colonial era, and the possible need for granting the United Nations new powers in this field.

Step 66: New methods should be developed for the further implementation of the United Nations Declaration on the Granting of Independence to Colonial Countries and Peoples, through the Committee of Twenty-Four or some other means.

Step 67: Arrangements should be made for a free expression of self-determination under United Nations supervision in all remaining non-self-governing territories, providing the people of each territory with such options as incorporation in, or association with, another State, self-government, and complete independence.

Step 68: The United Nations should be granted more effective powers enabling it to exert more pressure on States which refuse to comply with the wishes of the people of a non-self-governing territory under their control.

Step 69: The United Nations should assist newly independent States in achieving economic self-determination.

7.   Establishment of New International Regimes and Institutions

The Goal: To establish under the auspices of the United
Nations new procedures, regimes or institutions whenever new
circumstances or new developments in science and technology
indicate the need for international regulation of new areas in
the interest of all mankind, thus avoiding potential conflicts
and undue domination by the technologically more powerful or
geographically more fortunate States.

Comment: The United Nations should put under international administration the important waterways providing passage between seas and oceans, whenever their control by a
particular country has led to international conflicts. The United
Nations should also be more concerned in regulating international rivers, especially when no agreement can be reached
by the riparian States.   The disputes between some States
about a few small territories might be solved by placing them
under United Nations administration.   While problems of Antarctica have been temporarily solved without United Nations
participation, in the long run the United Nations can play a
constructive role in that area.

The powers of the United Nations need also to be
strengthened in various areas recently opened by science and
technology, and the United Nations should be given a built-in
capacity to deal effectively with any new problem which might
arise.

There is no doubt that the landing of two astronauts on
the moon has had a profound effect upon all of mankind.   The
great adventure was brought off with near perfection at a
time when the nations of the world were much less successful
in coping with many grave problems on earth.

The United Nations began assuming its responsibilities for
outer space in the late Fifties.   In 1959 a United Nations Committee speaking of outer space, found "that the great forward
surge of space activities will also tend to widen the gap
between the technologically advanced nations actively launching vehicles in space, and other nations watching and wishing
to take part in space activities but feeling incapable to do so."

The Committee went on to say, "The problem is to make available and to exploit the possibilities that exist for participation by nations at all levels of development, from supporting research or operation of tracking stations to launching small vehicles or joining with others in more advanced undertakings. A related problem lies in arranging the sharing of basic scientific information and topical data so that wide-spread participation is possible.

"In space activities, scientific and technological, there has been a great surge forward which opens new perspectives for human progress. Even more than in astronomy, they inherently ignore national boundaries. Space activities must to a large extent be an effort of Planet Earth as a whole."

The Commission agrees with the views expressed in that report and believes that they should be implemented through a United Nations space authority. As suggested by President Nixon, steps need to be taken to enable as many nations as possible to participate in future journeys to the moon and other celestial bodies.

The seabed beyond the limits of national jurisdiction is another area which is not, and should not be, subject to national appropriation. Its internationalization would open new fields for cooperation among nations and their citizens. The resources of seventy per cent of the earth's surface will soon become available and they should not be grabbed by a few strong powers or a few coastal States. (The Nineteenth Report of the Commission contained special recommendations on this subject.)

In the future, science is likely to open new areas for international cooperation, and one cannot even predict today where those areas might be. A broad grant of authority should be given to the United Nations to adopt the necessary regulations in such new areas as soon as the need might arise.

Recommendations: The Commission proposes the establishment of autonomous United Nations authorities to administer areas of special concern to mankind, to reconcile conflicting national interests or to open new fields to a collaborative effort. In the several areas discussed in this section the following steps might usefully be taken:

a.   *With respect to areas in which conflicts have arisen or might arise:*

Step 69:   The United Nations should establish special international authorities to administer international canals and straits, to regulate and develop international rivers, and to supervise small territories placed under direct United Nations jurisdiction.

Step 70:   The United Nations should take part in the supervision of the execution of the Antarctica Treaty and in due course should establish a new regime for Antarctica putting it under direct United Nations regulatory power.

b.   *With respect to outer space:*

Step 71:   The United Nations should establish an autonomous Outer Space Authority to enable all the peoples of the world to participate in space activities.   Such an authority should have the power to adopt regulations concerning all aspects of navigation in, and other uses of outer space, and all activities in the space environment, or on the moon and the planets, and to manage international cooperation therein.

Step 72:   The Outer Space Treaty should be amended to provide that whatever resources are found on celestial bodies and can be brought back to earth should be turned over to the United Nations, which should use them for the benefit of all peoples.

c.   *With respect to the seabed and the sea:*

Step 73:   The United Nations should proclaim the principle that the seabed beyond the limits of national jurisdiction is not subject to national appropriation and should be developed in the common interest of all mankind.

Step 74:   Pending the establishment of an international regime for the seabed beyond the limits of national jurisdiction, the United Nations should proclaim a freeze on any extension of national jurisdiction beyond a specified limit, which should be as narrow as possible.

Step 75:   The United Nations should establish an autonomous Seabed Authority with power to adopt regulations and issue licenses with respect to all activities on the seabed beyond the limits of national jurisdiction.

Step 76: The United Nations should establish an autonomous Living Resources of the Sea Authority with power to adopt regulations concerning all activities relating to living resources of the sea.

d. *With respect to future areas*:

Step 77: The United Nations should establish an autonomous Science and Research Authority to conduct research on the international level and to keep the United Nations abreast of research on the national level.

Step 78: Whenever the Science and Research Authority should certify to the General Assembly that a new area requires international regulation, the United Nations should be given the power to establish a special authority for the purpose.

8. Making the United Nations More Universal

The Goal: To increase the effectiveness of the United Nations by making its membership more nearly universal.

Comment: The United Nations is the first general international organization which is almost universal. But a few important States are still outside the framework of the United Nations, though some of them participate at least in the non-political activities of the United Nations and in most specialized agencies. The remaining gap needs to be bridged.

Both parts of divided States and all new States, with the exception of the very small ones, should become Members of the United Nations. New relationships must be devised for the so-called "microstates" and various semi-independent territories.

Recommendations: *The Commission wishes to reiterate its previous recommendations for making the United Nations universal in membership, except for certain small entities.* The following steps might be taken to achieve this objective:

Step 79: All independent States with a population of over 1 million should be eligible for membership in the United Nations, and all independent States with a population below 1 million should be eligible for associate membership with more limited rights and obligations. Special effort should be made to bring into the United Nations both parts of divided States, such as Germany, Korea and Vietnam, and to ensure that the Republic of China in Taiwan will not be deprived of its seat in the United Nations upon acceptance of the credentials of the People's Republic of China. Any admission of two separate "governments" of a State to the United Nations should be without prejudice to the possibility of future unification and without effect on the recognition policies of any State.

Step 80: Very small States not admitted to the United Nations and semi-independent territories should be provided with adequate protection, economic assistance and access to international institutions in situations affecting them or where they can make a special contribution.

9. Improving the Decision-Making Capacity of the United Nations

The Goal: To ensure that the decisions of the United Nations are made expeditiously and authoritatively.

Comment: It would be dangerous to increase the powers of the United Nations, as outlined in previous sections of this report, without at the same time strengthening the supervisory machinery of the United Nations and increasing the will of the peoples and governments of the world to maintain that organization. World law requires an institution for its enactment, interpretation and enforcement. An international peace force without adequate supervision might become a menace to the nations powerless to oppose it. Disarmament depends on the effectiveness of the machinery of the United Nations for maintaining peace. Courts cannot themselves decide about the means of enforcing their decisions; only a political body can make these decisions effectively. Not all international disputes can be decided by courts, and there should be a political body with power to determine how non-legal disputes should be settled. Moreover, the costs of the disarmament controls, of an international peace force and of an adequate development program would be much higher than the present United Nations budget, and it would be the duty of the United Nations to find the financial resources needed for these purposes. If the United Nations is expected to cope with these problems, its machinery must be strengthened, and—to use President Kennedy's phrase—we must "enlarge the area in which its writ may run."

Decisions of the United Nations need to be given universal scope, they should apply to all States whether they are Members of the United Nations or not, and all States should be entitled to participate in decisions affecting them. The decisions of the United Nations should be made by majorities speaking authoritatively for the world community and including those whose support would be needed to make the decisions effective, and should be arrived at by expeditious procedures.

Important changes need to be made with respect to the structure, mode of operation and voting procedures of various United Nations organs.

As far as the Security Council is concerned, the permanent members might be asked to accept certain restrictions on their right to veto the decisions of the Council.

The Commission has considered the question of revising the composition of the Security Council, especially with respect to permanent membership. It has discussed, among others, the following proposals:

a. That when the credentials of the People's Republic of China are accepted by the Security Council, India and Japan should be included at the same time among the permanent members of the Security Council; and that the Federal Republic of Germany should be given the same status upon its admission to the United Nations.

b. That all States with a population of over 40 million, other than the present permanent members of the Security Council, should be entitled to semi-permanent seats on the Security Council, rotating at two-year intervals. (This would include India, Indonesia, Pakistan, Japan, Brazil, Nigeria, the Federal Republic of Germany, Italy, and Mexico.)

c. That the ten States ranking highest by a formula taking into account population, industrial and commercial importance, and contributions to the United Nations budget should be entitled to permanent or semi-permanent seats on the Security Council. (This would include, in addition to the present permanent members, the following semi-permanent members: India, Japan, the Federal Republic of Germany, Italy and Brazil.)

d. That all States with population over 200 million or contributing more than five per cent of the United Nations budget (the People's Republic of China, France, Federal Republic of Germany, India, the Soviet Union, United Kingdom and the United States) should have permanent seats; and that all States with population over 40 million but less than 200 million (Brazil, Indonesia, Italy, Japan, Mexico, Nigeria,

Pakistan, and, though it does not yet fulfill the population criterion, the United Arab Republic) would have semi-permanent seat.

As none of these suggestions commanded wide consensus, the Commission decided to recommend no changes in the permanent membership of the Security Council at present.

Many changes are possible with respect to the General Assembly. Most of them do not require amendment of the Charter and can be introduced by resolutions of the General Assembly adopted on the basis of general consensus.

For instance, to give more weight to the attitude of the major powers, the voting rules of the General Assembly might be revised to require in the committees of the General Assembly (where voting changes can be made without a revision of the Charter) different majorities, depending on the measure of support received from the superpowers and other major powers. While the actual formula is likely to be the subject of long bargaining between the large and small States, the following table illustrates some of the possibilities.

United States	Soviet Union	20 other major Powers	Remaining UN Members
Yes	Yes	11	Two-thirds (67%)
Yes	Abstains	12	Three-fourths (75%)
Abstains	Yes	12	Three-fourths (75%)
Abstains	Abstains	14	Four-fifths (80%)
No	Yes or abstains	15	Five-sixths (83%)
Yes or abstains	No	15	Five-sixths (83%)
No	No	16	Six-sevenths (86%)

The actual figures, of course, do not matter here, but the idea of requiring more votes if the superpowers abstain from, or oppose, a decision would seem to have merit.

The General Assembly has already created several permanent committees dealing with specific subjects between sessions of the General Assembly. More work might be delegated to such committees thus diminishing the burden carried by the   General Assembly during its regular sessions. The work at the sessions of the General Assembly could be further expedited by establishing permanent working groups of limited membership for a more efficient exploration of possible consensus on various subjects on the Assembly's agenda.

The Commission also explored the possibility of establishing a World Parliamentary Assembly, the concurrence of which might be required for the exercise of the new powers to be granted to the General Assembly. This second assembly would represent the peoples of the world as distinguished from the governments. Though the preamble of the Charter acknowledges the fact that the United Nations was established in the name of "the peoples of the United Nations" there is no machinery available to bring the wishes of the peoples of the world directly to the attention of the United Nations. Perhaps in the next century "a parliament of man" elected by all the world's peoples will be created. In the meantime, however, we could establish at least indirect representation, through delegates elected by national parliaments.

We have already several international parliamentary assemblies in Europe; joint meetings of the delegates of the United States Congress with similar delegations of Canada, Mexico, the European assemblies and the countries of NATO; a Latin-American Parliament; and regional meetings of members of national parliaments of African, Arab and Asian countries. Finally, we have the Interparliamentary Union where parliamentary delegations from some seventy nations meet frequently to discuss political and economic problems of the world. In all these interparliamentary bodies nations are represented not by governmental delegates but by members of parliaments, the number of members representing a particular State varying usually in accordance with its population, though those numbers are in no case in an exact proportion to the population of each nation.

The next step in this evolution might be a United Nations parliamentary body which would assist the General Assembly in decisions relating to peacekeeping, financing and other important matters. Various formulas can be devised for the composition of such a body. All of them are likely to take into account the population of each nation. Some of them might also reflect the fact that national parliaments play an important role in approving appropriations of funds for international organizations, and that consequently parliaments contributing the largest share of United Nations resources might insist on additional representation. Finally, each nation should have a minimum representation, allowing representation of both the majority and the minority of its parliament. Thus, in the transition period before full acceptance of popular representation, one could envisage the following temporary formula:

Each national parliament would elect three members of the United Nations interparliamentary assembly. In addition, the parliament of any nation having a population exceeding one per cent of the total world population might be entitled to select one extra member for each full one per cent of that nation's share in the population of the world. Similarly, the parliament of any nation which contributes more than one per cent of the total contributions to the United Nations expenses might be allowed to select one extra member for each full one per cent of that nation's contribution. To prevent a too large discrepancy between the number of delegates from large and small nations and to provide equality between the superpowers a ceiling of 25 members might be established. If this method were adopted, the United States and the Soviet Union would have the maximum 25 members, India 18, the United Kingdom 11, France 10, Japan 8, Canada, Indonesia, Italy and Pakistan 6 members each, etc., while some ninety nations would have 3 members each. Should the People's Republic of China be represented in the United Nations, its "legislature" would also be entitled to appoint 25 members, while the Federal Republic of Germany upon its admission would be entitled to 11 members.

Such a World Parliamentary Assembly would enable national parliaments to become better acquainted with the work of the United Nations, and the members of parliament who have taken part in the Assembly would, on their return home, help in the execution of United Nations decisions by their own parliaments. A decision of the General Assembly supported by the World Parliamentary Assembly would have added strength, and the supplementary support received in national parliaments for such decisions would increase the pressure to behave in accordance with United Nations standards. The establishment of a second body in which the major nations would have an added weight would bring the United Nations closer to the one man, one vote ideal, and would constitute an important step toward giving the United Nations the peace-keeping and financial powers which it should have and toward ensuring that the powers thus conferred would be reasonably exercised.

Similarly, it might be useful to establish a World Youth Assembly, where the younger generation would be given a forum to voice its opinions and a chance to influence the policy-makers.

Recommendations: The Commission believes that the United Nations can become more effective through an overhauling of its procedures, an improvement of its voting rules and the development of new institutions for the expression of world public opinion. The following steps might be taken to achieve these objectives:

a. *With respect to the Security Council:*

Step 81: The permanent members should relinquish their right of veto with respect to recommendations relating to the peaceful settlement of disputes under Chapter VI of the Charter, and the voting rules of the Security Council should be changed to allow decisions by a concurrent vote of a majority of permanent members and a majority of non-permanent members.

Step 82: The veto should be removed with respect to decisions under Chapter VII of the Charter relating to enforcement measures not involving use of armed force by the United Nations.

Step 83: The new voting rules to be adopted with respect to decisions under Chapter VI (Step 81, above) should be extended later to decisions under Chapter VII, with the proviso that no State should be required to use armed force without its consent.

b. *With respect to the General Assembly:*

Step 84: In order to expedite the work of the General Assembly and thus save time and money, a sufficient number of working groups should be established at the beginning of each session of the General Assembly to prepare resolutions on subjects under discussion after the end of the general debate on each subject. Each Member State should be entitled to participate in at least one such working group.

Step 85: The General Assembly should establish more permanent committees for specific subjects, which would meet between sessions of the General Assembly and prepare matters more thoroughly for the Assembly's agenda.

Step 86: More rigid priorities should be established with respect to topics to be discussed by the General Assembly, and time should be divided among them in accordance with their importance. The number of speakers in the general debate at the opening of the General Assembly should be limited. They should be divided equitably among the regional groups, which should arrange for adequate rotation among their members.

Step 87: The powers of the President of the General Assembly and of the Chairmen of Committees to limit speeches to the topics under discussion should be increased.

Step 88: The Secretariat of the United Nations should be authorized to establish an autonomous Consulting Drafting Service, composed of experts on the work of the United Nations, on international law and other important subjects. The main function of this service would be to assist delegations in the preparation of resolutions and to provide them with factual and legal information for use in speeches to be made at the United Nations.

Step 89:   A Resolutions Committee should be established within the Bureau of the General Assembly. It should be composed on the one hand, of the representatives of the permanent members of the Security Council and other major powers, and, on the other hand, of an equal number of representatives from other States selected from various groups of States in accordance with a specified formula. This Committee would consider and, if necessary, by a concurrent majority of both groups of members, revise resolutions coming from various committees of the General Assembly in order to make them more generally acceptable. No substantive resolution would be submitted to a vote in the General Assembly unless it had been passed by the Resolutions Committee.

Step 90:   The voting rules of the committees of the General Assembly should be revised to take into account the need of majorities larger than a two-thirds vote in cases of special importance, if one or more of the superpowers or a majority of other major powers is opposed to a resolution, thus providing a variety of voting requirements depending on which major powers are in the majority, abstain or oppose a resolution. (For an illustration of this proposal, see Comment to this Section, above.)

Step 91:   A World Youth Assembly should be established by a resolution of the General Assembly. It should be chosen by various national and international youth organizations in accordance with rules to be adopted by the General Assembly. It should be consulted by the General Assembly on subjects of special interest to youth.

Step 92:   A World Parliamentary Assembly should be established (incorporating perhaps a Human Rights Assembly if it has been previously established), to be chosen in a manner to be determined by national parliaments, in proportion to a nation's population and to its contribution to the United Nations budget, with a specified maximum of representatives (e.g., 25 or 30) and a specified minimum (e.g., 3), and to be consulted by the General Assembly on specified subjects.

Step 93: Resolutions establishing rules of world law, adopted concurrently by the General Assembly and the World Parliamentary Assembly should be binding upon all States and individuals. (Similar binding force might be given to some of the resolutions adopted in accordance with the procedures suggested in Steps 89 and 90 above.)

10.   Financing

The Goal: To provide the United Nations with financial resources adequate for the many tasks which the increasing interdependence of nations continuously imposes upon it.

Comment: In the last twenty-five years the United Nations has gone through several financial crises. Some of its current operations depend on voluntary contributions by a few States. There is general agreement that the methods of obtaining contributions from States need to be improved, and that independent sources of revenue need to be found, especially for the United Nations activities connected with the maintenance of peace and for those related to economic and social development. Arrangements might also be made for collecting revenue for services rendered by the United Nations in maintaining order in various areas, preventing conflicts, and making and enforcing standards and rules.

Recommendations: The Commission has already dealt several times with problems related to United Nations financing. It recommends again that various methods be tried for increasing the financial resources of the United Nations. In particular, the following steps might be taken:

a. *To improve the collection of contributions from States:*

Step 94: If new Members are admitted, some of them (for instance, the Federal Republic of Germany) will make a large contribution to United Nations expenses, thus making the burden relatively smaller for other Members.

Step 95: A special United Nations fund should be established in each country to enable individuals, corporations and foundations to contribute, on a voluntary basis, funds for educational and humanitarian activities of the United Nations and the specialized agencies without diminishing the governmental payments under Article 17 of the Charter and under similar provisions in the constitutions of the specialized agencies.

Step 96: More effective measures should be devised for obtaining payments from Members whose capacity to pay is not in question. (For instance, the right of the United Nations to seize funds kept abroad by a State in arrears might be recognized.)

Step 97: A method might be developed for direct payment to the United Nations by individuals or corporations of a specified percentage of national taxes equal to an agreed portion of the contribution due to the United Nations from a particular nation. To avoid double taxation, all such taxes paid to the United Nations by individuals or corporations would be deductible from taxes payable by them to the State concerned.

b. *With respect to new sources of United Nations revenue:*

Step 98: The United Nations should receive an equitable share of the revenues from the exploitation of the resources of the bed of the sea beyond the limits of national jurisdiction, to be used for such purposes as may be agreed upon.

Step 99: The United Nations should receive an equitable share of the revenues from space communications.

Step 100: The United Nations should receive an equitable share of the revenue obtained from the exploitation of the living and mineral resources of the high seas, to the extent at least that new resources or methods of exploitation have been developed with the assistance of, or through regulatory action by, the United Nations.

Step 101: The United Nations should be given the power to grant charters to large international corporations doing business in several States. Such corporations would be subject to special regulations to be adopted by the United Nations, and the United Nations should have the power to impose reasonable taxes on them, and national taxes on such corporations would be proportionately restricted.

Step 102: A strictly limited United Nations tax might be imposed on international mail and telecommunications.

11. United Nations Communications System and World Understanding

The Goal: To assist the United Nations in developing a world point of view among all peoples through independent worldwide communications facilities and other educational and informational means.

Comment: No formal changes are going to remove the obstacles to United Nations success, unless there is a simultaneous improvement in the attitude of the peoples and governments of the world toward the United Nations. Very few persons in the world know what the United Nations can and cannot do, and how its activities affect them and their own countries. Even fewer are deeply interested in making the United Nations work better.

There is also the additional problem of increasing world understanding, replacing narrow national points of view with a global approach, visualizing mankind as an interrelated whole.

Much needs to be done to improve both the understanding of the United Nations and world understanding in the broader sense.

Recommendations: The Commission believes that better use should be made of existing media and a reasonable share of new media should be made available to the United Nations. Through increased cooperation between the United Nations family of organizations and national governments world literacy and world understanding should be promoted. In particular, it recommends the following steps:

Step 103: The United Nations should be provided with a more effective communications system reaching all areas of the world for transmission of messages between United Nations headquarters, offices and field personnel.

Step 104: The United Nations should have direct access to sufficient satellite broadcasting and television channels to ensure that the decisions of and discussions in United Nations bodies would be made known to all the peoples of the world without interference by any government.

Step 105: The United Nations should make adequate arrangements for enabling all nations to share with the rest of mankind their most valuable contributions to world culture, arts and ideas through the communications media of the United Nations, UNESCO and other specialized agencies.

Step 106: UNESCO, with the cooperation of other international organizations, should develop additional programs, to be implemented by national governments, to achieve world literacy and to promote world understanding through exchange of students and professors and through other appropriate means.

Envoi

The United Nations enters its second twenty-five years. A quarter of a century is scarcely a fraction of a second in the long time that man has been building political institutions on this planet. Why then is the present moment so crucial?

The answer can be found in the facts of the nuclear age. For the first time man has the capacity, literally, of total destruction of himself and the environment from which he has evolved. It is not inconceivable that before the end of this century, unable to organize itself to deal effectively with its problems, the world might break up in chaos and anarchy.

It is not unthinkable that the atomic powers, which have enough atomic bombs to destroy life on this planet, would find themselves in a nuclear confrontation which no one wanted but no one had prevented. Some time later a few human beings, stumbling out of shelters and caves, would try to rebuild life in such areas of the world as would be habitable.

Such a catastrophe can and must be avoided. Man has the capacity to direct to his salvation the forces which he has created. In the last twenty-five years he has made significant progress in building the law and the institutions of peace. He must strengthen these institutions, reject certain obsolete concepts of national sovereignty and establish a greater measure of justice for men and nations; he must use the United Nations to bring about a world of law and justice in which the human spirit would flourish anew.

It is in the spirit of this awesome challenge that the Commission has put forward what it hopes may be practical suggestions for strengthening the United Nations to meet the challenge of the next twenty-five years. Some of the steps can be taken immediately. Others may require the completion of previous steps in one or more areas. None of them is impossible, if there is sufficient will to make the United Nations work.

The following members of the Commission have signed this Report. Signature means approval of the general principles outlined in the Report, but not necessarily of all the details.

Arthur N. Holcombe, *Honorary Chairman*
Louis B. Sohn, *Chairman*
Clark M. Eichelberger, *Executive Director*
Luther H. Evans, *Chairman, Executive Committee*

Leonard P. Aries
Nelson Bengston
Clarence A. Berdahl
Donald C. Blaisdell
Jacob Blaustein
Roy Blough
David B. Brooks
Harrison Brown
James B. Carey
John Carey [1]
J. Michael Cavitt
Daniel S. Cheever
Ben M. Cherrington
Carl Q. Christol
Francis T. Christy, Jr.
Joseph S. Clark
Benjamin V. Cohen
John R. Coleman
Norman Cousins
Edward P. Curtis, Jr.
Thomas Curtis
Royden Dangerfield
Aaron L. Danzig
Malcolm W. Davis
Vera Micheles Dean
Oscar A. deLima
Rupert Emerson
Richard A. Falk
Charles G. Fenwick
Vernon L. Ferwerda
Roger Fisher
Thomas M. Franck

Gerald Freund
Wolfgang Friedmann
Richard N. Gardner
Arthur J. Goldberg
Leland M. Goodrich
Frank P. Graham
L. Allen Grooms, Jr.
Ernst B. Haas [2]
Donald Szantho Harrington
H. Field Haviland, Jr.
John H. Herz
Willard N. Hogan
H. Stuart Hughes
Philip E. Jacob [3]
Anne Hartwell Johnstone
Hans Kohn
Joseph P. Lash
Walter H. C. Laves
Gerard J. Mangone
Charles E. Martin
Marion H. McVitty
Donald N. Michael
Hugh Moore
Raymond D. Nasher
Leslie Paffrath
Josephine W. Pomerance
Charles C. Price
Walter P. Reuther
Roger Revelle
William R. Roalfe
J. William Robinson
Irving Salomon

James H. Sheldon
Eugene Staley [4]
C. Maxwell Stanley
Alonzo T. Stephens
Richard N. Swift
Obert C. Tanner
Howard Taubenfeld
Amos E. Taylor

David V. Tiffany
Richard W. Van Wagenen
Paul W. Walter
Urban G. Whitaker, Jr.
Francis O. Wilcox
Harris L. Wofford, Jr.
Richard R. Wood
Quincy Wright

[1] With reservations concerning steps 41 and 47.

[2] Mr. Haas cannot approve of steps 49, 51, 53, 54, 60 and 64 (referring to human rights) because he considers their implementation liable to cause more hostility than respect for human rights because of the increasing dissensus on underlying values. He also disagrees with steps 65, 66 and 69 (referring to self-determination) because their implementation is more likely to lead to ethnic and national exclusiveness than to increase international cooperation. Finally, he disagrees with steps 91, 92 and 93 because they are likely to contribute more controversy than constructive solutions to the problems this report really addresses.

[3] With explicit reservations regarding the section on world law (steps 1-8) and step 96 re financing.

[4] With reservations as to certain implications of steps 35, 40, 41, 47 and 69.

Supplementary Papers

One

Development of International Institutions Under The United Nations System

by

Quincy Wright

After each of the great wars of modern history new international institutions have been projected to meet the danger of recurrent war. After the Thirty Years War of the 17th century, religious war was renounced and the system of national states under international law was recognized by the treaties of Westphalia (1648). Permanent diplomatic missions were established and occasional conferences were held to administer this system. After the War of the Spanish Succession, the balancing of power was asserted in the Treaty of Utrecht (1713) as essential to stability and peace. After the Napoleonic wars, the treaties of Paris and of Vienna (1815) established the "Concert of Europe" under which the great powers were to adjust international political crises by conferences. The practice of dealing with legal problems by arbitration and of international river problems by international commissions was stimulated. After the Crimean War and the wars of nationalism in Central Europe in the mid-19th century several conferences met to codify aspects of international law. The Alabama and other important international disputes were settled by arbitration and a number of public international unions was established to administer general communication and humanitarian interests.

This activity and anxiety over the development of destructive military technology led to The Hague conferences of 1899 and 1907 designed to initiate periodic conferences to codify international law, to assure the pacific settlement of international disputes, and to promote disarmament. After World War I the Treaty of Versailles (1919) established the League of Nations and the International Labor Organization to coordinate and give teeth to these efforts by permanent institutions and economic sanctions. The members of the League were obliged to take collective security measures to prevent resort to war until all facilities for pacific settlement had been utilized. During the inter-war period the Permanent Court of International Justice was established, many states accepted the "optional clause" of the Court Statute and ratified the "General Act" requiring the pacific settlement of all international disputes. Several serious conflicts were settled by the League, the Kellogg-Briand Pact "outlawing war" was ratified by nearly all states, bringing the United States, which had not joined the League or the Court, into the system, and a General Disarmament Conference was convened. The purposes of the League Covenant seemed on the way to realization when the Japanese invasion of Manchuria and development of "the axis" with further aggressions in Africa, Asia, and Europe led to World War II. Before the war was over the United Nations Charter was signed at San Francisco (1945) to supersede the League by a stronger institution. The members of the United Nations committed themselves to refrain, except in defense against armed attack, from the use or threat of force in international relations and from intervention in matters within the domestic jurisdiction of any state; to settle all disputes by pacific means; to accept the authority of United Nations organs to enforce these commitments; and to see that non-members observed the same principles.

Although institutions to assure peace and world order were successively stronger after each of these crises of modern history, none of them achieved their objectives. Major wars occurred every half century with many smaller wars between and the course of events since World War II gives no grounds for belief that the pattern has changed.

After signature of the United Nations Charter the first atomic explosion occurred at Alamogordo, followed by the destruction of Hiroshima and Nagasaki by atomic bombs. Some people were convinced that a stronger international organization was necessary. This conviction has become more widespread as the "cold war", the succession of local wars, and the arms race have continued and the progress of science and technology has developed thermo-nuclear weapons, missiles, and satellites. This history has manifested the continued dominance of "power-politics" in international relations and the probability of a third world war of unparallelled destructiveness. The United Nations has had some successes in stopping hostilities and promoting the self-determination of peoples, but has been unable to maintain peaceful coexistence and cooperation among states, and to prevent their competition and conflicts from escalating into serious international hostilities on the frontiers of India with Pakistan and China, and in Korea, Vietnam, and the Middle East. Many instances of colonial and civil strife have threatened or precipitated international hostilities as in Greece, Indonesia, Indo-China, Hungary, Algeria, Congo, Cuba, Nigeria, and Czechoslovakia.

System change has been called for by students of international relations, by humanists and pacifists, and indeed by governments in formal statements. In view, however, of the continued dominance of the sentiment of national sovereignty among peoples, and the continued assumption by governments that a favorable military position is essential to national security or successful negotiations, no such change, although projected by the U. N. Charter, has actually taken place. There has been much controversy as to the nature of a system change which would be both feasible and effective. Strategic writers and general staffs have hoped to stabilize the balance of power by a system of mutual deterrence assisted by agreements for arms control. The super-powers have assumed responsibility to intervene individually or together to deal with critical situations. Federalized regional arrangements or integrated ideological blocs have been advocated, especially by those desiring to strengthen the NATO or Warsaw alliances. Greater activity of the functional organizations has also been advocated.

As discussion has continued, informed opinion has doubted whether power-balancing, great power responsibility, regional blocs or functional organizations can meet the problem. Such opinion has increasingly insisted that power politics must be superseded by an effective universal political organization. Some believe that this can be effected by gradual development of the United Nations through practice, interpretation, supplementary conventions or amendment of the Charter. Others believe it necessary to establish a world federation with central legislative, executive, and judicial power established by a world constitution, revising or superseding the United Nations Charter and capable of enforcing federal law upon individuals in all states. These opinions have tended to converge. The United Nations Association and the Commission to Study the Organization of Peace have continued to propose only such limitations of national independence as are essential to realize the purposes of the United Nations. World federalist organizations, on the other hand, have often insisted that effectiveness can be obtained only by a sudden change as in the United States transition from the Articles of Confederation to the Constitution. All groups, however, which perceive the need for effective universal political organization to meet the danger of general nuclear war in the next generation believe that, as a minimum, institutional and other changes are necessary to increase the power position of the United Nations relative to that of states (1) in opinion, (2) arms, (3) economic resources and (4) legal authority; (5) to develop U. N. procedures for performing its political functions; and (6) to extend the regulatory competence of the U. N. system into emerging areas of potential conflict. Brief attention will be given to these six requirements.

1. Public Opinion

Power does not refer exclusively to military power. In fact, in the age of potential nuclear war and actual guerilla war, the power of the sword is increasingly subordinated to the power of the word, the power of the purse, and the power of the law. In each of these types of power, the major states are today superior to the United Nations. The U.N. to be effective should improve its relative position in all of them and to do so it appears that it must first increase its power of the word—its capacity to influence world opinion.

Institutions should be established to enlighten public opinion among all the peoples, through the use of mass media and education, on the danger of nuclear war and the conditions of peace, including the image of a world order which would be capable of maintaining peace with justice and which could gain genuine acceptance within a reasonable time by all states of political importance. In view of the strong sentiment of nationalism throughout the world and the great diversity of peoples in language, culture, economic development and political institutions, that image cannot contemplate a world with a common culture or ideology but rather a world of peacefully co-existing and cooperating states with different economic and social systems, or, in the words of President Kennedy, "a world safe for diversity", a world which protects the individuality, security, and domestic jurisdiction of all states, great and small, under international law. Some common beliefs are, however, necessary. All must believe that there can be a world capable of giving such protection and also of maintaining at least the minimum standards of justice expressed in the Charter. All must, therefore, accept the value of international peace, of the self-determination of peoples, of respect for human rights, of cooperation among states for the economic and social welfare of mankind, and, particularly, because essential to all the others, the value of a spirit of toleration and good neighborhood, reducing mutual suspicion and increasing mutual trust among nations.

Although UNESCO and the United Nations have sought to educate all peoples along these lines, they have been hampered by the control of educational and mass media facilities by the national governments, and the usual effort of those governments to educate and propagandize their people for nationalism, sometimes even regarding education for internationalism as subversive.

International agreements should be concluded to assure that UNESCO and the United Nations Office of Public Information have direct access to the public of all nations through radio and television at favorable times and with suitable wave lengths. These agencies should also be assured of contact with national educational systems permitting them to distribute literature and to organize conferences with teachers and journalists. The National Commissions of UNESCO, the United Nations Associations, and other Non-Governmental Organizations have cooperated to these ends but they should do much more.

There can be little doubt but that education of the public of all nations towards a world point of view, toward awareness of the dangers of excessive nationalism, and toward understanding of the conditions of peace in the 20th century is the first step toward augmenting the relative power position of the United Nations.   There can also be little doubt that in so far as such education becomes effective, many governments will offer resistance.   They will seek to maintain exclusive loyalty to the nation.   The parochial attitudes, opinion, and loyalties of peoples are, however, the underlying causes of war.   The organization of peace requires much more internationalism in world opinion than now exists.

2.   Armaments

The establishment of a better balance between national armaments and United Nations forces is a second condition of peace.   The United Nations has recognized the need of general and complete disarmament, has recommended United Nations peace forces, and has established such forces in several critical emergencies.   The relationship between national disarmament and adequate United Nations forces for policing purposes has been recognized, especially in the United States-Soviet (McCloy-Zorin) "Agreed Principles for Disarmament Negotiations" of September 20, 1961. Various agencies to consider arms control and disarmament have been established in the field of both nuclear and conventional armaments, and an International Atomic Energy Agency has been established to regulate peaceful uses, and to prevent by suitable inspections military uses, of fissionable material which it supplies. Progress has, however, been slow. The general assumption that a strong national position in arms is necessary for security over-rides taxpayer pressure for reduced military budgets. Although the need for international inspection to assure compliance with agreements is recognized, some states fear that inspection would be used for espionage.

A permanent agency with competence in the fields of nuclear and conventional arms and U. N. forces should be established within the framework of the U. N. as recommended in the U. S.-Soviet "Agreed Principles". It should have authority to propose steps in national disarmament and the building of U. N. forces in order to inspire confidence in all states of freedom from attack. It should have full powers of inspection to assure compliance with agreements resulting from such proposals.

The success of such an agency would depend on the success of educational agencies in developing sentiments of internationalism and of political agencies in settling international disputes. The structure of such an agency would have to provide for weighting of votes in accord with military capability giving the major powers, whose consent is essential for disarmament, a dominant position, but as progress is made in disarmament and the building of the U. N. forces, the voting system might be adjusted.

3. Financial Capacity

Assurance of the financial capacity of the United Nations and the Specialized Agencies to perform their functions is essential to programs of education and of building U. N.

forces. The refusal of certain states to pay their share of the costs of U. N. forces as apportioned by the General Assembly in the regular budget of the U. N. is due to exaggerated sentiments of nationalism opposing increased economic power for the United Nations. Although the International Court of Justice has advised that functions such as the use of peace-keeping forces are clearly within the competence of the U. N. and can be financed through the regular budget, the General Assembly has considered it inexpedient to deprive delinquent members of their votes in the General Assembly as authorized by the Charter (Article 19). This situation has underlined the importance of discovering other sources of revenue for the United Nations, as well as of stimulating pressures of opinion upon members to observe their Charter obligations.

It is encouraging to note that states have actually increased their appropriations for international organization during the last century more rapidly than they have increased their military budgets. If a similar rate of increase should continue, the U. N. would have large financial resources in another century, but its present budget is less than one tenth of one per cent of the world's military budgets. Its power of the purse should be increased even more rapidly.

A United Nations financial agency to recommend the budget to the General Assembly, including new sources of revenue, might be established with such a weighting of votes as to alleviate the fear of the larger contributors of being overruled in appropriations and apportionments by groups of small countries that contribute little. A dual vote in the General Assembly on the budget and its apportionment might be established with such a weighting in one vote and equal vote for all members in the other. Such a change would require Charter amendment.

4. International Law

The development of international law and its application to international disputes of a legal nature is of major importance if world stability is to be assured.

The United Nations International Law Commission should meet continuously and should give more attention to codifying the principles of the United Nations Charter including the definitions of aggression, intervention, domestic jurisdiction and other key words in Article 2 of the Charter. It should reconsider international criminal law and the establishment of an international criminal court, dealt with in its early days but abandoned because of the "cold war". It should coordinate its work with that of the Human Rights Commission. It should develop international law in new areas such as outer space and the bed of the sea.

The International Law Commission should also recommend steps to increase acceptance without reservations of the Optional Clause of the Statute of the International Court of Justice and should propose a general treaty by which states should accept international law and treaties as supreme law of the land applicable in national courts superior to national legislation and executive orders.

Full acceptance of the optional clause might encourage states to require the application of international law in national courts to avoid being sued in the International Court.

A wider use of Advisory Opinions by all U. N. organs, especially in defining domestic jurisdiction of states, is of importance if a system of peacefully coexisting states is to be observed.

An increase in the power of law in the U. N. is essential if states are to have confidence in the world order as a substitute for national military power. Such confidence requires change as well as stability. Law must be continuously adapted to changing conditions.

The International Law Commission and the General Assembly should therefore develop procedures of peaceful change, as well as codify international law. They should propose rules which may become binding, even in the absence of treaty acceptance, by general recognition and acquiescence establishing customary international law. Charter amendments giving the General Assembly legislative power by a weighted vote should be considered.

5. Political Functions

The procedures of the U. N. to perform its political functions need strengthening. Its inability to solve major political disputes has been a source of disillusionment for the general public.

As the power position of the U. N. relative to that of states increases, its ability to discharge its primary political functions of peace-keeping, peace-making, peace-maintaining and peace-building will be augmented.

The U. N. has had some successes in peace-keeping by issuing cease-fire orders or obtaining armistice agreements stopping hostilities, but it has not acted in a number of serious cases and hostilities have continued.

A permanent U. N. peace force would contribute to this activity as would adoption of a voting procedure eliminating the veto in the Security Council.

The U. N. has been less successful in peace-making. It has not been able to settle many of the international disputes and situations which have developed since World War II and experience has shown that continuance of such disputes will in time upset cease-fire arrangements. In peace-making U. N. agencies have only recommendatory powers, in contrast to the Security Council's power of decision in peace-keeping.

Charter amendment or a supplementary treaty should give the U. N. power to make decisions for the settlement of disputes threatening peace after the parties have exhausted the procedures of diplomacy, mediation, conciliation, adjudication, and U. N. recommendation. A joint vote of the Security Council with the veto eliminated and a General Assembly weighted vote might be provided to make such a decision. Wider ratification of the General Act for the

Pacific Settlement of International Disputes would contribute to this end.

Peace-maintaining, contemplated by Article 14 of the Charter, to remove grievances and relax tensions before disputes have developed, may involve changes of treaties, boundaries, and other rights under existing international law. To give U. N. agencies authority to make such decisions is more difficult than to give them authority to settle actual disputes and situations. Recommendations of such changes may, however, have an effect if supported by vigorous world opinion.

The numerous resolutions of the General Assembly since its establishment recommending measures to reduce tensions might be brought together in a general code.

Peace-building is a legislative function. It involves action to keep international law up to date and to establish new institutions essential for peace in a rapidly changing world.

The establishment of the U. N. legislative power is essential for peace in a rapidly changing world but, except in limited fields provided for certain Specialized Agencies, it requires Charter amendment or supplementary treaty.

The development of a world opinion ready to subordinate national sovereignty to the United Nations and to build conditions of peace is a prerequisite to such changes. U. N. recommendations in this field may, however, have great weight if supported by studies of the International Law Commission and the Specialized Agencies, and may, as noted, establish new obligations of customary international law.

6. Regulatory Institutions

New administrative agencies should be established in the United Nations system to make and administer regulations in emerging fields of potential international conflict. The experience of the United Nations indicates the value of Specialized Agencies, each with a conference, council, and secretariat, relatively independent but subject to supervision by the U. N. Economic and Social Council. Such agencies should have procedures and voting power adapted to their special functions, as illustrated especially in the triple vote in the I. L. O. Among new regulatory institutions there is immediate need for agencies on outer space and the seas.

An outer space agency should be established to deal with problems of defining outer space; licensing outer space vehicles; providing for rescue operations; promoting exploration and scientific knowledge of the Cosmos; in cooperation with the International Atomic Energy Agency, preventing non-peaceful uses; and, in cooperation with the U. N. International Law Commission, developing general outer space law.

The procedures of such an agency would have to balance the special interest of states with a present capability in outer space activities with the interest of all states in observance of the law of outer space to assure peace, freedom of exploration and security from the fall of objects from outer space.

A sea agency should be established with competence in all uses of the sea and the sea-bed including fisheries, navigation and pollution, and exploration, exploitation and prevention of non-peaceful uses of the sea-bed. It should have powers of regulation and licensing to assure equitable distribution of the products of the sea and sea-bed, and competence to deal with disputes. Recommendation on the limits of territorial waters and of the continental shelf and the development of international law in all of these fields should also be within its competence in consultation with the U. N. International Law Commission.

In addition to new Specialized Agencies on armaments, outer space, and the sea; the problems of economic development; of pollution of the atmosphere, rivers, and the sea; and of population control are emerging as major human problems. All have gained attention in the United Nations and existing Specialized Agencies. New agencies devoted to each of these problems may prove desirable.

Two

World Order and Law

by

Carl Q. Christol

"The time has now come to take the initiative in the direction of establishment of the rule of law in the world to replace the rule of force." Vice President Richard M. Nixon, 26 *Proceedings of the American Academy of Political Science* 13 (May 1959).

Introduction

The life-style of world order and law, frequently considered under the heading of "the world rule of law," evokes a variety of responses. One view suggests that this idea affords no basis for legitimate attention—that it does not constitute a serious matter, since at best the concept can be but an ideal or utopian dream. Some hold that world order and law constitute a valid idea and a practical challenge, and, as such, deserve the serious and measured attention of all mankind. Others would go even further and urge that it is the primary political-legal issue of our times.

Central to a modern understanding of the universe is the world rule of law. Such primacy is based on the principle that justice within a legal framework is a fundamental need for any organized society. What, at this stage of history, can be done about it?

One can begin by accepting the view that world order and law are within man's reach. If his grasp is to be meaningful, it will be necessary to blend successfully both his practical capabilities and his utopian expectations.[1] As he seeks to meet this challenge he must go forward with the unqualified recognition that no matter what he does—acts affirmatively or remains passive—the future is in the vise of one ultimate certainty: there will be change.

From this it follows that the rule of law concept for Commission of Jurists, as consisting of "the complex of value the world can be identified, as it has been by the International acceptances and of practical institutions and procedures which experience and tradition in the different countries of the world, often having themselves varying political structures and economic backgrounds, have shown to be essential to protect the individual from arbitrary government and to enable him to enjoy the dignity of man." [2] It has also been identified as follows: "The rule of law means the rule of reason under the moral standards developed by the experience of man. Tradi-

---

[1] It has been said of lawyers that they must be on guard against both heritage and heresy. The contest between pragmatism and perfection is the life blood of the law. Its constant effort is to reduce the distance between the present fact and the ideal. It gives a dynamism identified by Justice Robert H. Jackson, when he said: "No alert lawyer doubts that the law he works with is constantly being reshaped and at any given moment represents a point at which contending forces have temporarily come to balance." *Jurisprudence in Action*, p. iv (1953).

Thus, a philosophy of law is as essential for the world rule of law as for any other aspect of law. For our purposes, law may be considered to be a means of sharing a vision of life—a vantage point from which to obtain the truest perspective of reality. It becomes the balance wheel on the machinery of peace. It is reason which has overcome force. It is common sense writ very large. It is a social value system. It is the ultimate basis of a progressive civilization.

[2] "The Rule of Law in World Affairs—An Introduction to World Law," 2 *Journal of the International Commission of Jurists* 7 (No. 1, Spring-Summer 1959).

tional moral values underlie law principles. These values have their roots deep in the conscience of humanity." [3]

For there to be a rule of law there must of necessity be an institutional framework. It must be capable of effecting change and of restraining the national exercise of uncontrolled power. This is particularly necessary where traditional moral values and ethical considerations supported in one community are rejected—possibly for ideological reasons—in another community.

The concept also has a primary function. This is "to strengthen the body, the machinery, the acceptance and sanctions of international law so that law will increasingly come to occupy the place in international affairs that it does in the domestic affairs of civilized nations." [4]

There is a school of thought which suggests that a distinction should be made between international law and the concept of a world rule of law.[5] The latter is designed to provide a regime for a new and emerging sphere of social reality. Such a reality would exercise a larger authority over sovereign nation-states than at present. By the same token it would reduce the vast areas of discretion now left to States

---

[3] C. S. Rhyne, "A Challenge to the Future Lawyers of America," 5 *The Student Lawyer Journal* 6 (April 1960). J. Stone has said that "The essence of the rule of law ideal lies, therefore, not in technical law as such, but rather in the supremacy of certain ethical convictions, certain rules of decency prevalent in the community, and in the psychological fact that those who are at the apex of power share those convictions and feel bound to conform to them." *Quest for Survival* 4 (1961). In commenting on the subject Henry R. Luce, suggests that through the rule of law society's highest values could be translated into the lower language of action and policy. "This act of translation is performed by law. For law functions on that middle ground between the spiritual and the material. For law is principle applied to fact. . . ." "Peace Through Law," 105 *Congressional Record*, Part 3, p. 3842, 86th Cong., 1st Sess., (March 11, 1959).

[4] A. Larson, *When Nations Disagree* 3 (1961).

[5] World law may be thought of as the constitutional law of an emerging world legal regime.

under the general rubric of "domestic jurisdiction." Such proponents accept the view that law is a process seeking to achieve socially desirable goals. Such goals include an enlarging and more effective protection of world community as well as individual and national values and benefits.

Present Strategies for World Rule of Law

A present strategy must include an action program. This is necessary so that all available resources can be most profitably utilized. At least three avenues may be explored for this purpose.

1. The first point of an action program is to distinguish the several levels of discourse affecting the world rule of law. In one instance there are the routine or lower level of discourse situations. These involve the regular and unspectacular resort to law in such technical matters as safety requirements on the sea or in the air, procedures and practices relating to the exchange of diplomatic representatives, the allocation of radio wave lengths, and a host of others too obvious and numerous to mention.

A more difficult level of discourse relates to those essentially political and security problems, which, nonetheless, fall within the proper orbit of the world rule of law. These situations are grouped around institutional efforts to assure international peace and security. Highlighted are such concepts as national self-defense, aggression, national sovereignty, political independence, outside intervention in the internal affairs of a State, and self-determination of peoples.

It is also safe to assume that there is an intermediary level of discourse, where, by and large, there is a tendency to accept the application of the rule of law. Thus, on relatively unimportant boundary disputes or where a dispute can be resolved through the payment of ascertainable damages on facts determined either by negotiations or through the offices of a judicial tribunal, there is a substantial practice to accept the rule of law.

The existence of these varying levels of discourse can be seen as an encouraging factor, for, with proper management it may be possible to move issues which were initially characterized as belonging to the highest or most volatile level into an intermediary or lower level. The important consideration here is that a realistic action program must admit of the different levels of discourse. Also one must take into account the fact that such problems are mobile and are able to be transferred progressively into situations and forums in which the rule of law can serve as the overriding consideration. This is not to suggest, of course, that law at the present time is irrelevant to a consideration of the upper level of discourse type problem. As is well known, the debates in and the actions of the Security Council and of the General Assembly consistently make reference to the legal meaning of Charter terms, and in particular to the provisions of Chapters VI, VII, and VIII.

2. The second point in an action program is to identify the reasons which induce nation-states to accept the dictates of reason and experience in permitting legal principles, standards, and rules to govern—and largely to control—their relationships. The strategy is to identify the means for transferring the usual favorable applications of such legal concepts from the routine to the more highly politicized problems. These latter are often asserted under the heading of rights pertaining to national sovereignty.

Reasons, which have long induced States to apply the rule of law to their world relationships, are readily identifiable. Included are the following: (1) Law may be regarded as a social value system, and, as such, it assures reciprocal benefits—or detriments—to those who are parties to the system. Regularization of the relationships of participants is seen as a value. Mutually agreed or customary standards can be produced through such expectations of benefit or detriment. (2) As implied, conformity to law may flow from a preference for consistency of relationships. This permits a degree of predictability in conduct, and this is desirable. (3) Law is a tough, taught tradition. It has become a system of practical reasoning. The reference of disputes to such an environment does, more often than not, permit conflict resolution. (4) When such a system is available with suitable processes and substances, it is probable that avoidance of the system by a recalcitrant entity may result in loss of esteem or prestige. There may be a fear of such loss in the event of a policy of non-conformity. (5) Further, departure from the system may cause either a fear of sanctions or the actual application of sanctions, physical or nonphysical. (6) Since law is so extensively interwoven with moral obligations, there is the strong urge of moral commitment to conform to rule of law concepts. This is heightened when there is a commitment to the view that law contributes to a condition of order in a society and that a substantial amount of order is essential to the presence of a large amount of liberty and justice. This factor is particularly important where the legal system is so constructed that it includes procedures for effecting peaceful change—where the law is sufficiently malleable so that it can provide effective responses to injustices which are patently present. In short, States are most readily persuaded to conform to the obligations of law when they perceive that an international legal system provides a realistic process for the realization of their legitimate national interests. If, at the time of the assertion of such interests, the community considers them not to be legitimate claims, it must also be the function of such law to supply sanctions against unacceptable claims. The fact that claims can be referred to as unacceptable or "unlawful" suggests the existence of a norm of lawful conduct.

Are such reasons adequate? We are again confronted with the basic problem of the applicability of law to international relations. This problem may be approached from several perspectives.

Some prefer to attack the subject from the vantage of a highminded Talmudic type of discourse. Others prefer to identify what they consider to be practical points of view. Neither need be exclusive, and an almost invisible blending of such approaches undoubtedly exists. Both acknowledge that today's trend is clearly toward a more integrated and even centralized framework for the conduct of international affairs. Neither can deny that there is an intense competition going on between the older nationalistic and newer community ideas.

Since the rule of law is so encased in human values it is possible to identify high-minded or "spiritual" concepts working in support of it. These concepts stress the importance of men and the need to protect personal dignity and human rights.

Such a perspective lays stress on the rational as well as the human quality of the individual, and makes a large commitment to human intelligence. This approach accepts the perfectible quality of man as a fact. It reflects a degree of faith in man's ultimate ability to resolve his problems in a sensible way. This school of thought accepts law as a cement which can bind individuals into viable social units and can merge nations into an integrated and purposeful world community.

With the binding together of the human elements of today's civilization, partisans to such an approach consider that law can unite the universal elements of a rapidly expanding and impacting world culture. There is a strong tendency to place importance on concepts of freedom, social justice, liberty, dignity, righteousness and to demonstrate a faith in man's capacity to achieve a rich and versatile quality in his interrelations. In those countries where these values have reached their highest acceptance, there has been the most complete dedication to the principles and programs of the world rule of law movement.[6]

---

[6] This has been captured by Justice W. O. Douglas who has said: "Mr. Justice Holmes said in 1895, 'Now, at least, and perhaps as long as man dwells upon the globe, his destiny is battle, and he has to take his chances with war.' That viewpoint has dominated men's thinking for centuries. Yet it deserves no enduring place in any decalogue. For man is capable of great cooperative efforts in peace as well as in war. Love and the instinct for preservation of life— these are even deeper in man's character than violence." "The Rule of Law in World Affairs," *Center for the Study of Democratic Institutions* 5 (1961).

This approach takes into account such considerations as faith, vision, and goodwill. Armed with these preconceptions there is a strong inclination to believe that it is the function of mankind to organize a universal society in which the foregoing values may be realized.

This approach assumes that the idea of the world rule of law ought to have universal appeal, since it is believed that through an understanding of law one can obtain a perspective of and understand the world in which he lives and of which he is a part. This relates to the inherent view that man is perfectible and that he possesses the ability to resolve his problems through legal processes. Yet if these expectations are too grandiose, it may still be asserted that support of the rule of law in world affairs can be a unifying force for democratically oriented nations and peoples. And, as has been experienced in the United Nations, it has been possible to conduct a dialogue on political as well as other matters through the use of legal concepts. Thus, there is reason to hope that the rule of law will provide an increasingly fertile means of obtaining a continuing dialogue between all ideologies.[7]

That the rule of law may produce a greater unity among States dedicated generally to Western values and culture may be both beneficial and dangerous. Its beneficial character is due to its ability to unify common expectations in a legal form. There is, however, the danger that opposing ideologies may conceive of the concept as separating them from the other members of the community and consequently in enhancing their insecurities. But this is a danger which may be readily overcome simply by recognizing it. Indeed, the rule of law concept can serve as a valuable instrument in creating a more precise understanding of the needs and problems of peoples residing within the orbits of opposing ideologies, and can also

---

[7] It is clear that a world rule of law strategy must distinguish between the substantive law principles and the processes whereby such principles are rendered acceptable.

help those who are now assuming the burdens of leadership in the developing nations.

Admittedly, these philosophic conceptions—important as they are—do not always prove to be of persuasive importance to many individuals and nations. For many they may be regarded somewhat akin to an admonition to a recidivist to behave himself. However, for the more mature, the more educated, the materially favored, and the more experienced, these intangible considerations have a profound impact on expectations and behavior.[8] And even for the sophisticated they constitute a challenge and a commitment to be both strong and faithful to their fundamental principles. These conceptions seek implementation through an awareness of the ideal justice and a respect for human intelligence.

On the other hand, since the rule of law is the product of historically tough reasoning applied to practical matters, it is possible to identify material considerations in support of a world rule of law. As an underdeveloped but developing force the rule of law is assertedly capable of replacing force as an all too frequently employed process in international relations. Thus, the central practical consideration is that law offers alternatives to both non-peaceful and totalitarian methodologies. The basic question from this perspective is "Will and does the rule of law pay off?" The assumption is that practical considerations will impact vigorously upon the world's diverse cultures and that the multitudinous attitudes of peoples will be suitably revised. The principal forces at work to secure such a revision of outlooks are the horrors of modern warfare and the gains or losses which will result from either properly or wrongly commiting man's human and economic resources. As with the spiritual or value approach, so also with the practical or material approach: much depends on the overriding

---

[8] Elihu Root once noted that "There is an indefinite and almost mysterious influence exercised by the general opinion of the world. The greatest and strongest governments recognize this influnce and act with reference to it." Quoted in C. C. Hyde, I *International Law* 14 (2nd rev. ed. 1945).

human faith which is brought to the intelligent management of the military and economic forces of the world social complex.

The presence of today's armaments has failed to provide nations and peoples with the security which they have sought. From the point of view of world order this means that it is quite absurd for any State to assert that it has the right to be a self-judge in matters which it considers of special importance to it. The exercise of the self-judging claim through resort to modern warfare is certainly counterproductive, and, indeed, is a calamitous misuse of human and material resources. Further, it is now generally recognized that atomic capabilities have produced such a superabundance of destructive power as to void the use of such weapons as effective instruments of aggressive policy.

There are additionally horrible risks inherent in an unlimited arms race. It seems incontrovertible that the direction of today's race has produced a "steady open spiral downward into oblivion." [9] The material costs of producing weaponry—both offensive and defensive—are currently under challenge as never before in man's history. The vast costs have not produced security. Further, there are increasing demands for a more humane expenditure of man's material resources. The world is aware of a vastly augmented environmental erosion—a degradation of both human and physical resources. Individuals are confronted with starvation and moral blight. The land and waters of the world suffer from contamination and disregard. Men and resources cry out for an orderly world under law, for as we know there is no other rational alternative. The risk is well known, for "mankind must put an end to war—or war will put an end to mankind." [10]

A fair and equitable use and efficient management of economic resources will also contribute to the emergence of an

---

[9] J. Wiesner and H. York, "National Security and The Nuclear Test Ban," 211 *Scientific American* 35 (October 1964).

[10] J. F. Kennedy, "Let Us Call a Truce to Terror," 44 *Department of State Bulletin*, 622 (October 16, 1961).

effective rule of law in world affairs. Foreign aid, when intelligently directed toward valid goals, and when managed in the interests of the entire community can contribute materially to a condition of world order. A larger allocation of such resources, especially to the educational and agricultural needs of the world, can move forward the cause of world law. Ascertainable and evenly applied world law in business and economic areas bears directly on the success or failure of business and economic matters. Thus, there is reason to believe that such law would do more to advance the flow of a profitable world trade and consequently raise the economic standard of living of many parts of the world than even the most inspired foreign aid. Recently significant challenges have been addressed to the private sector of the world's economy to assume its fair share of economic progress. If private investment is to assume its conceded responsibility there is a need for a sound and reliable framework.[11]

The most practical of all reasons for the acceptance of the rule of law is that it serves a utilitarian purpose. A disorderly world is a dangerous world, and a rejection of a lawful world invites one fraught with basic insecurities. The existence of law contributes to acceptable conduct by States, for when law exists, even though vaguely, States find it difficult to break it flagrantly or to deny the law publicly. Rarely does a State assert that its conduct departs measurably from the tenets of the law.

These reasons—philosophical or spiritual and practical or material—provide a basis for conformity to the rule of law.

---

[11] In his 1959 address entitled "The Rule of Law," Vice President Nixon urged that the rule of law be used as a way of settling disputes among nations as among individuals. He noted that "We should be prepared to show the world by our example that the rule of law, even in the most trying circumstances, is the one system which all free men of good will must support." "The advance of civilization, the growth of culture, and the perfection of all the finest qualities of mankind have all been accompanied by respect for law and justice and by the constant growth of the use of law in place of force." R. M. Nixon, *op. cit.*

With a well-founded rule of law the human intellect can be emancipated from a ravaging insecurity. Further, man's material well-being and his capacity to enjoy the fruits of intellect and labor are more completely assured. These reasons are adequate to assure the success of the rule of law in world affairs.

3. The third point of an action program is to note that there is room for many programs. Such programs must exist for both present and future needs. Within a present action program it is necessary to identify strategic priorities. Partisans of the democratic way of life assume that the most perfect of all perfect worlds would consist of democratically oriented nation-states, in which the human rights of all residents would be affirmatively assured and protected. In accepting this assumption one can conclude that States possessing such an orientation—though varying widely in their diversities—have a fairly broad social outlook. Trained and educated human resources and an abundance of food and other natural resources have contributed materially to a political orientation in which a high priority has been assigned to a life-style of law and order. Since there are more "have-not" than "have" States, there is clearly a need on the part of the developed States to take the lead in improving the condition of life throughout the world. Such a program cannot be meaningful simply through the expenditure of funds. To be utilitarian it must be organized, humanitarian, dedicated, and continuing. Such a program must be people to people, private enterprise to private enterprise, and public institutions—both national and international—must accept constructive roles. Despite cultural and other diversities it is clear that substantial communities of interest exist or can be created within narrower loyalties, and that as a result of such cross-frontier contacts there can be established the essential bases for a world rule of law.

In addition to broadening the democratic base of the world's nations and improving the material foundations of all States, a very high present priority must be assigned to the effective maintenance of the United Nations and the specialized agencies. Every effort must be made to secure the full use of procedures listed in Article 33 of the Charter. States in their policies and practices must learn to abide by decisions arrived at through such procedures. Full support must be given to the formal institutions charged with the active implementation and protection of human rights. It has been well said that one State can have very little faith in its dealings with another State if the latter is disrespectful of the human rights of its residents. Institutions such as the European Commission and Court of Human Rights must be extended on a world-wide basis, and even this prototype needs to be given more independence and managerial authority.

A fertile area of international conflict has been the exploitation of the oceans, including the sea-bed and ocean floor. Many disputes have also resulted from uncertainties as to fishing rights and a lack of precise identification of the boundaries of territorial waters and continental shelves. A high priority must be presently assigned to the resolution of these matters. States are even more sensitive about their national security, and immediate steps must be taken to ameliorate and control the current arms race, and in particular to assure that the sea-bed and ocean floor are used exclusively for peaceful purposes. Another high priority item is to assure to States full sovereignty over their natural resources, but at the same time make proper legal procedures available to claimants who allege a wrongful deprivation of vested rights existing in another State.

An often unmentioned priority is the need to engage in the research activity which is basic to the ascertainment of fact and the formulation of policy. With the increasing availability of computer technologies, there is every reason to believe that they can be used for a wider accumulation and dissemination of facts relating to important world law and policy matters.[12]

---

[12] Important suggestions and activity in these areas have been undertaken by the World Peace Through Law Center in Geneva and by the World Rule of Law Center at Duke University. The latter's work is entitled "Design For Research in International Rule of Law." The work of many other similar institutions is well known.

The central priority at the present is to accept the fact that measured by any standard the rule of law in world affairs "pays off." Present institutions must be used in their most effective manner. In this way attitudes of peoples and of their leaders will change. In such a way affirmative and constructive policies will replace those which still have some semblance of support even though they have long since been rendered obsolete.

Future Strategies for a World Rule of Law

Future strategies must be more imaginative and effective than those which exist at the present time. As the basic minimum a future strategy must encompass a willingness to propose the creation of new institutions. Attendant upon such a development there must be an inquiry into the prospective quality of their performance. Whatever the direction which may be taken in an institutional sense, the essential priority must be to find a way for preserving the diversities among peoples and nations while building up a world community based on a sharing of values and the emergence of a common respect, material satisfactions, and national security.

The suggestion for the establishment of new world institutions does not suggest that present institutions should be unthinkingly swept aside. A strategy for the world rule of law is obliged to take into account the qualities and contributions of present institutions in all of their ramifications.

Since world institutions provide the optimum conditions for the development of a universal rule, it is in the nature of things to place first emphasis on such bodies. However, both political and functional agencies exist at the world level. Additionally, there are the regional institutions. Among these are the freely federated and those in which there is a dominant hegemony. Although it is natural to assume that the UN, as a kind of universal "lookout" institution, can best serve present and future needs, some contend that either the development of regional confederations or the extension of powers of the specialized agencies will lead to a more highly integrated world community.

World institutions lead to the emergence of world law. They serve as forums for the identification and use of reason and experience. Further, they are able to implement those norms which are authoritatively imposed by a politically organized society, particularly when they seek the advancement of the welfare of a civilization.

Institutional trends pursue the pattern of incremental authority. New institutions are being created to perform new functions. Existing institutions are constantly enlarging those areas over which they have been given jurisdiction. Over time the world process of government has been strengthened and substantive provisions have been extended. These activities, though in flux, have resulted in a larger amount of order and stability in the world community. They have created conditions in which the concept of world rule of law has become increasingly meaningful. Future strategies must take into account the potential of such institutions. Realism requires acknowledgment that this is the era of international organizations and that they can serve great public purposes.

In taking into account the need for reform, it is clear that the world's existing major international organizations must be given more effective power. A sounder financial base is urgently needed, if there is to be a more closely integrated world community. At the United Nations this might be achieved by providing it with an income earning capacity. Instead of relying almost exclusively on national assessments, this organization should be entitled to revenues derived from licensing the right to exploit the high seas, or the deep sea-bed or ocean floor, or other suitable widely distributed resources. It should, like any large private corporation, engage on a profit making basis in multi-purposed activities. Perhaps it should be given a limited power of direct taxation with respect to suitable international transactions, the details of which might be worked out within the not too far distant future.

International organizations can perform some tasks more effectively than national bodies, and it is necessary to provide the financial and moral support for such institutions. As the major States give greater heed to their obligations flowing from membership in international organizations, the more powerful such institutions will become. It is probable that such organizations will be more independent of the influence of the Great Powers if new means are found to pay the financial obligations of such bodies.

Reforms in the legislative, executive, and judicial branches of present-day international organizations must be anticipated. The United Nations must be modernized through the enlargement of the power and authority of its legislative branch. The swift emergence of new and pressing international problems requires the development of a modern legislative capacity equal to the challenges presented to the universal international organization.

At the United Nations it is increasingly accepted that unanimous resolutions or declarations of the General Assembly and the Security Council should be accorded a law-creating quality. Such unanimous resolutions or declarations constitute a process for adding greater specificity to the meaning of the Charter in current or future situations. For such legislative decisions to constitute international or world law it would be essential to have approval of all the Great Powers.

One may expect that the United Nations will be obliged to assert greater authority. Such authority will be manifested in ever-increasing specificity—in the areas of political, social, military, and economic activity, and also in the area of human rights. More particularly one must look forward to a United Nations having the legislative and executive capacity to authorize sanctions in the event of proven aggression. Further, the United Nations will be required in the interest of operational effectiveness to set out legal rules placing limits on the authority of those who are assigned policing functions. There will be a need to determine if voting procedures in both the General Assembly and the Security Council will have to be modified. One such procedure would be to eliminate the veto. Going beyond present thinking, it is possible to contemplate the establishment of regional and world parliamentary assemblies subject to popular election within States. Such bodies might be representative of peoples rather than national entities.

With enlarged functions for international legislative and judicial bodies it will be necessary to augment the powers of the executive branch of international organizations. The enforcement of legislative and judicial decisions will require substantial delegations of authority, including the establishment of a standing and effective international police force.[13]

Many writers suggest the need to establish broader powers for international tribunals if the rule of law in world affairs is to achieve greater effectiveness. There is a clear tendency to propose the creation of new courts with new areas of jurisdiction.

While there is general agreement on retaining the World Court, it has been urged that it should be open to individual litigants as well as States. Should a body of regional courts be created, it has been thought this Court could become an appeals tribunal, as well as a court of original jurisdiction. Many believe that national reservations to jurisdiction have weakened this tribunal, and larger authority for the Court to determine its jurisdiction has frequently been recommended.

There are also proposals for the creation of international and regional courts possessing a criminal jurisdiction. Like the World Court, an International Criminal Court should have jurisdiction over appeals from the regional criminal tribunals. In some other instances, for instance in the case of violations

---

[13] The rule of law presupposes the need by the community to exercise force by and for the welfare of mankind. Legal restraint is implicit in such a power. The imposition of the community's violence is but one of the enforcement means open to the community.

of human rights, the court might be given ultimate review over the decisions of high national courts.

If the world rule of law is to come about within the predictable future, it will be necessary to fashion additional international institutions to meet the need. Attention should be given to the establishment of a specialized agency for legal matters, possibly patterned in its structure on the International Labor Organization. The International Law Commission should be retained in its present posture, but the new "World Legal Authority" would be novel and would benefit from representation of both governmental and private lawyers.[14] One large function for it to perform would be to communicate directly with the national lawyers of the world. Through their active participation, the world rule of law concept could be brought more directly to the attention of lawyers at the practicing or grass roots level, and they, in turn, would be more active as molders of public opinion and formulators of public policy.[15]

In no event should such a body be considered a substitute for existing private organizations which seek the advancement of the world rule of law. Through common memberships and purposes the public and private international legal bodies would coordinate their several, and often mutual, programs. The breadth of their participation would provide a greater credibility for progress. The imperative of such individual popular support in the establishment of a true credibility for the world rule of law cannot be overly stressed.

---

[14] This proposal does not suggest that lawyers only should be asked to formulate rule of law policies. As is well known, they sometimes move with the speed of turtles, while other policy makers soar on the wings of eagles. For the rule of law to receive effective acceptance its supporters must include highly placed statesmen, informed legal craftsmen, and the guiding elements of wise citizens.

[15] It is safe to say that the individual now has a greater and more majestic opportunity to influence the emergence of the world rule of law than at any prior moment in history.

It may be assumed that the "World Legal Authority" would grant a consultative status not only to international and national—including state and local—bar associations, but also to scholarly and professional groups within which there is an active interest in the world rule of law. Thus, such American institutions as the Commission to Study the Organization of Peace, or the American Society of International Law, or the International Studies Association might be given the opportunity to send observers and to submit proposals.

There is unquestionably a very large and very influential body of lawyers, judges, and scholars—to mention only those who may have a major interest—who understand the merit of having a larger body of world law and a more effective international legal system. The problem is to mobilize their strength so that their true importance can be known throughout the world. It is with this fact in mind that the creation of a "World Legal Authority" is put forward as a future strategy. Among its functions would be to conduct regular meetings. Its work product would consist of research studies, discussions, and draft treaties and conventions. It would maintain a world law library, be a general clearing house for world law materials, and serve as a law computer center. As a central institution it would be able to obtain world-wide support for acceptable drafts of treaties or conventions which had been produced by the International Law Commission or other international organizations. The existence of a "World Legal Authority" would make it more feasible for the General Assembly to require the International Law Commission to embark on a vigorous effort to codify and develop international law. Through it, a State could seek to advance its policy of giving preferred positions to such other States as were fully dedicated to rule of law concepts.

Further, the existing specialized agencies must be given extended legislative powers. Their law creating capabilities can be exploited with greater effectiveness if they exercise powers comparable to those already in use by the International Labor Organization. Thus, they should be required to monitor the ratification, interpretation, and enforcement of international conventions adopted in the exercise of their law-making function. Further, all of the specialized agencies should pattern their law-making activities on the practices of the International Civil Aviation Organization and the World Health Organization. The latter suitably have adopted a procedure whereby regulations approved by their legislative bodies become binding on a member if that member does not formally reject the proposal within a fixed time period.

Additionally, through a more effective utilization of the capabilities of nation-states, acting separately or in concert, the world rule of law can be significantly advanced. In keeping with the proposals made to meet the needs of the emerging States—especially through concentrating on their deficiencies in the educational and agricultural fields—it is expected that there should be a larger exchange of legal and other experts between the developed and developing States. It is common for national military schools to receive large complements of foreign students each year. The sense of community might be augmented by the establishment of interchanges between foreign service officers in the graduate foreign service institutes of the several States. Comparable, if not common, educational backgrounds—especially among individuals possessing a basic legal education—will undoubtedly serve well the development of a world legal system based on similar programs. And through such processes sharp ideological, cultural, and other divisive influences may be sufficiently ameliorated so as to permit a sharing of common values and policies. Thus, there is a need for greater cooperation and coordination through the use of existing national institutions.

It would be a mistake to downgrade the efforts and contributions of those States which have had the greatest international contacts and experience in the past. Such contacts have been measured in practice, custom, and treaty relations. The future can benefit from a suitable appreciation of past achievements and expertise. On the other hand, it is frequently charged that these are the States which are most prone to violate the law. It is clear that the Great Powers must

be the strongest supporters of the rule of law concept if it
is to be meaningful.[16]

The view is held by many that manifestations of power
politics will be minimized with the replacement of bipolariza-
tion by a multiplicity of power centers. This is based on
the belief that there is a greater chance for world stability,
and, hence law, if there could be a depolarization of competing ideologies and forces and a consequent larger equilib-
rium in the world. Further, such an approach acknowledges
a wider sharing of the world decisional process with a lesser
burden imposed on the Great Powers. Assuming the merit
of this contention, then a function of world law in the present
and in the future must be to advance a wider distribution of
power with a consequent reduction in the mass destruction
weapons capability of States.[17] In such a situation the interaction of law and stability would measurably improve the
condition of each. In such a situation the more influential
members of the world community would be obliged to make
it clear to the smaller and component elements that force
was not open to them to satisfy their grievances.

---

[16] It has been suggested that the credibility of the United States
in this area would be improved by: (1) the negotiation of disarmament
agreements going beyond the present test ban agreement and the non-
proliferation convention; (2) the planning of an orderly transition from
an economy in large part built on military expenditures to one more
supportive of non-military expenditures; (3) the promulgation of policies
involving greater openness in space and ocean floor activities; (4)
the early acceptance of negotiated human rights conventions; (5) the
domestic implementation of national civil rights statutes; and (6)
the repeal of the Connally amendment affecting World Court jurisdiction.

[17] Such an assumption must depend on (1) the evolution of an
advanced and clearcut structure of world legal order, (2) common
knowledge of and general reliance on law and legal processes, (3) the
existence of an atmosphere in which States are dutifully aware that
they are expected to conform to the prescriptions of the community,
and (4) the existence of a strong inclination among the members of
the community to invoke suitable sanctions to prevent the emergence
of conflict and to promote conflict resolution.

The rule of law concept may also be regarded as an energizing or directive power. This is true because it provides a basis for hope for a more orderly society. When accepted by nations it perhaps may also provide a greater coherence for their respective foreign policies. It is believed that world law provides principles which do condition and circumscribe the emotions of States and of their respective leaders. Equipped with a strong appreciation of an existing rule of law for international affairs, such leaders may be induced to depart from traditional power practices and militant expectations. In such fashion human minds and skills may be unchained from the narrow influences of the past and permitted to challenge the forces of social disorganization.

Viewed from the perspective of nation-states, a major future strategy must be to improve the quality of the international legal system. This goal may be accomplished by accepting a long-term policy orientation on the part of the participants in the system. Their best interest can be served through emphasis on anchoring down the system. They must give less attention to the formulation of unsubstantial argument. They must forego the assertion of dubious claims in order to obtain a hoped-for victory on a given day. There is the need for the emergence of the view that rejection of an international claim in an international legal forum does not cause a loss of face to a national claimant. Surely this condition exists among private litigants, and such an attitude is well within the scope of national and international law and politics. The world system will be immeasurably strengthened through the gracious acceptance of loss in a controversial matter. Further, through the emergence of such a climate of reason there very probably would be a diminution of the traditional reliance on balance of power. This practice has proven to have very little lasting utility, and in many instances has been at odds with law and reason.

A strategy for the future must also take into account the possibility of systemic change. It can be assumed that an effective world rule of law system would produce—in the not distant future—a more closely coordinated world community.

Excessive claims should not be made. Yet, if the rule of law is going to produce a higher degree of universality, one should at least consider the possibility of changes in the system. This might result in a world federal system of quasi-sovereign States. It could emerge in the form of new, highly interrelated regional complexes. It could take other directions.[18] Such integration could be general in highly sensitive areas such as security, peacekeeping, and economic matters. It could result in more technical integration, for example, communications, transportation, flow of goods, or a treaty on proof of foreign judgments. Current experiences have demonstrated institutional defects or limitations. They may help to point the way to possible changes.

Any future strategy must highlight the fact that a world order system is capable of preventing conditions of social disorganization from arising. Its secondary purpose is to manage or eliminate differences, unhealthy diversities, and conflict. This can be done in a legal system by diverting or directing situations involving conflict resolution into community oriented needs and expectations. Preventive law must, therefore, constitute a primary strategy.

A further strategy for the future must be to identify substantive goals, and within such confines to identify priorities. It is clear that such goals must be both general and specific. Perhaps the basic strategy is to work for a change of attitude so that the world rule of law concept takes on an assertive ring. However, this may lead some to expect only such general goals as peace, liberty, freedom, justice, equality, and the like. Without diminishing the importance of such an approach, it is necessary to identify more specific goals. Among these certainly must be the following: precise legal rules for the use

---

[18] G. Clark and L. B. Sohn, *World Peace Through World Law* (1958). It is clear that it is not necessary to have a superstate in order to have world law. However, an efficient world State would undoubtedly produce a body of formal world law without difficulty. Conduct based on consensus would remain more important than sovereign command.

of the oceans including the sea-bed and ocean floor, outer space, disarmament and arms control, human rights, peace-keeping, promotion of material—with emphasis on economic and financial—benefits, etc. The list is long and the challenge great.

Effective strategy must also allay concerns that certain rule of law goals are mutually exclusive or even hostile. It will be necessary to gain support for the view that the task of the rule of law to obtain peace does not result in compromising such goals as order, freedom, and justice.[19]

Another strategy must be taken into account. It is the factor of urgency in an era of exponential change. The initiation of world rule of law programs cannot be pondered or debated or deliberated without end. An overly large concern for problems and complexities becomes unproductive. Opportunities may be lost in the backwash of unremitting debate. The distinction between contemplation and activism should not be lost. However, an urgent approach would go a long way to dispel the myth that law is the armor of conservatism. The urgency will bring its own dynamism in support of the changing needs of society.

In the strategy of the future it would be a serious mistake to downgrade past and present efforts for the world rule of law. The progressive development and codification of an enlarging body of law continues to manifest itself in many forms. From a formal point of view the decisions of courts and arbitral bodies offer much, as do the unanimous resolutions of the United Nations Security Council and General Assembly. The practices of the Secretary-General and the work of the International Law Commission are manifestly of a high order of importance. The decisions of regional bodies and specialized

---

[19] *Pax Justitiae Opus.* Peace is the work of justice. The difficulty of moving freely from such basic principles to a practical distribution of tangible benefits as a result of the application of specific rules cannot be discounted. However, when this is accomplished through a world rule of law system, such difficulties as there will be are bound to be minimized.

agencies contribute substantially to the formal accumulation of legal prescriptions. Today the most important and by far the largest number of treaties emanate from these public organizations. The less formal, but not necessarily less important, practices and usages of nations and international organizations will continue to provide substance and direction for the rule of law at the world level. Future strategies while emphasizing changes of structure or function must also stress the more effective use of reasonable and available procedures.

Conclusion

With the widespread and popular dissatisfaction with man's seemingly uncontrollable involvement in world violence and instruments of mass destruction, the time is propitious to suggest a new world outlook. Perhaps the life-style of a world rule of law can provide an acceptable alternative.

The validity of such an alternative depends on several considerations. Dissatisfaction with international violence depends in part upon the conviction that law is alive to human needs, that law is being accepted, and that reliance can be placed in it. Credibility in the rule of law also requires that the concept be simple enough so that it can be popularly comprehended. It must, at least, be related to the common and uncomplicated experiences of the great mass of individuals. In measuring the acceptability of this concept it is entirely possible that the world's peoples are more ready for a rule of law in world affairs than has been generally assumed.

The fashioning of social change has always been achieved only at enormous costs. It has resulted only from an embattled, step by step, pragmatic process. Even when dissatisfactions are rampant and when courageous leaders are dedicated, the path of change—and of progress—is strewn with difficulties and delays. This has been particularly true when the required form of change may be more than a modification of existing national and international persuasions and preconceptions. Such difficulties are particularly troublesome when a wholly new and systematic change may be required. Yet, when such change is seen in an historical context—where an identifiable beginning and end is perceived and where a meaningful relationship exists over time—then individuals and their institutions are found ready to support social objectives.

Under these circumstances it is fair to ask what is the distinguishing mark of today's civilization. Can we identify the critical values and can the energies and imaginations of men be mobilized to attain them?

Success or failure will not depend so much upon the merits of the world rule of law—for its advantages appear to be quite obvious as it seeks its goal of making the world the lawful habitation of mankind—or upon the strategies which may be contemplated. More important—in fact, all that is of importance—will be man's firm conviction,[20] his profound faith,[21] his essential reason,[22] his bold action,[23] and a suitable awareness [24] that a rule of law is possible even though it will not by its mere presence bring an end to world violence.

---

[20] Justice Robert H. Jackson once noted that "We may go forward on the assumption that reason has power to summon force to its support, confident that acceptable moral standards embodied in law for the governance of nations will appeal to the better natures of men so that somehow they will ultimately vouchsafe the force to make them prevail." "The Rule of Law Among Nations," 1945 *Proceedings of the American Society of International Law,* p. 17.

[21] The settlers of Colonial Williamsburg, aware of the newness of their condition, adopted as their guide: "That the Future may Learn from the Past."

[22] Plato considered man to be perfectible and equipped with reason. His assumption is accepted rather than that of Protagoras. The latter conceived of man as essentially evil and destined to self-destruction.

[23] Free men exist to cope with crises engendered by the forces of man and nature—not to be overwhelmed by them.

[24] The 20th Report of the Commission to Study the Organization of Peace is designed to promote such an awareness.

Three

Steps to Advance the Legislative Capacity of the General Assembly

by

William R. Roalfe

Although the Charter provides for six primary organs (Article 7) the General Assembly has, by the full exercise of the limited powers granted to it, and through a process of evolution, emerged as the central organ of the United Nations. The new and emerging states look to the United Nations hopefully for assistance and support and many regard it as instrumental in helping them to achieve and maintain their independence. For them, and indeed for all members, the General Assembly is the major forum and, whatever its limitations may be, every member in one way or another is affected by the course it pursues. Accordingly, the General Assembly is in some respects in a better position today, than at any time in the past, to play an important role in the world community. However, the increase in the number of members, particularly through the addition of the smaller states, has had a greater adverse effect on the General Assembly than on any other organ in the United Nations. Size alone has impaired its effectiveness, but more serious is the fact that the

---

* In this connection see also "Reconciling Power and Sovereignty" by Urban G. Whitaker, Jr. in the Seventeenth Report of the Commission entitled *New Dimensions for the United Nations: The Problems of the Next Decade* (1966).

participation of many small states in Assembly voting further aggravates the discrepancy between the legal fiction of sovereign equality and the uneven distribution of de facto power. Decisions made in disregard of this political reality are not likely to command the respect of the members or provide the sound basis for such implementation as the decisions may require.

Although this is no doubt the principal obstacle that impedes the further development of the General Assembly there are procedural and structural deficiencies which have the same inhibiting effect. As will be perfectly apparent in the following pages, these deficiencies are in their effect sometimes closely related and, together, they frequently impair and sometimes altogether prevent responsible action on the part of the General Assembly.

That the difficulties involved in bringing about an improvement in the performance of the General Assembly are formidable, no one will deny. However, the problems are primarily political rather than formal in character and a great deal can be done without amending the Charter, although this may eventually be necessary. In this chapter consideration will be given to a number of steps that may be taken to strengthen the General Assembly and, at the same time, enhance its legislative capacity.

First, however, it is important to consider the General Assembly as it is actually functioning today, to determine to what extent its activities are consonant with the exercise of the legislative function. In the first place, the General Assembly has broad powers in meeting a need common to all legislative bodies, namely, the securing of information. It may freely initiate studies of its own and it regularly receives reports from the Security Council and the other organs of the United Nations. It can and does call upon the United Nations staff and relies upon it constantly for assistance. In the second place, the General Assembly alone reflects the entire membership. Hopefully, membership will eventually be universal, an important question that is discussed elsewhere in this volume. In the third place, the General Assembly's area of general responsibility is extremely wide and extends in one form or another to virtually all of the fields of activity with which the United Nations is concerned. In the fourth place, the General Assembly may adopt resolutions concerning this wide range of subject matter. Viewed as a legislative body the only significant formal deficiency is that its decisions are, with few exceptions, such as in financing and trusteeship matters, declared by the Charter to be recommendatory only and are not legally binding on the members.

So much for the organization of the General Assembly and its functions broadly considered. From our immediate point of view the procedure followed, and what might be called "products" of the General Assembly, are also of the utmost importance.

Every delegate, regardless of his ideological background and the national self-interest he represents, must accommodate himself to the parliamentary procedure of the General Assembly, a procedure that through debate requires the consideration of every question from a much broader point of view. Thus, the General Assembly provides a process for the orderly achievement of a consensus on substantive issues—a process that plays an important role in the development of international law and a process typical of full-fledged legislative bodies.

The "products" of the General Assembly of interest at the moment, are the declarations and resolutions. What is the significance of a General Assembly declaration or resolution, which is the outcome of proposal, discussion, mustering of support, pro and con, by all the means employed in legislative bodies, and, finally, adoption by a qualified majority? Before attempting to answer this question it may be well to consider a few examples.

One example is the General Assembly Resolution on "Permanent Sovereignty Over Natural Resources," dealing with a most controversial subject. After a decade of debate, which involved the consideration of voluminous materials—facts, legislation, treaties, and administrative practice—the General Assembly adopted a declaration of principles by an affirmative vote of 87 to 2 with 12 abstentions.

Another example of the process is the resolution proposed by the United States on cooperation in outer space. This resolution recognized the application of the principles of international law to "outer space and celestial bodies" by all states "in conformity with international law." Although in a formal sense it may not be proper to say that these principles are the international law of outer space, this action, by the most universal international organization, carries great weight. At the moment what is more important than matters of detail is the exclusion of territorial claims, with all their attendant rivalries and dangers, from this vast area of space.

Another notable and especially interesting example of the influence of a General Assembly action is the Universal Declaration of Human Rights, adopted without a negative vote. Although it did not secure the approval of the communist bloc, including Yugoslavia, or Saudi Arabia and the Union of South Africa, these members preferred to abstain rather than go on record as voting in the negative. The President of the General Assembly at the time, Mr. H. V. Evatt of Australia, said this was "a remarkable achievement" and the passage of time has fully confirmed his initial appraisal. This Declaration has, in spite of flagrant disregard on many occasions, had a tremendous impact around the world. In it, the preamble and several other provisions of the Charter have been articulated in a separate document, to which men on every continent frequently repair in their struggles for freedom and human dignity.

One more example is the Declaration on the Granting of Independence to Colonial Countries and Peoples. The tremendous impact of this Declaration has been evident to all. The fact that independence has been achieved without sufficient preparation in some instances, and that the leadership and other conditions requisite for the creation of a viable state have not always been present, does not alter the fact that the Declaration played a prominent part in the great change that has taken place. Indeed, it is doubtful if an enactment, with all the formal requisites of legislation, would under the existing conditions, have had any greater effect. As these and many other actions demonstrate, in practice, resolutions adopted by a large majority are generally respected and, if not immediately, at least with the passage of time, they acquire by custom and practice, the status of generally binding obligations. That they play an important part in the lawmaking process is beyond question.

Surely, the most realistic and constructive approach to the problem of improving the performance of the Assembly involves (1) taking full advantage of the existing situation in so far as it contributes to the development of a more effective decision-making organ, (2) minimizing the disadvantages, if they cannot be eliminated, and (3) moving forward by taking steps that will promote greater effectiveness. The belief that such forward steps cannot be taken, and, especially the assumption that the principal obstacles are formal, is without foundation. As the following discussion will clearly indicate there are a number of constructive steps that can be taken immediately. Others are perfectly feasible within a reasonable length of time and together these could, within the next twenty-five years, transform the General Assembly into a body capable of performing the legislative function at the international level in a manner far more in keeping with the pressing demands of the world community.

Procedure

Procedural reform, something that is clearly within the competence of the General Assembly under Article 21, is long overdue. This authority can and should be exercised to effectuate modifications in procedure that would at once enhance the performance of the General Assembly. For example discussions in the General Assembly should be governed by more rigid priorities as to the topics to be discussed, and the time allocated to each topic should be in terms of its relative importance. It would also be highly desirable to limit the number of speakers in the general debate at the opening of the

General Assembly. Surely the many days devoted to this more or less routine feature could, for the most part, be put to better use in debating specific issues which call for General Assembly action. Some limitation could be readily achieved by dividing speaking assignments equitably between regional groups under an arrangement for a rotation among the members. Furthermore, the President of the General Assembly should have greater authority to limit the discussion to the topic under consideration. When advisable as, for example, when other topics have a higher priority, a question should be postponed for later consideration and some topics could, perhaps, be discussed on a biennial basis. There should be more general referral of questions to a committee or another organ of the United Nations for consideration without debate. This would be particularly helpful when the topic requires study before a decision can be made. Finally, a much greater emphasis should be placed upon debate for the purpose of reaching agreement rather than for the purpose of taking a vote on the question in order to establish a record in a contest.

These and other procedural changes alone would not only facilitate the work of the General Assembly but they would as an inevitable consequence tend to minimize existing frustrations and, therefore, promote and encourage a greater sense of responsibility on the part of the delegates in the performance of their duties as such.

Committees and Working Groups

The improvement in the performance of the General Assembly that could be achieved by taking the foregoing procedural steps, could be further enhanced by increasing the role of committees of limited size and placing less reliance on committees of the whole. The value of such a practice has already been demonstrated and it merely has to be expanded. Through these committees the General Assembly could be further relieved of some of the burdens it carries during regular sessions.

Permanent committees, to supplement those already functioning, should be established to deal with specific subjects that are of a continuing interest. In addition, the General Assembly could substantially facilitate its work if, at the beginning of each session, it created such additional special committtees or working groups as are necessary to deal with topics not assigned to regular committees. The function of the committees should be to thoroughly prepare the matter for later consideration by the General Assembly, including the drafting of a resolution for submission at the end of debate on the subject. Participation in the work of committees should of course be distributed among the members with each member being entitled to serve on at least one committee.

A Resolutions Committee should certainly be included among the new committees. This committee should consider and, when necessary, revise resolutions coming from other committees for the purpose of making them more acceptable to the General Assembly as a whole. The Resolutions Committee should consist of the permanent members of the Security Council, a number of other major powers, and a number of other states equal to a specified percent of the entire membership as, for example, fifteen percent. The latter should be selected so as to represent various groups of states in accordance with a specified formula. If no resolution were to be considered by the General Assembly unless it had been approved by the Resolutions Committee, the quality of the resolutions would improve and their disposition by approval or rejection facilitated.

Various criteria could be used for the selection of the committees similar to those taken into consideration when dealing with weighted voting to be discussed hereafter. These could and should no doubt vary, depending upon the subject matter with which the committee is concerned. However, the following should no doubt be included: (a) general weighting by population, financial contribution or other evidences of power and influence; (b) geographical areas; and (c) general political association. However, such criteria should be used as general guides and need not be rigidly applied. The important thing is to create a committee that can function effectively and command the confidence of the members. To this end a committee to advise on nominations for committee assignments could play an effective part. Application of these criteria involves no novelty within the United Nations for they have been applied by several of the specialized agencies. For example, the members of the Permanent Executive and Liaison Committee of the Universal Postal Union are elected on a geographical basis and, because entirely different considerations are involved, in the International Bank for Reconstruction and Development the selection of Executive Directors takes special account of the five members having the largest number of shares of stock but leaves the selection of the majority to the other members. The International Civil Aviation Organization provides another approach. In ICAO its Assembly must, in electing members of the Council, give adequate representation to (a) the member states of major importance in air transport, (b) members not otherwise included which make the largest contributions to the provision of facilities for international civil air navigation and (c) those members not otherwise included whose election will ensure that all major geographical areas of the world are represented. Also suggestive is the pattern laid down for the selection of members of the Economic and Social Council. It provides for twelve from Africa and Asia; three from Eastern Europe, five from Latin America; and seven from Western Europe, including the United States and Canada. In this manner, geographical distribution by broad areas is ensured while leaving considerable room for flexibility within each area, including the rotation of membership.

The fact that special criteria are successfully in use within the United Nations family strongly suggests their more general application to committees—committees limited in size and exercising initial responsibility for special areas of General Assembly concern.

The work of committees could be further facilitated if provisions were made for majorities larger than a two-thirds vote, in regard to matters of special importance, and when one or more of the superpowers or a majority of the other major powers is opposed to a resolution. In this manner, it would be possible to provide several voting requirements, depending upon which major powers are in the majority, abstain or oppose a resolution. Such voting rules could be adopted without amending the Charter as they do not affect the voting procedure of the General Assembly as a whole.

Such committees provide several advantages. One advantage is that of being able to meet as frequently as is required, whether the Assembly is in session or not, and they are small enough to transact business efficiently, especially if the chairmen are given the authority to limit the discussion to the topic under consideration. Equally important is the fact that, in the selection of members, added weight can be given to the major powers and to blocs. This practice would serve to reconcile the uneven distribution of power with the universal demand for equality among members and would at the same time improve the work of the Assembly. And even these committees could more generally delegate to subcommittees the conduct of hearings and the drafting of documents.

Such committees would provide a better forum for the consideration of controversial issues, for the careful examination of the various factors involved and for the reconciliation of differences. And approval of a proposal by the committee would generally give it a sounder status when submitted to the Assembly as a whole. And yet, in the Assembly, all members would have an opportunity to pass upon it. When so adopted, a proposal would represent consensus based upon the vote in the committee as well as in the plenary body. The "product", whether it be called a recommendation, quasi-legislation or legislation would obviously be qualitatively superior and would be recognized as such.

Subsidiary Organs

The General Assembly could substantially improve its performance through the greater use of existing subsidiary organs and the creation of new ones to perform important functions of a continuing nature. An example of the former is the International Law Commission, which consists of twenty-five members who serve in their personal capacities as experts in international law and not as representatives of governments. This important organ, established to assist the General Assembly in fulfilling its responsibility under Article 13 of the Charter to encourage "the progressive development of international law and its codification", has already made a good beginning in both directions. Among its achievements are drafts of a Declaration on Rights and Duties of States and a Code of Offenses Against the Peace and Security of Mankind. No final action was taken, however, on either of these drafts. They may nevertheless be considered as "major pieces of international legislation" because, even if they did not result in multilateral conventions, everyone confronted with a treaty law question will turn first and will almost certainly give priority to the International Law Commission draft. Other examples of its constructive work are concerned with the law of the sea and the monumental task of formulating the law of treaties.

The Commission should be substantially strengthened so as to be in a position to assume an even greater responsibility for the development and codification of international law. Although its major emphasis has been on the preparation of draft conventions, it has prepared texts in other forms. It might well play a constructive part in the legislative or quasi-legislative processes by being requested to submit recommendations on, or drafts of, proposed legislation.

In order to strengthen the Commission, consideration might well be given to the advisability of (1) providing for longer sessions, (2) putting the Commission on a full time basis, (3) providing more adequate compensation for the staff, (4) securing greater support from the Secretariat, and (5) possible modifications in geographical representation.

The work of the International Law Commission could and should be augmented by the creation of a World Law Commission authorized to prepare for General Assembly consideration, declarations developing rules of world law which are needed to implement the provisions of the Charter. Probably the most practical way to accomplish this purpose is to convert the Special Committee on Principles of International Law Concerning Friendly Relations and Cooperation Among States, into such a body.

This Committee, with a present membership of thirty-one, was created by the General Assembly to further aid it in carrying out its responsibility for the progressive development and codification of international law. Altogether, the General Assembly has identified seven principles as being embraced within the area of the Committee's responsibility. These are (1) the principle that states should refrain from the threat or use of force in international relations, (2) the principle of the peaceful settlement of disputes, (3) the duty not to intervene in matters within the domestic jurisdiction of a state, (4) the principle of sovereign equality of states, (5) the duty of states to cooperate with one another in accordance with the Charter, (6) the principle of the equal rights and self-determination of peoples, and (7) the principle that states shall fulfill in good faith the obligations assumed by them in accordance with the Charter. The Committee is at present charged with the responsibility of preparing a report in order to enable the Assembly to adopt a declaration concerning these principles.

The Committee's limited size is conducive to meaningful collaboration and yet permits the reflection of the views of a representative cross-section of the entire membership of the General Assembly. Its present assignment is obviously consistent with its conversion into a World Law Commission with broader responsibilities and with an increased capacity to serve the General Assembly in the development of world law.

Finally, there is a great need for a periodic review of the work of the subsidiary organs and their relationship to each other in order to avoid unnecessary duplication of effort and effectuate a greater degree of coordination.

Voting

As has already been indicated, the present method of voting in the General Assembly is the most important barrier in the way of making it a more effective and responsible body. There is no doubt but that the greater use of committees organized and operating as has here been suggested would go a long way toward resolving this problem. However, there is also no doubt about the fact that modification of the voting procedures of the General Assembly itself would be highly desirable and would contribute to its effectiveness. For many purposes the present practice of counting votes on the basis of one-member-one-vote is satisfactory or at least presents no serious problems. The same is true of the present practice of deciding "ordinary" questions by a majority vote and "important" questions by a two-thirds majority vote. This is because on many occasions there is no sharp division of opinion or because "hidden weighting" plays an important part in all General Assembly decisions. The vote of a major power obviously carries more weight in and of itself, and, on most issues, a certain although fluctuating number of members line up with one or another of the major powers. But the extent and effect of such weighting will vary from issue to issue. For example, on a question involving the expenditure of substantial funds the support of major contributors such as the United States is essential. Implementation is impossible without their participation. And an overwhelming majority, minus several of the major powers, or a number of the states primarily concerned may be almost meaningless. Such actions tend to debase the effectiveness of the General Assembly to the detriment of all the members. A much greater emphasis should be placed upon reaching a broad measure of agreement, upon achieving realistic majorities than on merely winning votes. In this way only, can the General Assembly acquire and maintain the confidence and respect that will enable it to speak with authority.

One approach to this problem which does not involve an abandonment of the one-member-one-vote formula, is dual voting. This can be achieved by providing that, on certain specified questions—questions that require a more realistic consensus, decisions must be reached by obtaining the requisite majority both by the one-member-one vote method, and by some form of weighted voting which would take account of such factors as population or economic strength as indicated by national income, and contributions to the United Nations budget.* For example, votes may be distributed in accordance with the populations or the national incomes of the members or a combination of both. But weighting need not, if indeed it can, be determined with precision because power reflects both tangibles and intangibles, varies from issue to issue, and fluctuates with the passage of time. International organizations have already demonstrated that weighting can be satisfactorily based upon such measurements to provide practical limits within which changes in power status are absorbed by political rather than legal adjustments..

Under such a method the vote can of course be taken simultaneously but recorded separately. By restricting dual voting to certain questions, where the composition of the vote is crucial, much of the activity of the General Assembly could be carried on with votes taken as at present. And weighting could, if thought desirable, be based on different criteria for different classes of decisions. However, the availability of an alternative method as a recognized feature of General Assembly procedure could facilitate the reflection by vote of a consensus much more likely to achieve widespread acceptance and effective implementation.

Two House System

Another method of recording a broader consensus is through a two house system analogous to the two house system in the United States. Although consideration of this alternative may not at first appear to be within the purview of this paper, which is concerned with the General Assembly, its primary thrust is that of advancing the *legislative capacity* of that body. Certainly a shared responsibility merits consideration if it will increase the legislative capacity of the General Assembly.

---

* For a fuller consideration of weighted voting see discussions by Louis B. Sohn and Catherine Senf in the Ninth Report of the Commission entitled *Charter Review Conference* (1955).

One application of this proposal is to require the concurrence of the Security Council on certain questions. Such a step would of course not be without precedent, for the Charter provides for such joint action in the ratification of amendments to the Charter; in the admission, suspension or expulsion of members; in the election of the Secretary-General; and in the election of judges to the International Court of Justice. To be practicable the concurring vote in the Security Council on such questions would have to be by a prescribed majority and excluding the veto of the five major powers.

Another example of participation by the Security Council and the General Assembly is a proposal by Richard Hudson *
for peacekeeping questions. Under his proposal a decision on peacekeeping would require a majority constituted as follows: (1) ten members of the Security Council and (2) two-thirds of the members of the General Assembly, including (3) 51 percent of the world's population. However, his plan also includes an injunctive vote by the International Court of Justice which, by a majority of ten of its fifteen members, could prohibit any peacekeeping action.

A third approach is one proposed by Louis Sohn. Under his proposal the United Nations would establish permanent direct liaison with National Parliaments which are in fact the source of the United Nations financial support. He proposes the creation, by the Assembly, of a Consultative Parliamentary Conference, to include three representatives from each parliament and additional representation to a maximum of twenty-five, based on population and contributions to the United Nations. The Conference would meet concurrently with the Assembly, advise it on budgeting and financial matters, consider the annual report of the Secretary-General and maintain liaison with national parliaments and the International Parliamentary Union.

A final step would involve the establishment of a World Parliamentary Assembly to share responsibility with the Gen-

---

* *War/Peace Report,* February, 1964.

eral Assembly in the exercise of the legislative power concerning matters of special importance. This could be achieved by requiring the concurrent votes of both bodies in respect to specified matters. The Parliamentary Assembly would represent the peoples of the world directly rather than the governments but the General Assembly would still play an important role in which legislation at the international level would be an important factor.

Legislation

So far very little has been said about legislation, notwithstanding the fact that enhancing the legislative capacity of the General Assembly is the objective of this discussion. This is because, as was pointed out in the beginning, the basic problems today are not formal legal limitations. That the General Assembly has the authority to make important decisions is beyond question. That it has legislative authority in certain limited areas and, that some of its decisions are quasi-legislative in character, are also beyond question. With all its limitations, it has in fact contributed significantly to the development of international law. The foregoing discussion has been concerned with the removal of some of these limitations, because this will improve its decision-making capacity, and, as one important consequence, lay a firmer foundation for the development of its role as a legislative body.

However, helpful as these steps will be, it is not necessary for the General Assembly to wait until they have been realized, either in whole or in part, in order to move forward in the development of its lawmaking function. Relying on past achievements that are a matter of record, it can and should at once come to grips with the problems now facing the world community. It is this affirmative approach that has made possible the excellent beginnings in dealing with the problems of outer space, and that gives promise of a similar role in the development of a regime for the constructive utilization of the resources of the sea and the seabed. But the General Assembly must also deal far more effectively with the ever mounting problems in the more traditional areas of activity as to which international solutions are indispensible. Crises, if responsibly met, are the very stuff out of which growth emerges. In this manner, the gap between quasi-legislation and legislation can be progressively narrowed, with full legislative capacity in certain specified areas of obviously international concern as the ultimate outcome. If, at some point, as is likely, amendment of the Charter becomes necessary, this will at that time not present an insuperable obstacle.

Viewed in this light the prospect is not without promise. Some significant steps are possible now. If these are taken promptly, others will then also become feasible. Among the steps that may be taken now or in the immediate future are the following, but they are not necessarily discussed in the order of priority or feasibility.

1. In the first place, the General Assembly should promptly take steps to improve the procedure applicable to the processing and adoption of international conventions. The cumbersome and time consuming treaty process upon which so much reliance is now placed, and a process that will undoubtedly continue to play an important role in the development of international law, can and should be simplified and improved.

At present, whenever a treaty or convention is involved, one of the important shortcomings in the procedure followed is that, even after the usual arduous and time consuming process of drafting and adoption, there is further delay, or even failure, at the stage of ratification. Although the member state may be opposed to the convention in question, the delay is often due to inertia and the complicated machinery involved in the ratification process. In addition, governments and their parliaments are disposed to consider international conventions as of less immediate political importance than domestic matters. If a convention is regarded as a matter that can wait, postponement may follow postponement. In addition, governments are inclined to wait to see how other states respond, thus creating a situation in which further delay is inevitable.

Although the individual states themselves could and no doubt should improve their ratification procedures, the General Assembly could in effect put pressure upon the members to act more promptly by the adoption of a general recommendation to the effect that all conventions be submitted to the proper national authorities for consideration within a specified time as, for example, one year. Such a recommendation might also include a provision calling for a report to the General Assembly on the status of the matter at the expiration of the time specified, if by then the convention had not been ratified. This procedure is of course not novel. Not only is it common among the specialized agencies but it has been applied by the General Assembly itself to specific conventions. What is here suggested is action to apply such a procedure to all conventions promulgated by the United Nations. This could be effectuated by a recommendation of the General Assembly addressed to all members, and to non-members. The absence of political implications suggests that such a recommendation might well receive general approval and be followed in practice.

As a further step in the improvement of the treaty process the General Assembly should have the power similar to that of some other international organizations, to monitor compliance with, and the interpretation and enforcement of, international conventions adopted under its auspices. The well established practice of the International Labor Organization for facilitating the ratification of conventions and for monitoring their implementation is an instructive example.

Briefly stated the ILO procedure is as follows: Member states are required to bring every convention adopted by the ILO conference before their competent national authorities within one year or, in exceptional cases, not more than eighteen months after its adoption. They are also required to inform the ILO Director-General of the measures they have taken to comply with this requirement and, when a convention is ratified, to so advise the Director-General. Member states which have not ratified a convention within the specified time are requested to report periodically indicating the difficulties that are preventing or delaying ratification or the extent to which their law and practice has given effect to any of the provisions of the convention.*

2. The foregoing steps give the General Assembly an opportunity to improve one of the important traditional methods of creating international law. It can also move forward significantly in reliance on the provisions of the United Nations Charter. To begin with it should adopt a declaration specifically calling attention to the fact that the Charter of the United Nations (under Article 103) prevails over all other international agreements and also over conflicting provisions of national constitutions and laws. Members who have not as yet conformed their domestic laws to the provisions of the Charter should be reminded of their obligation to do so.

3. The General Assembly should declare that regulations when duly adopted are binding on all the member states which have not specifically rejected them within a specified time. The well established procedures in the International Civil Aviation Organization and in the World Health Organization clearly indicate their practicability and their effectiveness. In ICAO a regulation adopted by a two-thirds vote of the Council becomes effective within a specified time after submission to the members, unless a majority register their disapproval with the Council within a specified time. In WHO regulations adopted by the Health Assembly come into force for all members after due notice of their adoption, except for such members as notify the Director-General of their rejection or of reservations within the period stated in the notice.

4. A good beginning has been made in the field of human rights. A comprehensive Human Rights Code, giving protection to all individuals throughout the world should be prepared and adopted. The code should include all previously

---

* For a fuller discussion of ratification procedures see Roberto Ago, (A/CN. 4/205/Rev. 1; 29 July 1968.)

adopted provisions and any additions needed to fill existing gaps.

5. The drafts of the Code of Offenses Against the Peace and Security of Mankind and the Statute for an International Criminal Court, should be completed and adopted. These highly significant documents were prepared for the Assembly by the International Law Commission and a special committee respectively, and have since been considered by a succession of committees of the General Assembly. However, to date, outstanding difficulties, including a definition of aggression, have not been resolved. There can be no doubt that a renewed and determined effort should be made to resolve the problems involved so the Statute and the Code may be considered by the General Assembly and adopted.

6. The General Assembly should proclaim that it has the power to adopt declarations for the development of rules of world law necessary to implement the provisions of the Charter, after they have been prepared and submitted by the World Law Commission. To become binding such declarations would of course require adoption by large majorities as, for example, a unanimous vote or a four-fifths majority, including the permanent members of the Security Council. The General Assembly should also declare that the rules of world law should be binding not only on States but, where appropriate, on all self-governing communities, international organizations, public and private associations and individuals.

Four

Peaceful Settlement of Disputes
by
Louis B. Sohn

I. Introduction

The practice of the United Nations distinguishes between peacekeeping and peacemaking. One of the objections to strengthening the peacekeeping arrangements of the United Nations is that the result would be to perpetuate the *status quo,* to freeze many unjust situations, and to deny redress to those who wish to change inequitable conditions imposed upon them by force in the past and who have to resort themselves to force in order to achieve the desired results.

To prevent the use of force as a means for change in international relations, peaceful methods must be devised for obtaining change and for settling international disputes before they lead to a breach of peace. The Charter of the United Nations provides parallel obligations in Article 2 with respect to the use of force in international relations and the settlement of international disputes by peaceful means "in such a manner that international peace and security, and justice, are not endangered." In a similar parallel fashion the Charter lists as the primary purpose of the United Nations the maintenance of peace through effective collective measures and through adjustment or settlement of international disputes or situations which might lead to a breach of the peace "by peaceful means, and in conformity with the principles of justice and international law." To implement these provisions, the Charter empowers the General Assembly and the Security Council to recommend various measures (Articles 11, 14, 33-38). But the basic obligation of the Charter is directly imposed on the parties to any dispute the continuance of which is likely to endanger the maintenance of international peace and security. Under Article 33 of the Charter they "shall, first of all seek a solution by negotiation, enquiry, mediation, conciliation, arbitration, judicial settlement, resort to regional agencies or arrangements, or other peaceful means of their own choice."

It is not possible to explore in this essay all these methods of settlement. It seems, therefore, most important to concentrate on the possible improvement in those methods which can lead to a binding decision which may then be enforced on the recalcitrant party. In addition, in view of the current interest in methods of fact-finding, investigation and conciliation, some suggestions will also be made with respect to these areas.

Obligations for peaceful settlement of disputes may be accepted by a variety of means: through accepting the optional clause in the Statute of the International Court of Justice; through accepting a multilateral treaty on peaceful settlement of disputes, such as the 1928 Geneva General Act on the Pacific Settlement of International Disputes which was slightly revised by the United Nations in 1949; through a bilateral treaty on peaceful settlement, similar to those concluded recently by Switzerland with several States of Africa; or through a so-called compromissory clause in a bilateral or multilateral treaty which submits to peaceful settlement disputes relating to the interpretation or application of that particular treaty.

While each of these methods has its merits, the most comprehensive way for providing a variety of methods for a variety of disputes is that pioneered by the Geneva General Act, mentioned above, and followed by several regional instruments such as the American Treaty of Pacific Settlement (Pact of Bogota) of 1948, the European Convention for the Peaceful Settlement of Disputes of 1957, and the Protocol of the Commission of Mediation, Conciliation and Arbitration of the Organization of African Unity of 1964. It would seem desirable to systematize the various procedures outlined in these and other treaties as well as those developed by various international organizations, and to embody them in one comprehensive instrument. The revision of the Geneva General Act in 1949 was merely formal and took place at a time when the United Nations membership was much smaller than today. The preparation of a new General Act would not only result in a more modern instrument including new means for the settlement of disputes developed since 1928, but also would acquaint the new Members of the United Nations with the problems involved in peacemaking. Such a new Act should permit a step-by-step approach; it should provide many options from a minimum step to a most comprehensive approach. In providing a whole series of procedures, it should permit selective acceptance of only some of them, and should allow further options with respect to the types of situations to be included in the obligation, and with respect to States or groups of States to which a particular State would be bound by a particular procedure. Some of the many possible options are explored below.

II. Judicial Settlement

The most effective means for a definitive settlement of certain types of international disputes is a binding decision of an international court. Though there are a few regional tribunals with restricted jurisdiction, there is only one tribunal with universal jurisdiction—the International Court of Justice. The jurisdiction of that Court is limited to legal disputes between States, the four basic categories of which are enumerated in Article 36 of the Statute of the Court, as relating to the following questions:

"a. the interpretation of a treaty;

"b. any question of international law;

"c. the existence of any fact which, if established, would constitute a breach of an international obligation;

"d. the nature or extent of the reparation to be made for the breach of an international obligation."

At present less than one-third of the Members of the United Nations and a few non-members have accepted the jurisdiction under the optional clause contained in that Article, and many of them included crippling reservations in their declarations of acceptance. For instance, the United States has excluded from the jurisdiction of the Court disputes "with regard to matters which are essentially within the domestic jurisdiction of the United States of America as determined by the United States of America"; and the United States has actually invoked this reservation in the Interhandel Case brought by Switzerland against the United States. While States should retain the option to accept this broad jurisdictional clause, it is obvious that the categories listed in it are too extensive and many States seem to be reluctant, in particular, to accept the jurisdiction of the Court with respect to "any question of international law." Other options need, therefore, be opened to States, permitting more limited acceptance of the Court's jurisdiction, without need for nullifying reservations. Four lines of approach might be explored in this connection:

1. Acceptance of the jurisdiction of the International Court of Justice over disputes relating to the interpretation and application of treaties.

2. Acceptance of the jurisdiction of the International Court of Justice over specified areas of international law.

3. Acceptance of the jurisdiction of the Court through regional arrangements.

4. Granting to the United Nations the power to make a binding request that parties to a dispute refer the matter to the International Court of Justice.

1. *Disputes concerning treaties.* Some five hundred treaties, including many multilateral ones, have already conferred on the International Court of Justice or its predecessor, the Permanent Court of International Justice, jurisdiction to decide disputes relating to their interpretation or application.[1] Prac-

---

[1] International Law Association, *Report of the Fifty-first Conference* (Tokyo, 1964), p. 83.

tically every State in the world, including most of those States of Africa, Asia and Eastern Europe which have not accepted the jurisdiction of the Court under the optional clause in the Statute of the Court, has accepted that jurisdiction under several of these treaties. It should be possible, therefore, to persuade most States to approve a jurisdictional clause limited to the interpretation and application of international agreements to which they are parties. It is generally accepted that questions relating to the interpretation and application of treaties do not raise issues of domestic jurisdiction, and there would be no need, therefore, to make any reservations to an agreement conferring jurisdiction on the Court to interpret treaties only. As treaties in a sense codify international law as understood by the parties to them, no strong disagreements can arise with respect to the question whether a particular rule has been accepted by the parties to the dispute. Current controversies concerning the existence of more or less definite rules of international law in various areas should not prevent the approval by States of an agreement which is limited to treaties voluntarily accepted by States.

In drafting the clause relating to treaty jurisdiction, several supplementary options are possible. States might be permitted to exclude disputes relating not strictly to the interpretation of an international agreement but to its validity or to the right to terminate because of a change in circumstances. Some States might wish to limit their acceptance to interpretation of treaties only, excluding questions of their application. Another option might allow distinction between old and new treaties. Some States might accept the clause with respect only to future treaties, others might exclude those concluded before a specified date such as, for instance, the date of coming into force of the United Nations Charter (24 October 1945).

2. *Disputes concerning specified areas of international law.* The emphasis on the treaty option need not preclude additional options in the vast area of customary international law. But in that area also a selective, gradual approach might be preferable to a stark all-or-nothing alternative. The reluctance of States to accept the jurisdiction of the International Court

of Justice is often due to some special problems about which they are worried. Almost every State has some skeletons in its closet and might not wish to have them exposed before the Court. Even if States could avoid some difficulties through reservations, they are usually afraid that they might have forgotten something important or that some new problems might arise which could not have been covered by specific reservations. It is this fear of unforeseen consequences which has led some States in the past to a refusal to accept the jurisdiction of the Court or to its acceptance with sweeping, open-ended reservations.

Perhaps it might be easier for States to accept the jurisdiction of the Court if they could be given greater freedom to select more precisely the areas of international law in which the Court would acquire jurisdiction over them. If a list of subjects covered by international law could be prepared, the States would have a chance to pick and choose; they might accept the jurisdiction of the Court with respect to some subjects without hesitation, and would be able to postpone their acceptance concerning other subjects. Thus, in sensitive areas where the views on law differ greatly among States, there would be no acceptance of the Court's jurisdiction, while in other areas it might be accepted immediately by most States of the world.[2]

Such a list might include only a few broad topics or it could deal with many specific topics such as the following ones:

1. Recognition of States
2. Recognition of governments
3. Succession of States
4. Succession of governments
5. Acquisition of territory
6. Boundaries of States
7. Leased territories
8. International servitudes

---

[2] For a summary of similar proposals, see *ibid.*, pp. 87-89.

9. Inviolability of national territory
10. Ports and inland waters
11. International rivers and lakes
12. Territorial waters
13. Contiguous zones
14. Continental shelf
15. International canals and straits
16. Regime of the high seas
17. Fisheries
18. Whaling and sealing
19. Air navigation
20. Polar regions
21. Regime of outer space
22. Nationality and status of ships
23. Piracy
24. Slavery
25. International traffic in women and children
26. International traffic in narcotic drugs
27. Nationality and statelessness
28. Admission of aliens
29. Position of aliens
30. Expulsion of aliens
31. Treatment of foreign corporations
32. Violations of contracts between States and aliens
33. Asylum
34. Extradition
35. Responsibility of States for injuries to aliens
36. Denial of justice
37. Commercial relations
38. International communications
39. Protection of minorities
40. Protection of human rights
41. Immunity of States, and of their agencies and subdivisions
42. Privileges and immunities of heads of States
43. Privileges and immunities of foreign ministers and their deputies
44. Diplomatic privileges and immunities
45. Consular privileges and immunities

46. Status, privileges and immunities of international organizations
47. Status of armed forces on foreign territory
48. Jurisdiction over nationals abroad
49. Limits of criminal jurisdiction
50. Enforcement of foreign judgments and commercial arbitral awards
51. Validity of international agreements
52. Interpretation and application of international agreements
53. Termination of international agreements
54. Validity and interpretation of international arbitral awards
55. Pacific blockade
56. Reprisals
57. Indirect aggression and subversion
58. Relations between belligerents
59. Relations between belligerents and neutrals
60. Violations of the laws of war

This list is, of course, not an exhaustive one and many additional subjects could easily be listed. Should a State be willing to make its acceptance cover not only the subjects listed above but also all remaining subjects, so much the better. A question might arise with respect to the dividing line between international customary law and international treaty law, and in some cases acceptance of the jurisdiction of the Court over a particular subject might extend not only to international customary law but also to relevant treaties. It may also be noted that some categories overlap; for instance, the subject "Responsibility of States for injuries to aliens" includes as well such topics as "Denial of justice", "Treatment of foreign corporations", and "Expulsion of aliens". Some States might find the broader subject unacceptable to them at the beginning, but might be willing to accept the jurisdiction of the Court over expulsion of aliens; on the other hand, those accepting the broader one would find no difficulty in accepting at the same time the other ones, so that the Court would have jurisdiction with respect to both groups of States over subjects covered by their declarations of acceptance.

Again a variety of further options is possible. As a minimum, one could require that each State, on becoming a party to the agreement, should accept the Court's jurisdiction over a specified number of areas (for instance, ten out of the sixty areas here suggested). There might also be an obligation to consider from time to time (for instance, at ten-year intervals) the possibility of accepting the jurisdiction of the Court with respect to further subjects and to report to the United Nations in case of a negative decision. As States do not like to submit such negative reports whenever they can avoid it, this procedure would put additional pressure on them to make a positive decision extending their acceptance of the jurisdiction of the Court to new areas.

A greater commitment might also be considered. The parties might bind themselves in the initial agreement not only to accept at least ten subjects in the initial declaration, but also to accept at least ten more at stated intervals (for instance, at the end of each ten-year period after the coming into force of the agreement). In this manner, assuming an initial acceptance of ten subjects, the whole area of the above mentioned subjects would be covered after the expiration of five periods (in our example, after fifty years).

Under either alternative, States would have a chance to select first subjects which are least likely to involve a danger to their vital interests, and to postpone more "dangerous" areas until later. Though the jurisdiction of the Court over each pair of States would be based on the acceptance by both of them of at least one common subject, it is likely that many States will put the same value judgment on various categories of subjects and that from the very beginning the Court will acquire jurisdiction over many pairs of States in several areas. With additional acceptances in later years, the jurisdiction of the Court would constantly broaden, and the likelihood that the Court would not be able to exercise jurisdiction in a particular case would progressively diminish.

3. *Disputes with a specified group of States.* In antici-pating "dangerous" international disputes, governments worry not only about the subject-matter of the possible disputes, but also about the parties to them. It is relatively easy to contem-plate going to the International Court of Justice in a dispute with a friendly State, and a government does not mind being able to bring to the Court a good case against an adversary. It is the other side of the coin that scares governments: the possibility that an unfriendly State would use the Court to harass the government which has accepted the Court's juris-diction with respect to all other States, without excluding in some way all potential enemies. Some States might prefer, therefore, to limit their commitments to go to the Court to States with which they have long-standing ties of friendship and as to which no bitter disputes should be anticipated.

While the United States might be afraid to have disputes brought to the Court against it by Communist nations (assum-ing they ever accept the Court's jurisdiction), it cannot in good conscience object to a decision by the Court in a case involving one of its closest allies. The only thing which is nec-essary here is to forget the old-fashioned notion that it might endanger our relations with our friends if we bring cases against them, or if they bring cases against us, to the Court. In most legal disputes, the points involved do not concern any vital interests of either side, but both sides believe that they have a valid legal point which they do not want to give up in bilateral negotiations. For instance, neither the Congress nor the people of the United States would rise in arms if the United States and the United Kingdom should submit the long-standing dispute about Christmas Island in the Pacific to the Court for final decision; or if the United States and Canada would submit a question of interpretation of an extradition treaty to the Court.

It would seem useful, therefore, to give States an option to accept the jurisdiction of the Court over all (or some) legal disputes, not with respect to everybody but with respect to selected groups of States (for instance, partners in various alliances or parties to certain treaties) or with respect to specified States only. Each State accepting this obligation might be bound to list at least ten States to which this obligation would apply, and there might be the additional option of agreeing in advance to increase the list by at least ten more States every ten years after the original acceptance. In this way, the circle of States with respect to which the obligation will be binding would extend slowly to most of them. Of course, such an obligation would apply only to States accepting the same obligation, and, to confer jurisdiction, it would be necessary that the names of the parties to a particular dispute appear, respectively, on the lists of both parties to that dispute.

4. *Disputes referred to the Court by the United Nations.* Article 36, paragraph 3, of the Charter of the United Nations provides that, in recommending appropriate procedures for the settlement of a dispute referred to it, the Security Council "should also take into consideration that legal disputes should as a general rule be referred by the parties to the International Court of Justice." Such a recommendation was in fact made by the Security Council in the Corfu Channel Case, and that recommendation seems to have contributed to the acceptance by Albania of the jurisdiction of the Court. There is, however, no general obligation to accept such a recommendation of the Security Council, or a similar recommendation of the General Assembly under Articles 11 and 35. While the International Court of Justice found it unnecessary to pass on that question in its judgment in the Court Channel Case, a separate opinion by seven judges pointed out that the contention of the United Kingdom that Article 36 of the Charter conferred jurisdiction on the Court was unjustified.

It would be an important step forward, if States could be given an option to accept a recommendation of the Security Council under Article 36 (3) of the Charter as binding upon them. Only if both parties to a dispute should accept such a clause, one of them could ask the Security Council to recommend that the case be referred to the Court; and such a recommendation would constitute a sufficient basis for the Court's jurisdiction because of the prior acceptance by the parties of this optional provision. As between those who have accepted this option, the recommendations of the Security Council would thus acquire an additional force not conferred upon them by the Charter.

While the Charter does not expressly provide that the General Assembly has the power to request the parties to refer a legal question to the International Court of Justice, it can be safely assumed that, if a dispute is referred to the General Assembly under Article 35 of the Charter, and the Security Council is not simultaneously exercising in respect of that dispute the functions assigned to it in the Charter (Article 12 of the Charter), the General Assembly can make any recommendations to the States concerned which it considers appropriate (Article 11, paragraph 2). Consequently, if an important legal question is involved in a dispute, the General Assembly would be entitled to request the parties to refer that question to the Court and to postpone the consideration of other aspects of the case until the matter is decided by the Court. As in the case of the Security Council, it would help if States were willing to accept in advance such requests of the General Assembly as binding upon them and as constituting a sufficient basis for the jurisdiction of the Court over them. [3] It might be a condition of such an acceptance that the General Assembly should consider any such reference to the Court as an "important question", requiring a two-thirds majority of the members present and voting (Article 18). If even such a majority should not be considered as a sufficient safeguard by some of the parties to this optional provision, they might condition their acceptance of the obligation to go to the Court on such other majorities as may be specified in their declarations of acceptance. For instance, to give to the decision of the General Assembly a greater weight, it might be specified that the two-thirds majority should include the

---

[3] It might be recalled that in the Italian Peace Treaty the parties agreed to accept as binding the decision of the General Assembly with respect to the future of the former Italian colonies. 49 *United Nations Treaty Series*, pp. 214-15.

concurring votes of a majority of a certain group of States (for example, a majority of the five permanent members of the Security Council or a majority of the fifteen members of the United Nations having the largest populations).

The option to accept a recommendation of the General Assembly may be a separate one from that relating to the recommendations of the Security Council; States might be given the option to accept as binding the recommendations referring a matter to the Court made by either the Security Council or the General Assembly or both. It is quite conceivable that some States would be willing to confer such power on the Security Council but not on the General Assembly and *vice versa*.

An agreement accepting the jurisdiction of the Court in case of a recommendation of the Security Council or of the General Assembly would remove the possible fear of some nations that, by accepting the present optional clause in the Statute of the Court, they would open themselves wide to many frivolous claims by other States which would bring before the Court any grievances they may have regardless of their legal merits. The proposed agreements would require a preliminary determination by the Security Council or the General Assembly that the dispute is serious and that important legal issues are actually involved. It is not likely that either the Council or the Assembly would make such determination without carefully considering the whole situation, including the possibility that one of the parties might not accept the decision of the Court. After a while, a line of precedents would be established for determining which types of cases might most usefully be referred to the Court and in which ones other means of settlement might prove more fruitful.

III. Arbitration

Until the establishment of permanent international courts, arbitration served as the basic method for settling international disputes, with an emphasis on legal disputes. Even after the establishment of the Permanent Court of International Justice at The Hague, and its successor, the International Court of Justice, arbitration continued to be used for the decision of legal controversies. It has been considered more suitable for the settlement of groups of small international claims by individuals, of minor disputes and of disputes not involving an important legal issue. Proceedings before arbitral tribunals are usually less expensive and take less time than those before the International Court of Justice. Normally, they entail less publicity, and the parties have the option of not publishing the award. Finally, the parties to a dispute have more freedom in selecting the members of an arbitral tribunal, while they cannot tinker with the composition of the International Court of Justice, with only some minor exceptions.

Should one wish to retain arbitration as a means of settling legal disputes, a few meaningful distinctions might be established between cases to be referred to the International Court of Justice and those to be submitted to an arbitral tribunal. It might be possible to reserve the Court for major, important disputes, while smaller disputes would be referred to an arbitral tribunal. A distinction might also be made between truly interstate disputes and those involving, in fact, rights of private persons rather than States. In particular, where there are many small disputes relating to private claims, especially those resulting from war or revolution, an arbitral tribunal or a claims commission might seem to be a more suitable device. But even here one could distinguish between important issues of international law (such as those relating to denial of justice, exhaustion of local remedies, expropriation, law of treaties, or the regime of the high seas, territorial waters or international rivers), which should be referred to the Court, and the question of the extent of damages to be paid in each individual case which could be better handled by a claims commission or an arbitral tribunal. As the International Court of Justice is not accessible directly to private individuals or corporations, any disputes arising out of international development agreements between States and large international corporations should be brought before an arbitral tribunal. Both the Permanent Court of Arbitration and the new dispute settlement procedure established by the International Bank for Reconstruction and Development provide special facilities for this purpose. Arbitral tribunals or special international courts may also be established to deal with special technical or economic legal questions.

Since the 1920's, especially since the General Act of 1928, a new dividing line has been established. That Act and many other treaties give priority in legal disputes to the Court and reserve an arbitral tribunal primarily for non-legal disputes to be decided *ex aequo et bono* (in accordance with what is equitable and just).[4] Some forty States have by now accepted this formula in one or more agreements, and the same principle has been embodied in all the multilateral treaties on peaceful settlement concluded since 1945.

It would be desirable, therefore, to provide in the new General Act several options for States with respect to the settlement of disputes by arbitration. In the first place, parties to a legal dispute should be allowed to send such a dispute to an arbitral tribunal of their choice. In the second place, various arrangements might be made for non-legal disputes. Parties might accept a tribunal's jurisdiction for all such disputes or for specified categories of them or with respect to a particular group of States. As in case of the jurisdiction of the International Court of Justice, a list of principal categories of disputes might be prepared, and States might accept the jurisdiction of the tribunal for a specified minimum number of categories and might agree to make additional selections from time to time.

In addition, it might prove possible to authorize the General Assembly and the Security Council of the United Nations, to refer, under Articles 14 and 36 of the Charter, any dispute or situation likely to impair the general welfare and friendly relations among nations or likely to endanger the

---

[4] For a list of treaties embodying this formula, see Sohn, "The Function of International Arbitration Today," 108 *Recueil des Cours de l'Académie de Droit International* (1963-I), p. 1, at 36-40.

maintenance of international peace and security, to an arbitral tribunal. The States accepting this option would agree to accept as binding upon them a recommendation of the General Assembly or the Security Council that a particular dispute between them be submitted to arbitration, and would authorize the establishment of the tribunal and the modalities of the arbitration in accordance with a procedure agreed upon in advance and to be embodied in the new General Act. This procedure might follow either the provisions of the 1949 General Act or those of the Model Rules of Arbitral Procedure prepared by the International Law Commission in 1958.

It would simplify the arbitration problem greatly if the United Nations could be authorized to establish one permanent arbitral tribunal to which could be transferred all jurisdiction to arbitrate disputes already existing under many arbitration treaties and under special arbitral clauses in various multilateral and bilateral treaties. In addition, the General Assembly or the Security Council could refer to that tribunal the disputes mentioned in the previous paragraph.

It has been also suggested [5] that another optional clause might empower such a permanent arbitral (or equity) tribunal to render advisory opinions with respect to disputes referred to it by the General Assembly or the Security Council of the United Nations. States would have thus an option to have a case referred to the tribunal for a binding decision, as discussed above, or for an advisory opinion. Another option might permit the General Assembly or Security Council to ratify the recommendations for the settlement embodied in such an advisory opinion and to enforce them as if they were decisions of the International Court of Justice, by analogy to Article 94 of the Charter. At present, there is no express provision for the executions of the international arbitral awards, and the decisions of the General Assembly and the Security Council under Article 11, 14 and 33-38 of the

---

[5] For a summary of various proposals, see International Law Association, *Report of the Fifty-Second Conference* (Helsinki, 1966), pp. 347-56.

Charter are merely recommendations. The new procedure would result in a binding decision, provided three conditions had been fulfilled: the General Assembly or the Security Council has decided that a particular dispute can best be settled by the arbitral tribunal, the tribunal has investigated the matter and approved specific recommendations for the settlement of the dispute, and the General Assembly or the Security Council has found the proposed settlement satisfactory.

Here again various additional options are possible with respect to the scope of the jurisdiction to be thus conferred on the tribunal. In addition, States might be permitted to restrict the power to approve the tribunal's recommendations to the General Assembly or to the Security Council, and might specify the vote in these bodies which would be required to render a final, binding decision.

It would be premature to speculate at this time as to the composition and procedure of the proposed tribunal, but the hope may be expressed that the tribunal would be closely connected with the Permanent Court of Arbitration, and that the members of the tribunal would be chosen from the members of that Court, perhaps by a process similar to that used in the election of members of the International Court of Justice.

The proposed tribunal could investigate carefully all the relevant facts and prepare a decision or an advisory opinion which would try to balance the interests of both sides. In a case in which one side would have to make a greater sacrifice than the other, the tribunal might arrange for a reasonable compensation or for some other benefit, either temporary or permanent, which would make it easier for that side to accept the award or opinion. The proposed solution might also require some other States not directly involved in the dispute to take certain action in the interests of peace which would make the suggested settlement more acceptable to the parties.

It needs to be stressed, in conclusion, that the proposed tribunal would not be imposed on anybody. Its jurisdiction with respect to any particular State would depend on that

State's voluntary acceptance, made in accordance with its own constitutional processes. The establishment of the tribunal would, however, provide all the States of the world with an additional means of solving their disputes, and they might find it useful to resort to it in cases in which the legal issues are submerged in the political ones or in which a question of peaceful change is raised rather than a problem of interpretation of existing rules of international law. At the same time, the Security Council and the General Assembly of the United Nations would have available to them a new method for finding an objective basis for any decision they might be entitled to take with respect to a dispute under the existing provisions of the Charter. If some States should be willing to go even further and allow these United Nations bodies to make a final determination based on the tribunal's advice, this option would bring us even closer to a world in which the rule of law will be tempered by justice.

IV. Fact-finding, Investigation and Conciliation

Most treaties on the pacific settlement of international disputes provide not only for judicial settlement and arbitration but also for conciliation, and there are in addition special treaties providing only for inquiry and conciliation or for investigation or fact-finding. In many disputes the United Nations has established special investigation commissions or has resorted to conciliation and mediation. A large number of treaties provides for permanent conciliation commissions, usually composed of five members. The General Assembly of the United Nations established in 1949 a panel for inquiry and conciliation, from which members of future commissions were to be chosen. A center for international fact-finding has also been suggested.[6]

The options in this area can thus include acceptance of conciliation for the settlement of all or certain disputes, with respect to all States or only some of them. In addition, the

---

[6] Schurmann, *A Center for International Fact Finding: A Review and a Proposal* (New York, Columbia University, 1963), pp. 26-28.

United Nations might be authorized to establish a Permanent Conciliation Commission, composed of eminently qualified persons, such as former Presidents of the General Assembly or former permanent representatives of States to the United Nations with long periods of effective service and with experience in United Nations investigative procedures.

Should a dispute arise between two Members of the United Nations who are not bound to submit that dispute to arbitration or judicial settlement, and should the parties fail to agree within a certain period on the composition of a conciliation commission, the Permanent Conciliation Commission should be able to step in on request of one of the parties or of the General Assembly or the Security Council of the United Nations (under Articles 14 and 33 of the Charter of the United Nations). In particular, it might be possible to transfer to this new Commission, by a clause similar to Article 37 of the Statute of the International Court of Justice, the jurisdiction conferred on conciliation commissions by several hundreds of treaties now in force, and thus avoid the need for a constant stream of appointments to membership of the bipartite commissions which are required under the existing system.

During the consideration of a dispute, the Commission should be entitled, if nationals of one or more of the parties are not members of the Commission, to co-opt one or more members of the panel who have been appointed to the panel by the parties to the dispute. Such a commission, with a permanent core but sufficient flexibility, should be able to accumulate the necessary experience and prestige which would make its use more frequent and its work increasingly effective.

V. Conclusions

It is the important characteristic of modern international law that it is flexible and amenable to change. In recent years, we have seen a great flourishing of new ways for applying traditional methods for settling international disputes. This paper has tried to explore the many suggestions which have been made and to extract those which would add further flexibility to the existing system. A variety of possible options has been considered with respect to three principal means for dispute settlement. Other means are, of course, available, and many additional options are possible. The crucial point is to realize that by broadening the range of possibilities encouragement is given to States, however timid they might have been in the past, to take tentative steps in the right direction. Should they find that these steps did not get them into grave danger, they might be willing to take further steps, until in due course they should find it possible to accept most of the options and to join a comprehensive and effective system for the settlement of international disputes.

Five

Peacekeeping And Peacemaking
by
Richard N. Swift*

The Problem Is Urgent

From the information . . . available to me as Secretary-General, [I can only conclude] that the Members of the United Nations have perhaps 10 years left in which to subordinate their ancient quarrels and launch a global partnership to curb the arms race, to improve the human environment, to defuse the population explosion, and to supply the required momentum to world development efforts.[1]

The Secretary-General, in making this statement did not wish to seem "overdramatic," but even if he was indulging in some rhetorical flourishes, no one can deny that such apocalyptic visions, once discounted as hallmarks of religious fundamentalists, now command a hearing in far wider quarters. The technical know-how to bring the world to an end is at hand; the chances of accidents are great; and political acumen is in short supply.

Strictly speaking, though, the world does not want so much for political acumen as for the will to use knowledge already available, knowledge that has in fact been available for a long time. In 1930, for instance, David Davies had already adumbrated all the peacekeeping proposals that have followed in

---

* I wish to acknowledge the assistance of the Center for International Studies of New York University in preparing this Chapter.
[1] U Thant, UN Press Release SG/SM/1109-DD/21, 9 May 1969, p. 2, and *New York Times*, May 10, 1969, p. 3.

noting that though it might be possible to produce "a host of proposals," they would all probably be variations of one of three schemes:

> Under the first scheme the international police force would be constituted by the provision of quotas drawn from each State-member, and organized under the supervision of a general staff at the headquarters of the international authority. In peace time, national quotas would remain under the direct control of their respective governments, and would be maintained by their national exchequers, whilst on mobilisation they would automatically come under the command of international headquarters. Their strength and equipment would be determined by the requirements of the authority, and not on any basis of self-defence prescribed by the national governments.
>
> The second scheme is the establishment of a complete self-contained international army, navy and air force, and the abolition of all national forces except those required for the maintenance of internal order. This scheme carries to its logical conclusion the idea of a central force and removes the necessity for maintaining national armaments. It suggests a single unified police force under the direction and control of the international authority.
>
> The third scheme consists of a composite international force embracing the national quotas and specialised contingent enlisted, equipped and controlled by the international authority.[2]

As D. W. Bowett says, Davies' analysis shows "uncanny acumen" in describing the pattern of subsequent analyses of international forces, even down to the models with which the United Nations itself has experimented.[3] Davies' first type is that provided for under Article 43 of the United Nations

---

[2] David Davies, *The Problem of the Twentieth Century: A Study in International Relationships* (London: Ernest Benn Limited, 1930), pp. 368-369, 373, 376.

[3] W. Bowett, *United Nations Forces* (New York: Frederick A. Praeger, 1964), p. 313.

Charter and also embraces those organized to serve in Korea, Palestine, the Congo, West Irian, and in the various observer groups.[4] The second type is that envisaged by Grenville Clark and Louis B. Sohn,[5] and the third, which Lord Davies himself preferred, is something of an amalgam of the first two.

Taking the experience of the League of Nations and the United Nations together with the writings on peacekeeping since the 1930's, there is a plethora of plans from which to choose. Over the years, we have learned so much about peacekeeping that we can no longer present what we know in capsule form, and we lack neither for analyses or prescriptions. The availability of so many studies shows that UN Members are short not so much of theory and recommendations as they are of commitment and will to act. This failure of will is more serious than mere ignorance, however, because we know far better how to dispel ignorance than to create volition. One approaches the problem of peacekeeping in the 1970's, therefore, with some sense of futility and desperation. One despairs, not just because goals so confidently enunciated at Dumbarton Oaks and at San Francisco have not been realized; most of them, after all, were long range. One despairs because, even knowing why nations have not realized the Charter goals does not help us take those first important steps towards a more rational world. The world still prefers to take known risks, great as they are, than run unknown risks, no matter how much greater security is implied. As one member of this Commission and his colleague have said, UN Members are unwilling "to commit themselves in advance to use their armed forces in a future contingency when they may not be certain that their national interests will require such action."[6] Twenty-five years after they signed the UN Charter, most Members who count (in a military sense) still have provided little evidence that they believe in its Purposes and Principles, as con-

---

[4] Bowett and also David W. Wainhouse, *International Peace Observation* (Baltimore: Johns Hopkins Press, 1966), both *passim*.

[5] *World Peace Through World Law* (3d ed., Cambridge, Mass.: Harvard University Press, 1966).

[6] Leland M. Goodrich and Anne P. Simons, *The United Nations and the Maintenance of International Peace and Security* (Washington, D. C.: Brookings Institution, 1965), p. 620.

tained in Articles 1 and 2, or in the specific military provisions of Article 43.

The United Nations Experience

One could argue, moreover, that past UN experience and the present political situation do not augur well for any initiatives, no matter how limited, to improve UN peacekeeping. The difficulties that have plagued past UN efforts are not insignificant: the need to arrange every force on an *ad hoc* basis; the lack of continuous staff planning; the uncertain political direction; the way the Secretary-General has often been left exposed by other UN organs and by UN Members unwilling to exercise their responsibilities under the Charter; uncertain and unsatisfactory financing; the way that present practices have brought the UN into serious financial and constitutional crises; and the dilatory or non-existent efforts of the United Nations, despite the time its forces have gained for peacemaking, to reach "final" settlements.

This recital is not pleasant, but rather than conclude that the UN has failed, one might more accurately suggest that observers will have to trim past optimistic assessments to meet today's realities. The General Assembly is not in the future going to play a major role in peacekeeping; future Secretaries-General will not enjoy (if that is the word) so free a hand as Dag Hammarskjöld had in the Congo; the Security Council role is going to be central; and the need for the United States and the Union of Soviet Socialist Republics to agree on future peacekeeping patterns will be more crucial in the future than in the past.[7]

---

[7] Studies of UN peacekeeping made before the 1964 "Article 19 crisis," which stress a role in peacekeeping for the General Assembly, must now all be read with the lessons of that crisis in mind. See, for instance, Herbert Nichols, "An Appraisal," in Lincoln P. Bloomfield, ed., *International Military Forces* (Boston: Little, Brown, 1964), pp. 105-25, and Bowett, whose conclusions, written in 1964, also refer somewhat optimistically to an Assembly role in peacekeeping, pp. 561-69. *Cf.* Lincoln P. Bloomfield, "Peacekeeping and Peacemaking," *Foreign Affairs*, XXXXIV (No. 4, July 1966), 671-82, where he observes that in future peacekeeping discussions, the United States will have to sacrifice the right to make emergency appeals to the General Assembly as the price of making any further progress in improving UN machinery for keeping the peace.

Caution is always indicated in prescribing for the future, but we need not assume that the lessons of the *Organisation des Nations Unies au Congo,* the present financial stalemate, or the slow movements of the Committee of 33[8] mean that useful initiatives related to peacekeeping do not exist. Even while staggering from one three- or six-month extension by the Security Council to another, the UN Force in Cyprus continues to play a useful role; UN Forces are still in Korea and the UN Military Observer Group in India and Pakistan; and an on-again-off-again mission directed by Sweden's Ambassador to Moscow, Gunnar Jarring, continues after a fashion in the Middle East. All indicators about the Working Group established by the Committee of 33 suggest that the U.S. and U.S.S.R. are closer together now than in the past in thinking about the UN peacekeeping role. But even if no consensus emerges about what the UN should do generally about peacekeeping, Members could always arrange something again, *ad hoc.*

Nor should one ignore the success side of the UN peacekeeping ledger. Most observers agree that, despite weaknesses revealed in UN experience with peacekeeping, UN observers and forces to date have had some success. These groups have proved feasible militarily, they have kept combat confined geographically and in intensity, separated contenders, and gained time for peacemakers. The UN "presence" has been useful in observing, reporting on, mediating with, and restraining combatants. UN experience has shown, too, that the organization's founders were correct in assuming that great power unanimity is in fact a precondition for enforcing peace and that the permanent members of the Security Council them-

---

[8] This Special Committee on Peace-keeping Operations, is reviewing the whole question of peacekeeping. Under General Assembly Resolution 2451 (XXIII), 19 December 1968, the Committee is pursuing its current objective, a study of UN military observer missions "established or authorized by the Security Council for observation purposes pursuant to Security Council resolutions." The Committee is to suggest other peacekeeping "models" and report its progress in making a comprehensive review of peacekeeping in all its aspects.

selves are not easily amenable to UN discipline. As Leland Goodrich has noted,[9] when the great powers agree, or, at least, do not actively disagree, the UN has been able to bring hostilities to an end. UN experience, especially in the Congo,[10] has shown, moreover, that "vesting discretionary power in a Secretary-General who has demonstrated outstanding qualities as a public servant is not an adequate substitute for agreement of the major powers on critical issues." [11]

If one goes back, then, to Charter fundamentals, positive values emerge from past UN experience. At the same time, the political situation today may well be more favorable to new initiatives than one might at first glance assume. The Cold War world has passed into history. Bi-polar descriptions of world politics must now yield to appreciations of a tacit Soviet-American consensus on the dangers to world peace arising from the attitudes and behavior of the People's Republic of China and from the possibility that small states, especially those with nuclear potential, may act irresponsibly. Moreover, the United States is progressing toward liquidating the Vietnam war, and the end of the conflict there may well remove

---

[9] Leland M. Goodrich, "The Maintenance of International Peace and Security," *International Organization*, XIX (No. 3, Summer 1965), 429-443.

[10] Ernest Lefever, *Crisis in the Congo: A United Nations Force in Action* (Washington, D. C.: Brookings Institution, 1965), p. 181, offers this assessment of the UN's most controversial peacekeeping operation: "The Congo peacekeeping effort was a novel, controversial, and a less-than-efficient enterprise. It sometimes fumbled. It made many small mistakes. It was assailed on all sides. It precipitated a financial crisis for the United Nations. But in the final analysis the U.N. Force must be judged by its contribution to international stability, regardless of what other interests it might have served. So judged, the mission succeeded. It contributed to peace and security in Central Africa and in the wider world.

"As the largest and most complex internationally authorized and administered operation in history, the Congo peacekeeping effort is rich in lessons and warnings for the future."

[11] Goodrich, p. 481.

some of the international ill will that the Secretary-General has long felt to be poisoning the international atmosphere.[12]

The millennium is not at hand, but neither do we need to resign ourselves to Armageddon. With both cautionary and diagnostic elements in mind, this report addresses itself not so much to articulating elaborate schemes for peacekeeping, but to the narrower, although more intractable problem of how to push the major powers, and especially the United States and the Soviet Union, closer together in efforts to breathe more life into Article 43 and Chapters VI and VII of the Charter. This paper does not consider technical problems, which, because they are easy to understand, have received so much attention. As Ruth Russell has put it:

> Even if all the technical improvements were put into practice tomorrow, the toughest problem—the political problem—would remain. This is not so much a question of strengthening the ability of the *Organization* to promote peacekeeping and, even more important, peaceful settlement. It is rather a matter of overcoming the resistance of the *Members* to making the political concessions required to settle their disputes.[13]

Following this line of thought, this paper does not set out yet another elaborate peacekeeping scheme or formulate visions of the world as it might be *if* . . . . The big *if*—*if* only the United States and the Soviet Union could appreciate their common interest in developing a larger role for the UN in peacekeeping—does indeed impede dramatic progress. But we already know about what could be *if* . . . ; what we need more, at this juncture, is the key to unlock the door to the knowledge we already have. The best service we can render now is to suggest places in which to look for the key.

---

[12] See his *Annual Report on the Work of the Organization,* UNGA *OR,* Supp. 1A, for the years since 1964-1965.

[13] Ruth B. Russell, *The United Nations and United States Security Policy* (Washington, D. C.: The Brookings Institution), p. 210.

The United Nations search is essentially cautious—a request to the Committee of 33 to study past observer missions which the Security Council authorized.[14]   When the Committee completes this study, it may well go on to study UN Forces, not just observer missions, which the Security Council established. Outsiders have been more adventurous, but they would be well advised to heed the Members' desire to move slowly and to think only in terms of relatively modest proposals.   But even if one restricts oneself to reviewing those suggestions that the powers could implement immediately, one need not settle for the *status quo*.   The United States itself could act without waiting for any other state; and interested parties could urge the United Nations to take other steps.   Recommendations addressed to the United States, which the United States could take unilaterally, should be relatively easy to implement; multilateral steps, of course, require negotiation.

Some Proposals Considered

One proposal would urge the United States to give a higher priority to UN peacekeeping and "consider it under appropriate circumstances as a substitute for US action."[15]   This suggestion would require no more than a Presidential declaration of American intent and policy.   Perhaps, in the wake of the Vietnam war, the idea would command support, especially since it would provide an alternative to a policy of unilateral involvement, which, in Vietnam, even American decision-makers now generally concede to have been disastrous.   Allowing one man in the Department of State to spend full time thinking out the implications for UN peacekeeping, as Arthur Cox suggests, would not seem an extravagant use of U.S. manpower, and taking comparable steps in the Department of Defense and in the U.S. Mission to the UN to escalate thinking about UN peacekeeping would do a great deal to accustom senior policy makers to thinking of UN action as one option they should always consider.[16]

---

[14] See n. 8 above.

[15] Arthur M. Cox, *Prospects for Peacekeeping* (Washington, D. C.: Brookings Institution, 1967), p. 137.

[16] Cox, pp. 139-140.

Another underdeveloped American policy to which several writers have alluded is the U.S. failure to use the Foreign Assistance Act to enable recipients of aid to participate in UN collective measures. Lincoln Bloomfield points out that representatives of UN permanent missions were not even aware that this legislative authority existed. Since much of the military aid given developing countries is intended to develop just the kinds of skills a peacekeeping mission needs (border control, paramilitary training, civilian policy functions), the United States could emphasize this aspect of its aid programs.[17] The United States could also redeem its promises to strengthen the peacekeeping capacity of the United Nations, either by earmarking a portion of its forces for UN call-up or by establishing a volunteer "First Brigade" of U.S. non-combatant logistical experts and other technicians maintained specially for the United Nations.[18] It could accompany these steps by an invitation to the Soviet Union to follow suit. Problems posed for the United Nations or Member States disinclined to have either U.S. or U.S.S.R. troops on their territory are mitigated because the Secretary-General or a military staff would ultimately decide which UN earmarked troops to call upon and would presumably build upon the Hammarskjöld principles that only troops from states acceptable to the parties concerned would participate in any UN action.

The United States could also encourage friends of the United Nations to submit reports, modeled on those submitted by the United States and others, on the availability to the United Nations of troops within the several national military establishments. Private diplomatic pressure might well pro-

---

[17] Lincoln Bloomfield, "Peacekeeping and Peacemaking," p. 680; Cox, p. 142; Russell, p. 215.

[18] The original proposal for the "First Brigade" appears reprinted in *Congressional Record*, CXI, pt. 10, 89 Cong. 1st sess. (1965), pp. 13826-27. The initials were an acronym for "Forces for International Relief on Standby." The proposal more often now appears as a call for the more familiar *Fire* Brigade.

vide the United Nations with a wealth of information, where formal efforts to request this information have failed.[19]

The most important step that the United States might take is to make still one more generous gesture in an effort to carry out the commitment made under the Article 19 settlement of August 1965, by which the Committee of 33 reported that "the financial difficulties of the Organization should be solved through voluntary contributions by Member States, with the highly developed countries making substantial contributions."[20] Since then, the United States has had occasion to observe that "there has been a thunderous silence" from states which were expected to contribute voluntarily.[21] The United States has clearly been expecting the U.S.S.R. to move first to make good on promises that it would contribute to a "Rescue Fund," whereas the U.S.S.R. has maintained that all states, including the United States, were bound to make voluntary contributions. The U.S.S.R. has even questioned the good faith of the Americans and argues that the United States has actually maintained that it was not bound by the Assembly's adopting the report of the Committee of 33.[22] In turn, the United States has reminded everyone that it has paid all its assessments for UN peacekeeping, insisted that in view of its previous contributions it was not bound to contribute just then, and noted also that no state had argued that its own contribution was conditional upon the United States' contributing first.[23]

---

[19] The General Assembly did not put to a vote in 1966 a proposal by Canada and others to require states to report on troops earmarked for the UN. See UN Doc. A/SPC/L.130, quoted in A/6603, "Report of the Special Political Committee," GAOR. XXI (1966), Annexes: Agenda Item 33, pp. 15, 21. Several states later volunteered such reports.

[20] UN Doc. A/5916, August 31, 1965, in GAOR. XIX (1964-1965), Annex No. 21, p. 85.

[21] UN Doc. A/AC.121/PV.26, May 16, 1967, p. 23, quotes Ambassador Arthur Goldberg's remarks on November 22, 1965, in Committee V (1098th mtg., p. 186, par. 22), relating to Assembly adoption of Res. 2053 (XX).

[22] *Ibid.*, pp. 32-35, 38-41.

[23] *Ibid.*, pp. 23, 37.

In short, each state has been insisting on giving pride of place to the other. The Soviet Union undoubtedly has refused to contribute first to avoid the stigma of confessing to a delinquency. But the Soviet position provides a good opportunity for the United States to demonstrate some diplomatic magnanimity. Since, as the United States is quick to proclaim, no one can accuse it of being in arrears, it could afford, both financially and for prestige, to contribute first to the Rescue Fund. If the Soviet Union then keeps its word, the deadlock will be broken, and the UN can go on to other matters; if not, blame for the deadlock will rest without question upon the U.S.S.R., and every stone will have been turned. If the U.S.S.R. does nothing, the U.S. gains a propaganda advantage, one which it may not want, but, at least, in Cold War terms, it will have received something for its money. As matters now stand, it is allowing the Soviet refusal to pay to determine the level of UN peacekeeping activity.[24]

As a guide to the actual amount the United States might contribute, one should bear in mind the Canadian example, when, in 1965, Canada contributed $4 million to the Rescue Fund. As Miss Russell points out,

> Ottawa's share of the regular U.N. budget is 3.17 percent and Washington's is 31.91 percent, or about ten times that of Canada. A comparable United States contribution to the rescue fund would on this basis come to some $40 million. If, however, the contributions were based more strictly on gross national product, the comparable United States contribution would be over $60 million since its gross national product is more than 15 times that of Canada.[25]

Although the United States alone could do much to get peacekeeping off dead center, it cannot itself do everything

---

[24] Ruth B. Russell, "United Nations Financing and the 'Law of the Charter'," *Columbia Journal of Transnational Law,* V (1966), 68-95, makes this point very strongly at p. 95.

[25] Russell, *United Nations and United States Security Policy,* pp. 442-43.

that needs to be done. With others, though, it could take the initiative in the United Nations by sponsoring a resolution in the Security Council, calling for the UN to take the first step towards establishing a peacekeeping force somewhat along the lines of Dr. Bowett's formulation, eschewing only his now dated reference to a peacekeeping role for the General Assembly. The basic idea would be to have the Secretary-General reactivate the post of Military Adviser,[26] by appointing a UN Chief of Staff, and in consultation with this Chief of Staff, to begin recruiting a permanent UN Headquarters Military Staff of approximately fifty experienced military officers. They would serve for five to seven years and would include experts in communication, transportation, ordnance, intelligence, civil affairs, and medical services.[27]   In Dr. Bowett's words:

> The Military Staff, when constituted, would undertake the following tasks:
>
> (1) A study of the different kinds of peace-keeping operations likely to be undertaken by a United Nations Force composed of national contingents and of the ideal composition and command structure for such a Force in any given type of operation.
>
> (2) A survey of the operational, logistical and administrative problems (including standardisation of equipment and of operational procedures, joint civilian-military operations) encountered in the past and likely to be encountered in the future.
>
> (3) Liaison with the Member States which have declared their willingness in principle to provide contingents for a United Nations Force, such liaison to include a periodic inspection of any such contingents by the United Nations Headquarters Military Staff.

---

[26] Major-General Indar Jit Rikhye resigned from this position on December 18, 1968 (see UN Press Note No. 3491, December 18, 1968) beecause the "peace-keeping operations of the United Nations are going through a phase of re-examination and restricted activity." The Secretary-General has appointed no successor.

[27] Bowett, p. 563. Bloomfield believes that this work should go on outside the organization, which is, in the terms presented here, a fall-back position. See "Peacekeeping and Peacemaking," p. 680.

(4) The organisation of joint exercises in which contingents assigned for United Nations duty by several Member States could participate under United Nations Command.

(5) The formulation of plans for a United Nations Staff College and of training schemes to be undertaken by such a College for the instruction of senior officers drawn from the armed forces of States declaring their willingness to provide contingents for the United Nations.

(6) The formulation of model Regulations for the Force, Status of Forces Agreements and Stand-by Agreements for submission to the political organs of the United Nations for discussion and adoption.

(7) The negotiation of contracts and charter parties with public and private associations designed to ensure that the Staff could call on supplies and transport as and when needed.[28]

Bowett goes on to spell out roles of the "political control organs," including one for the General Assembly, but, in light of the Article 19 controversy, it might be best to think in terms only of having the Security Council receive all the reports of the Military Staff and adopt all such regulations as they might devise. Moreover, even though Bowett suggests further stages through which a UN Force might evolve, sponsors of the first stage do not have to commit themselves to go any further at this time than to formulate the theoretical design and structure needed by UN forces. That would be ample progress for the moment.

It would have to be clear from the outset (and would presumably find specific place in the preambular material to

---

[28] *Ibid.*, pp. 563-64. In connection with Bowett's first point, note the warning by Charles Burton Marshall that questions about how to train UN forces and for what objectives have political implications for world politics. See his "Character and Mission of a United Nations Peace Force under Conditions of General and Complete Disarmament," *American Political Science Review*, LIX (June 1965), 350-64. These problems would have to be faced in time, but they are no worse than those we face now.

the proposed Security Council resolution or in an accompanying report) that the Military Staff, if created, would operate in the framework of *peacekeeping* and not *enforcement*. That is to say, plans would assume that:

> There is no enemy, there is no one to be defeated, there is no intention of eliminating and . . . it is not enough to neutralize one opponent—it is necessary to neutralize all belligerents without using force, solely by being present. Freedom of movement throughout the area occupied by both sides is therefore necessary.[29]

Or, as Miss Russell puts it, "A Peacekeeping Force is not a sanctions force writ small, but a truce-supervision team writ large."[30] As such, the force must undertake defensive actions only and, as indicated, must be guaranteed freedom of movement.

At the same time, the Committee of 33 should probably do more to explore the possibility of establishing the armed forces called for in Article 43 of the Charter. Western states should pay closer attention to the Soviet Union's offer of 1964 to make troops available for UN use under this Article, to a comparable Czech offer made in 1967, and to indications that the Soviet Union has recently come to think again of UN force being used as part of a general Middle Eastern settlement.[31] Thus, the present international situation may offer possibilities of moving quietly forward towards goals that have long been elusive. Moreover, Members should give thought to enlarging the existing Military Staff Committee to include

---

[29] Per Frydenberg, *Peace-Keeping: Experience and Evaluation — The Oslo Papers* (Oslo: Norwegian Institute of International Affairs, 1964), p. 191.

[30] Ruth B. Russell, "Development by the United Nations of Rules Relating to Peacekeeping," *Proceedings* of the American Society of International Law, 59th Annual Meeting (1965), p. 55.

[31] UN Doc. A/5721, July 13, 1964, contains the U.S.S.R. Memorandum of July 10, 1964 on UN Peacekeeping, in GAOR. XIX (1964), Agenda Annex 21, pp. 2-4. The Czech letter is in S/7852, April 13, 1967, Letter to the President of the Security Council. See also *New York Times*, September 26, 1968, p. 1.

all members of the Security Council plus the states now on the Committee of 33. Here the Council could discuss the possibility of having members agree to make contingents and facilities available to the Council in terms both of peacekeeping and enforcement.[32]

If these new initiatives find favor, Member states should consider the possibilities of peacemaking more seriously in the future than they have in the past. To quote Miss Russell again:

> In the strange and unsettled world in which we live . . . , fear of the unknown consequences is at times sufficient to bring about enough consensus to call a halt to open violence; and even to maintain for years on end an odd sort of twilight situation between war and peace —as in Kashmir, Palestine and Korea—under the more or less powerless supervision of the United Nations. But we have yet to learn how to generate enough either of fear or of civilized self-restraint to get us over the hurdle from the state of suspended violence and into the frame of mind and spirit that makes possible true settlement.[33]

Here an old plan to revivify a "Panel for Inquiry and Conciliation," established by the General Assembly in 1949, is worth reconsidering.[34] The Panel, to be composed of persons who, because of their training, experience, character, and standing, might serve as conciliators or mediators, was used only once, to select Dr. Frank P. Graham to serve in Kashmir. If the Members take to heart UN experience, especially in the Middle East, which dramatically illustrated in 1967 the dangers of allowing unsettled political problems to fester, they would do

---

[32] Russell, *The United Nations and United States Security Policy*, p. 405.

[33] Russell, *Proceedings*, pp. 57-58.

[34] Elmore Jackson, "Developing the Peaceful Settlement Functions of the United Nations," *Annals* of the American Academy of Political and Social Science: "The Future of the United Nations: Issues of Charter Revision," Vol. 296 (November 1954), pp. 27-35.

well to reassert the importance of intensifying efforts to settle political disputes and not just to contain them militarily. Reactivating such a Panel might well serve this purpose. Alternatively, the UN could create a "Peace Observation Corps," whose members it could call upon to establish a UN "presence" anywhere it might help preserve the peace. States could agree (by UN resolution, if by no more formal means) to admit such a presence to their territory when called upon by the Security Council (or better yet, by the Security Council, General Assembly, or Secretary-General). The Assembly ought also to reconsider the British proposal of 1965, to study peaceful settlement of disputes in all its aspects, taking into account "not only methods of peaceful settlement relating to the solution of legal disputes, but also the political aspects of the problem."[35]

Summary of Recommendations

To recapitulate, then, this paper recommends that the United States:

1) give a higher priority in the future than in the past to UN peacekeeping and consider using UN machinery as a substitute for U.S. action wherever appropriate, and, to this end, strengthen the administrative and policy-making machinery related to peacekeeping in the Departments of State and Defense and in the U.S. Mission to the United Nations;

2) vigorously undertake to encourage states receiving assistance from the United States to participate in UN collective measures and to use American funds to help states willing to do so prepare units for service with the United Nations;

3) earmark a portion of its forces for UN service or establish a volunteer "First Brigade" in accordance with proposals already made in Congress;

4) voluntarily contribute a sizable sum to the UN "Rescue Fund" in an effort to take a new initiative toward resolving the UN financial crisis relating to peacekeeping;

---

[35] UN Doc. A/5964, August 20, 1965, in GAOR. XX (1965), Annexes, Agenda Item 99, pp. 1-2.

and that the United States or other Member States of the United Nations:

5) sponsor a resolution in the Security Council calling upon the Secretary-General to appoint a UN Chief of Staff and, after consulting with him, to begin recruiting a permanent Headquarters Military Staff of experienced military officers to undertake preliminary planning for a UN peacekeeping force;

6) ask the Committee of 33 to explore more vigorously the possibility of establishing UN armed forces under Article 43 of the Charter;

7) revive the "Panel for Inquiry and Conciliation" established in 1949 in an effort to improve the organization's capacity for peacemaking;

8) create a "Peace Observation Corps" authorized to establish a UN presence wherever required to help preserve the peace; and

9) study peaceful settlement procedures in both legal and political aspects.

Time has not lessened the urgency behind Adlai Stevenson's call for "a reliable system of order with the capacity to induce peaceful change where change is needed."[36] Nor should we forget Arthur Goldberg's warning that the "risks of a United Nations without the capacity to act were far greater than the risks of a United Nations with that capacity."[37] It may well be that the Members will pay no more attention in the future than in the past to such advice and warnings. Before we resign ourselves to that conclusion, however, we should make a renewed effort to move forward along the lines developed above in the hope that, in an improved international climate, even old proposals may flourish as they never have before.

---

[36] "Strengthening the Machinery for Peace," Department of State Bulletin, L (1964), 969-970.

[37] GAOR. XX (1965), SPC 465th mtg., p. 3, par. 19.

Six

Disarmament
by
Marion H. McVitty

The Primary Objective

In 1959, the United Nations General Assembly unanimously agreed that the objective of disarmament negotiations should be the elimination of all national military establishments in their entirety. Prior to that time, disarmament negotiations under UN auspices had been directed toward a balanced reduction of national arms and armed forces to some more tolerable level of danger and cost. The difference between that prior goal and the new one of "general and complete" disarmament was not merely a difference in degree, but a difference in kind.

The earlier disarmament concept was predicated upon the assumption that the nation State would remain primarily responsible for its own defense and for the protection of its own national interests. The earlier concept was also predicated upon the intention to retain a balance of national military power as a major adjunct to international security and stability.

The new concept of general and complete disarmament was understood to mean that at the end of the disarmament process, nation States would have only sufficient internal police forces to maintain domestic order. As United Nations delegates pointed out at the time the proposal was made, this concept of disarmament envisaged "a warless world". To envisage a warless world in terms of the total disarmament of nation States it would seem necessary to assume, either that all conflicts of national interests would be eliminated with the elimination of national military establishments, or that an international peace and security system would be created for the equal protection of all States and their legitimate rights.

Since the first of those assumptions is preposterous, the second must be taken to be essential. It is, therefore, necessary to conclude that general and complete disarmament cannot be realistically pursued in isolation from the establishment of international peace and security forces, and from the institution of prompt and reliable means for the peaceful settlement of international disputes. These inalienable adjuncts to general and complete disarmament would be ineffective or subject to abuse, if they were not under the control of a representative and impartial world authority directed by law and devoted to justice.

When the Member Governments of the United Nations adopted the revolutionary change described in the approach to disarmament, it is probably fair to say that many governments accepted the goal in theory with varying degrees of reservation as to the possible and desirable outcome in practice. The very wording of the 1959 Resolution allows for some flexibility of attitude. That Resolution calls upon governments "to make every effort to achieve a constructive solution of the problem of general and complete disarmament."

During the next few years general and complete disarmament remained a live issue. In 1962, a Soviet draft Treaty and a United States draft Treaty Outline were presented to the 18-Nation Disarmament Committee. The two plans were incompatible with each other and inadequate to the purpose to be served. The U.S. draft Outline was detailed with respect to Stage I, but the two succeeding Stages were only very roughly sketched out. The Soviet draft offered a full Treaty text, but must also be considered incomplete, since it made no adequate provision for international security forces or peaceful settlement procedures.

Since 1964, these documents have remained static in content, and no other comparable proposals on the subject have been submitted by any other nation or group of nations.

Even before general and complete disarmament became the stated objective of the United Nations, comprehensive disarmament proposals had been dropped in favor of isolated arms limitation measures which might be more easily achieved. Because some progress has been made on such measures, and because the general and complete disarmament plans of the major Powers were seen to be irreconcilable as they stood in 1964, the step-by-step approach has been pursued almost exclusively in recent years.

Nevertheless, general and complete disarmament remains the ultimate objective of the United Nations, and lesser goals have come to be known as "collateral measures" to that end. Furthermore, some success with isolated steps and serious consideration of further arms limitation measures have tended to create new incentives to pursue the larger aim. Agreements reached, or currently in prospect, being fragmentary, may lack equity in sacrifices or risks among States, and may not long endure apart from other more far-reaching solutions to the disarmament problem. Thus the final objective remains primary as the end to which limited means are directed, and as the solid structure within which fragile gains may be made permanent and consonant with the positive needs of small and large nations alike.

The Commission to Study the Organization of Peace may wish to reaffirm its original belief in disarmament. In doing so it should probably use the current expression "general and complete disarmament". In making such an endorsement of the goal, the Commission should stress the need to link disarmament integrally with international peace and security forces, and with effective means for peaceful settlement of international disputes.

The Commission might further wish to recommend that the Soviet Union and the United States review their general and complete disarmament proposals with a view to perfecting their terms and reconciling their differences.

The non-aligned Members of the Conference of the Disarmament Committee, individually or collectively, might be urged to prepare general and complete disarmament proposals, or treaty drafts of their own. These might serve to reanimate serious negotiations on the subject and contribute to resolving differences between the plans of the major Powers.

The tragedy is that general and complete disarmament was pigeon-holed as an intractable issue, when the surface of the subject had barely been scratched. Possible solutions for some of the central problems are not far to seek, and other difficulties might yield to a modicum of innovation.

The question of the timing of the disarmament process is a case in point. The Soviet Union has insisted upon commitment to the whole program in advance, and to automatic progression from Stage I through Stage III within five years. The United States proposes commitment to a detailed Stage I, with no fixed timetable for the completion of Stages II and III, and the U.S. plan counts heavily on experience during Stage I to determine the amount and kind of progress to be made during the latter two phases of the process.

It would seem logical to suppose that if the United States would flesh out its whole plan in detail comparable to that now available for the first Stage, this would increase confidence that the United States intended to go on to achieve the full objective. In that event, the Soviet Union might be more willing to provide more flexible transition periods between one Stage and the next.

The difficulty over international inspection is also susceptible of accommodation. Inventive solutions to this problem have been worked out which would divide national territories into a number of inspection zones to be inspected in sequence over a period of time. Thus it would be possible to assure the international community that arms reductions were being carried out, while still permitting the nations to retain some military secrecy, which would grow progressively less as armaments reached lower levels and confidence grew.

Preoccupation with inspection has tended to overshadow the purpose of inspection as a safeguard. Inspection is necessary for timely detection of violations. Thereafter, it is important that violations be halted. Many violations might be voluntarily corrected as a result of exposure. If, however, serious and determined non-compliance should arise toward the end of the disarmament process, or after the process was completed, then the international response would need to have "teeth" in it. To avoid general rearmament, or coercion of the recalcitrant State as a whole, it could be agreed that arms regulation violations are international crimes for which individuals would be held responsible.

Other problems which have arisen with respect to international peace and security forces might be greatly ameliorated by an equitable representation system. Such a system would need to avoid a veto by any single nation, however powerful, and to take account of differences in size, population and economic responsibility in the apportioning of votes.

The points outlined above may serve to indicate the extensive areas for accommodation which have not as yet been formally explored by disarmament negotiations. Those noted by no means exhaust the list.

To pursue the essential goal of general and complete disarmament need not impair a simultaneous pursuit of promising arms limitation measures currently in the forefront of attention.

Arms Limitation Measures

Arms limitation measures already taken, and others under active consideration, have some intrinsic merit, serve to provide momentum toward further steps, and tend to emphasize the need for general and complete disarmament. Current arms limitation measures fall roughly into two categories, although there is some overlapping between the two. One group of such measures pertains to areas, or environments, which have not yet been militarized. The other deals with various means for the containment of nuclear weapons.

Unmilitarized Areas

The Antarctica Treaty, which came into force in 1961, was the first international instrument designed to "reserve exclusively for peaceful purposes" an area which had not been militarized. This Treaty has been ratified by the United

States and the Soviet Union, as well as by other governments having an interest in Antarctica.

Under the terms of this Treaty all military installations are ruled out of the area, and military weapons, maneuvers and weapons experimentation are prohibited. The Treaty provides for a system of mutual inspection by observers appointed by the States Parties. The observers have free access to all installations and equipment, and aerial inspection is permitted.

In addition to thus ensuring that Antarctica is fully demilitarized under agreed safeguards, the Treaty includes measures designed to deter conflicts in the area. Specifically, the Treaty limits sovereign claims, and affirms the right of all mankind to share freely in scientific exploration of the territory.

It is also noteworthy that this Treaty defines precisely the extent of the area to which it applies. The area is described as that "beyond 60° south latitude, including all ice shelves." It is, however, provided that the terms of the Treaty shall not prejudice the freedom of the seas within the zone of its concern.

The Antarctica Treaty having served its purpose well without giving rise to controversy in the years since its adoption, was taken as a model in framing certain parts of the Treaty on Outer Space, which was signed in 1967. The Space Treaty lags behind the Antarctica precedent in some respects and outstrips it in others.

Under the terms of the Outer Space Treaty, arms limitation provisions applicable to the moon and celestial bodies are very similar to those pertaining to Antarctica. In space, *per se,* however, only nuclear and other weapons of mass destruction are affected. Such weapons may not be orbited around the earth or "stationed in space in any other manner."

Restrictions on weapons in space itself are not subject to international verification, since they can be identified by nationally operated instruments. With respect to arms restrictions on the moon and other celestial bodies, this Treaty provides for "visits" by representatives of States Parties to installations and equipment of other States Parties after due notice and by arrangement.

While arms limitation measures for Outer Space are thus seen to be more limited than those for Antarctica, the Space Treaty goes further than the earlier document in other respects. It entirely rules out national claims to sovereignty in outer space and on the moon and other celestial bodies. The Treaty declares outer space to be "the province of all mankind" and the right of all nations to its benefits is affirmed. These principles decrease to a considerable degree national incentives to militarize the area.

The Outer Space Treaty does not define the boundary between air space, which is subject to national jurisdiction, and outer space, which is free to all. Satisfactory criteria for determining the lower limit of outer space proved to be technically difficult, or politically controversial, so that it was finally agreed that no definition is presently necessary.

Outer Space law is incomplete, and is under negotiation for further development in the United Nations Committee on Outer Space. Additional Articles to the present document or supplementary Treaties may be expected to be agreed upon in due course.

The Nineteenth Report of the Commission to Study the Organization of Peace deals comprehensively with the whole question of the seabeds beyond national jurisdiction. Since that Report covers the reservation exclusively for peaceful purposes of that environment, it is not necessary to analyze here the particular arms limitation problems and possibilities being considered in relation to that area.

It may, however, be useful to stress the very close relationship between the demilitarization of the seabeds and their exploration and exploitation for the benefit of all mankind. Being far larger in area than Antarctica, being far less remote than celestial bodies, and having resources expected to be more valuable and more exploitable than either, the future of the deep ocean floor appears to be more imminent and more momentous an issue to UN Member Governments. As a result, the need for legal principles, for legal definition of the limits of national jurisdiction, the sharing of economic benefits and the control of armaments in that environment, all seem to require more radical international action than has been embodied in the two earlier Treaties.

The Nineteenth Report of the Commission recognizes the magnitude of the seabed question as a whole. Specifically with respect to reserving the area exclusively for peaceful purposes, the Commission recommends in that Report:

"A *Declaration of General Principles*

"8.) The seabed, and subsoil thereof, should be used for peaceful purposes only. In particular, no military bases and fortifications should be established on the seabed; no nuclear weapons or other weapons of mass destruction should be emplaced on it, implanted in it, or affixed to it, and no such weapons especially designed for use on the seabed should be deployed thereon. Use of military personnel and equipment for scientific research should not, however, be prohibited."

The Containment of Nuclear Weapons

Three international Treaties have been promulgated which seek by different methods to contain the spread of nuclear weapons to nations which do not yet possess them. No one of the three has fully accomplished its objective, but each represents a progression in the amount of arms limitation involved. The partial Nuclear Test Ban Treaty, the Latin American Treaty Prohibiting Nuclear Weapons in Latin America, and the Non-Proliferation of Nuclear Weapons Treaty were all completed in the five years between 1963 and 1968.

The Nuclear Test Ban Treaty prohibits the testing of nuclear weapons in the atmosphere, in outer space and under water. No provision is made in the Treaty for verification of compliance with its terms, since violations could be nationally detected. The Treaty is described as "partial", because it does not include a ban on underground nuclear tests. The major Powers were unable to agree on the question of whether, or to what degree, international verification was necessary to distinguish between possible illegal underground tests and earthquakes.

The Test Ban Treaty must also be described as "partial" in application, since neither France nor the People's Republic of China have acceded to its terms. Indeed, both France and Peking China continued nuclear testing in the environments forbidden by the Treaty, after the Treaty came into force for the other nuclear Powers.

On the other hand, it is important to note that 96 governments, in addition to the original Contracting Parties, have acceded to the Test Ban Treaty. Among the 96 are included those nations with the greatest potential capacity to produce nuclear weapons at an early date. Unless those States can develop nuclear weapons without testing, or by testing underground, they may be deterred by the terms of the Treaty from proceeding to make these weapons for themselves.

When the Test Ban Treaty was adopted it was hoped that the improvement of seismic instruments would eventually obviate the need for international verification of compliance with a prohibition of underground nuclear tests. The Swedish Government, having undertaken technical studies, proposed during 1968-69 that adequate verification could be provided by a network of national seismological instruments plus provision of a "right to challenge", if identification were occasionally in doubt. The United States has differed with the Swedish conclusion and so has not responded positively to this proposal. The supposed Soviet willingness to halt underground tests on those terms has therefore not been put to the proof.

While the partial Test Ban Treaty was quite successful in reducing the hazard to human health from nuclear tests in the three prohibited environments, it had only a limited effect in preventing the spread of nuclear weapons. In 1962 no international agreement had yet been achieved which would prevent the geographic spread of nuclear weapons, either by transfer from nuclear Powers, or because additional nations could produce their own nuclear weapons.

In the wake of the Cuban missile crisis, the concept of regional de-nuclearization caught fire in Latin America. When the Soviet Union agreed to remove its nuclear weapons from Cuba, the immediate emergency passed, but some anxiety remained as to whether the USSR would actually remove all of those weapons as agreed. Furthermore, it was feared that other countries in Latin America might fall victim to Soviet influence and be similarly used as strategic outposts for the USSR in the Western Hemisphere.

Four Latin American States introduced a Resolution in the 1962 UN Assembly designed to prevent all countries and territories in Latin America and the Caribbean from manufacturing, receiving, storing or testing nuclear weapons. The creation of a "nuclear-free zone" in Latin America was not acted upon until the subsequent Assembly session. At that time, the United Nations gave its blessing to that objective, but left it to the States of Latin America to work out the terms for its achievement.

Seventeen Latin American States undertook preliminary work for an American Treaty Prohibiting Nuclear Weapons in 1964. The Treaty which resulted is an admirable document, well-defined, comprehensive in its terms, and envisaging inspection by the International Atomic Energy Agency. However, as the Treaty took shape, two major problems arose: 1.) the countries and non-self-governing territories to be included to insure its effectiveness; 2.) the nature of assurances to be obtained from nuclear Powers that they would respect the Treaty terms. These problems were solved by the inclusion in the final Treaty Text of two Additional Protocols. The first of these Protocols would apply to nations administering territories in Latin America and the Caribbean. If signed by such nations that Protocol would bind them to apply within their territories the very strict obligations of the Contracting Parties. The second Protocol, applicable to nuclear Powers, would obligate them not to violate the provisions of the Treaty, and not to use, or threaten to use, nuclear weapons against Parties to the Treaty.

The Latin American Treaty has been signed by 21 States in the region, and has been ratified by 11. The Treaty provides that 11 States shall be sufficient to bring the Treaty into force, to establish the control Agency and to seek inspection arrangements from the IAEA, provided those 11 agree to waive conditions respecting the Protocols. However, it is questionable as to how effective the Treaty will be unless the Protocols are adhered to by those nations to which they are intended to apply.

Only the United Kingdom has ratified the Protocols thus far. The U.S. has signed Protocol No. II. The Netherlands has signed Protocol No. I.

Adherence to Protocol No. I presents a serious problem to the United States. In particular, adherence by the United States to the first Protocol would seem to obligate the U.S. not to store nuclear weapons in such territories as Puerto Rico, the Canal Zone, etc., and not to permit its planes or ships to carry nuclear weapons through national air space or territorial waters in the Latin American region. The effect of such curtailment of U.S. defense arrangements in the Western Hemisphere would no doubt be considerable.

Adherence by the USSR to the second Protocol would presumably preclude any repetition of the Cuban missile type of military intrusion into the region. At this juncture the U.S. is unlikely to feel that the Soviet obligation would represent a sacrifice comparable to that which would be assumed by the U.S. should it adhere to both Protocols.

The immediacy of further action on the Latin American Treaty has been overshadowed by promulgation of the Non-Proliferation of Nuclear Weapons Treaty. That Treaty with its wider applicability has come into force, and has been ratified by the United States and the U.S.S.R.

When the super Powers completed a draft Non-Proliferation Treaty to their own satisfaction, and the text was presented to the UN General Assembly, it ran into a sea of opposition, which seemed not to have been anticipated by its sponsors. Basically, antagonism to the Treaty draft derived from what non-nuclear-weapon States felt to be the inequality of sacrifice implicit in the Treaty obligations. Specifically, the objections raised by non-nuclear countries were the following:

1.) The retention of the nuclear monopoly by the nuclear Powers with no reduction or limit to their own nuclear arsenals;

2.) International inspection stipulated for non-nuclear Parties to the Treaty, but not applicable to nuclear Parties;

3.) The prohibition of peaceful nuclear explosions by non-nuclear nations;

4.) The lack of security guarantees for non-nuclear States against nuclear attack, or threat of attack.

The terms of the final Treaty sought to overcome some of these objections by the following provisions:

1.) Under Article VI all Parties to the Treaty, including nuclear Powers, would undertake a solemn obligation to "pursue negotiations in good faith on effective measures relating to cessation of the nuclear arms race at an early date and to nuclear disarmament, and on a treaty on general and complete disarmament under strict and effective international control."

2.) Article V provides for bilateral or international arrangements for peaceful nuclear explosions to be undertaken for non-nuclear Parties at relatively low cost, and without discrimination.

The question of security guarantees was not resolved in the Treaty itself, but a special Security Council Resolution was passed at the instigation of the U.S., the USSR and Britain. The Resolution is somewhat ambiguous, and the ability of the Security Council to enforce it in an emergency is doubted by many non-nuclear States.

Despite the unresolved objections which have been raised by non-nuclear-weapon States, the Non-Proliferation Treaty could be a real barrier to the production of nuclear weapons by a dozen or more States which could readily manufacture some nuclear weapons of their own. As a number of those States are involved in conflict areas of the world, the danger of nuclear war would be greatly increased if the Non-Proliferation Treaty is not accepted by them. As of now, India and Brazil have responded negatively, and the position of Israel and the U.A.R. are in some doubt.

The Brazilian opposition is due to the prohibition of peaceful nuclear explosions. (It should be noted here that the Latin American Treaty expressly permits peaceful nuclear explosions.) India and the Middle Eastern States appear to be hesitant primarily for security reasons. In this connection, declination by the People's Republic of China to accede to the Treaty is obviously an important factor for India and certain other non-aligned States.

The reluctance of certain significant non-nuclear nations can probably best be overcome by speedy implementation of Article VI of the Treaty pertaining to further serious disarmament negotiations. It is important in this regard, to recognize that disarmament progress must be made within five years, if the Treaty is to endure. The Treaty is subject to automatic review after five years, and failure to make further progress in disarmament, as stipulated, might well threaten the Treaty's continued existence.

As far as the United States is concerned the Non-Proliferation Treaty would seem to be a more useful and acceptable instrument, than the Latin American Treaty. However, should the NPT fall short of its major objective, the U.S. might want to reconsider accession to Protocol No. 1 of the Latin American Treaty; particularly if that accession were offered on a reciprocal basis with Soviet accession to Protocol No. II.

Pressures for compliance with Article VI of the NPT are likely to be exerted on arms limitation proposals which have been given the highest priority by the UN Assembly and by the Conference of the Disarmament Committee. Among these are bilateral U.S.-Soviet negotiations on strategic offensive and defensive missiles; and completion of the Test Ban Treaty to include underground nuclear tests.

Prevention of the deployment by the two major Powers of anti-ballistic missiles (ABMs) has been urged in order to prevent a sharp upward spiral in the arms race. Central to the ABM issue is the understanding that development and deployment of new offensive weapons are likely to cause development and deployment of new offensive weapons capable of evading them.

The Soviet Union had by 1966 placed a few anti-missile missiles around Soviet cities. The United States responded by proposing that the two governments negotiate in an effort to agree that neither would proceed further with ABMs. The Soviets, however, contended that its ABMs were defensive weapons, and therefore represented no threat to the other side.

After considerable delay, and after both sides had undertaken further development of more sophisticated weapons, the USSR expressed willingness to hold bilateral talks with the United States on both offensive and defensive strategic missiles. The UN General Assembly in 1968 passed unanimously a Resolution urging the two Powers to negotiate on strategic missiles as a matter of priority. These bilateral talks began in February, 1970.

Meanwhile, the UN Assembly and the Disarmament Conference have continued to seek a ban on underground nuclear tests. It is increasingly difficult to believe that such a ban is impeded solely by military-technical problems respecting verification. It seems more likely that the usefulness to both countries of underground tests in the further development of nuclear weapons accounts for their continued unwillingness to take the further step indicated.

This might account for Soviet unwillingness to accept any form of international verification, even by those portable instruments known as "little black boxes". Alternatively, it could account for U.S. insistance on international verification. If this is, indeed, the real issue, then the U.S.-Soviet bilateral negotiations on strategic missiles might, if successful, facilitate a ban on underground tests.

The bilateral negotiations on strategic missiles must be successfully concluded as soon as possible in order to halt the impending upward spiral in the arms race. There is also possible real value in completion of the Nuclear Test Ban Treaty. If that were accomplished, peaceful nuclear explosions might then have to be placed under the control of the IAEA, whether conducted by nuclear or non-nuclear nations.

Arms limitation measures achieved thus far have not represented any reduction in armaments, but have been rather, attempts to prevent the arms race from intensifying. Another proposal in this same category deals with a cut-off of production of nuclear material for weapons purposes. Agreement between the U.S. and USSR to "freeze" the manufacture of nuclear weapon materials would undoubtedly raise again the difficult issue of international inspection.

Nuclear production for weapons and for certain peaceful uses are very much the same, and, as the Non-Proliferation Treaty has demonstrated, prohibition of the one requires supervision of the other. It should also be noted that the possibility of commercial espionage by an international inspectorate has been raised by non-nuclear States in considering the Non-Proliferation Treaty. It, therefore, seems likely that the USSR might consider commercial, as well as military, espionage to be a risk inherent in international verification of a cut-off in nuclear materials for weapons.

It may be more practical to consider first the proposal for dismantling a given number of nuclear weapons by each side. The United States has proposed that nuclear material recovered from a limited number of dismantled weapons should be contributed by both sides for the benefit of developing nations. When this proposal was put forward, the U.S. suggested that it contribute a somewhat larger percentage of nuclear material than the USSR in recognition that the U.S. had a proportionate superiority in nuclear weapons.

This plan for dismantling some nuclear weapons has certain advantages over the kindred proposal to cut off production. Dismantling in the manner suggested, could probably be carried out under mutual observation by the Powers concerned of the particular weapons affected. The recovered material would benefit developing States. However, unless the dismantling of some weapons is coupled with a "freeze" on manufacturing materials to replace them, this measure would not necessarily represent an actual reduction in nuclear arsenals.

Important Measures Not Under Active Consideration

Since 1957, disarmament negotiations have been concerned almost exclusively with nuclear weapons. It is, perhaps, natural that the frightfulness of these weapons has tended to the popular belief that it is *nuclear* war which is intolerable. Nevertheless, all wars since World War II have been fought with conventional arms, all wars with conventional arms involve the potential risk of escalation into nuclear war, and nuclear weapons cannot be reduced very much without upsetting the power balance, unless conventional arms are also reduced.

That neglect of measures to limit and reduce conventional armaments is a serious omission in the step-by-step approach to disarmament is illustrated by the situation now pertaining in the Middle East. A series of possible steps to limit conventional arms could be devised. These might range from agreements among major nations not to transfer such weapons to conflict areas, to undertakings coupled with UN observation or peace forces to insure that no such weapons from any source reached any of the Parties in conflict areas. Measures of the kind might range from registration of conventional arms transfers to international licensing of such transfers. Finally new disarmament proposals combining nuclear and conventional arms reductions for all States might be put forward.

The concern of the United Nations and of the Disarmament Committee with the problems of chemical and bacteriological weapons must be characterized as tardy and timid. However, the UN Secretary-General was authorized to prepare, with the help of experts, a report on the nature and effect of such weapons and their possible use. The presentation of that Report to the UN General Assembly has served to enlighten the UN Membership as to the danger of this kind of warfare, and as a goad to the initiation of appropriate measures to control it.

Certain chemical weapons have been characterized as "merciful" in the control of domestic riots, in the conduct of modern war, and possibly in the future conduct of UN peacekeeping operations. Bacteriological, or micro-biological weapons which produce diseases, on the other hand, cannot be similarly justified.

Without forming any judgment as to the possible humane usefulness of some types of chemical weapons, it might be useful to consider separating "disease" weapons from others in this class. It is possible that agreement might then be reached to permit WHO to play a role in controlling "disease" weapons both with respect to detecting deliberate dissemination, and with respect to medical measures to counteract the effect.

Experience has amply demonstrated that the People's Republic of China will not associate itself with arms limitation measures promulgated without its participation. There is, of course, no assurance that Peking's position on disarmament would be any more positive if that government was able to take part in the proceedings. It is, however, undeniable that general and complete disarmament cannot be contemplated without the concurrence of the People's Republic of China. Thus far, no serious effort is being made to involve China in the continuing dialogue, or to provide for China's participation in more extensive disarmament plans.

Surely rapprochement with the People's Republic of China must be regarded as an initial step towards general and complete disarmament. That rapprochement might be initiated by any or all of the following means: by the holding of a world-wide disarmament conference outside the United Nations framework; by efforts to include China in the present Conference of the Disarmament Committee; by new and more realistic approaches to provide for the representation of the People's Republic of China in the United Nations.

Arms limitation measures which have been taken, or which are under active consideration, have been reviewed in this report on their merits. Even such minor efforts should be encouraged in the difficult search for a solution to the problem of war. Nevertheless, it should be restated that these arms limitation measures are based on fragile agreements and are of doubtful durability. While it is hoped that each step taken will "buy time" in which further steps can be negotiated, it must be noted that every small step taken has been enormously time-consuming in its slow progress toward acceptance. Should any measure which has been adopted be subsequently repudiated, public and official disillusionment could result with the effect of slowing, or impeding, new efforts. The question should be raised as to whether preoccupation with such limited efforts distracts negotiators, governments and peoples from the primary objective of general and complete disarmament. The question should be raised as to whether the piecemeal approach to disarmament will make easier or more expeditious progress toward general and complete disarmament than a comprehensive attack upon the subject as a whole.

Seven

Trade, Aid, And Money: Guidelines For American Policy in the United Nations

by

Ernst B. Haas

This year marks the twentieth anniversary of the first major United Nations enterprise in world economic development: the Expanded Program of Technical Assistance. The Program owes much to the initiative of the United States. But it took shape in a world setting in which the United States was still hopeful of dealing with the aspirations of the developing nations as something apart from the main lines of American foreign economic policy. Our hopes were pinned to a vision of steadily growing world trade based on low tariffs, stable and freely convertible currencies, free competition, and a global division of labor, maximizing the initiatives of free enterprise. International institutions, such as the International Bank (IBRD), the International Monetary Fund (IMF), and the General Agreement on Tariffs and Trade (GATT) were to make possible the realization of this vision. Aid to developing nations was to enable them to play their role in the division of labor; hence American policy did not favor regional trading arrangements that would discriminate against third countries and commodity agreements that distorted free trade in primary goods. Multilateral development aid was confined to financing the technical assistance activities of the UN specialized agencies. Trade, aid and money, then, were regarded as separate policy items, treated separately.

Much has been learned since 1949. The lesson does not add up to a coherent and consistent new vision but it reflects a recognition that the original objectives are not attainable in the modern world. Moreover, the separate incremental lessons learned make up the current approach to global economic interdependence; they constitute our present institutional wisdom. What has been learned?

1. In general, trade among developed countries did grow in line with American ideas. Successive negotiating sessions in GATT, linked with the GATT arbitration procedure for settling trade disputes, resulted in dramatic cuts in tariffs among industrial countries and equally dramatic increases in their mutual trade. But the United States realized that the cardinal principles of the most-favored-nation and reciprocity of concessions are acceptable only to industrialized nations. Further, the United States learned that increasing trade dependence on industrial partners requires more responsiveness than anticipated, especially with respect to agricultural commodities. It also taught the United States that regular discussions and frank "confrontations" dealing with domestic economic and financial policies are essential if trade interdependence among developed nations is to continue. Hence the United States agreed to the use of the Organization for Economic Cooperation and Development (OECD) for this purpose.

2. GATT and OECD proved ineffective in helping the trade of developing nations, either with each other or with the industrial nations. The Third World countries demanded the creation of a new world trade-and-aid organization that would take up their development problems *in toto*, instead of in separate compartments as was done by the UN. One response, reluctant on the part of the United States, was the creation in 1964 of the UN Conference on Trade and Development (UNCTAD) as a "continuing" institution. Another was the reform of GATT that eliminated the principle of reciprocity as a condition of tariff bargaining and liberalized the

rules governing trade discrimination on the part of customs unions and regional arrangements.

3. The United States gradually agreed that trade itself should be regarded as a means for spurring economic development, possibly under auspices other than free trade, free enterprise, and free private investment. Hence we accommodated ourselves to the creation of common markets among developing nations and other regional arrangements designed to limit imports from the industrial countries. We also grudgingly consented to participate in some multilateral regulation of the commodity trade and to the principle of compensating developing nations for losses in earnings suffered as a result of falling commodity prices. Finally, the United States agreed to give tariff preferences to the industrial exports of developing nations, provided other industrial countries did the same on a basis of global competition rather than separate regional deals. Most of these lessons were learned in the institutional context of UNCTAD.

4. The world monetary system ceased to be regarded as optimal when the United States began to suffer from balance of payments difficulties and when the demand for dollars created the liquidity crisis. We cautiously approached the possibility of a true world central banking system when we joined in reforming the IMF by creating the system of Special Drawing Rights, with its implication of increased IMF control over national currencies in trouble — including the United States dollar. It appears that the curtain has just risen over the drama of world monetary reform and centralization.

5. The free enterprise-free private investment approach to world capital transfer issues was quietly curtailed when the United States sought to head off Third World demands for large UN capital aid institutions by reforming the IBRD. The demands were not stilled; they continue to be voiced in loud tones. But the IBRD was changed in several ways. It agreed to finance social and economic infrastructure projects formerly not considered bankable; it encouraged effective national economic planning; it created two subsidiaries — the International Development Association to make "soft" loans to the

poorest countries and the International Finance Corporation to invest in specific institutions and firms in the developing countries.

6. Technical assistance to developing nations was stepped up with the creation of the "pre-investment" approach to technical aid pioneered by the UN Special Fund. When the Fund absorbed other UN technical assistance programs and became the UN Development Program it acquired a good deal of control over the separate technical aid activities of the specialized agencies in such fields as agriculture; manpower training, public health, and technical education. Control over technical assistance was centralized under auspices that feature parity of representation for donor and recipient countries.

7. The over-all flow of technical assistance was stepped up in that the contribution to development became the major reason for being of the specialized agencies. However, they continued to follow their individual ways whenever they were not compelled to pull together by the UN Development Program. American opposition did not succeed in preventing the creation of a major new aid agency, the UN Industrial Development Organization (UNIDO).

8. Despite original opposition to the idea of global economic and development "planning," the United States has accepted the forecasting and analysis designed to pull all these scattered activities together under the aegis of the Second Development Decade, to begin in 1970. It also accepted the "planning" of scientific and technological knowledge and its diffusion to spur the development of the Third World, through the UN Advisory Committee on the Application of Science and Technology to Development (UNAC).

But the resulting policies remain unclear. The institutions go their separate ways. And the benefits from the lessons learned are likely to be minimal unless much greater vision is shown. No new set of trade and money rules has emerged and, while a shift in institutional enmeshment can be gleaned from the welter of activity, no consensus on aid policy can be seen as the Third World continues its demands for dramatic global income and resource redistribution. Trade and aid still go their separate ways, undoing each other's tasks on occasion. The United States is uncertain *why* aid is desirable and *how* trade practices and aid objectives can be linked. Nor does it know *when* and *where* multilateral channels should be preferred over bilateral ones.

Ambiguity of Foreign Economic Policy

American officials favor a doctrine that explains economic aid as furthering "political development" in recipient nations; but they cannot agree on whether "political development" means anti-communism, pro-Americanism, or attachment to peaceful change. Further they cannot explain *how* economic aid is able to realize these political objectives as long as it is evaluated largely in economic terms; in practice, the objectives of a given country program come to mean "economic growth in the short run." Sometimes a pragmatic consensus seems to be much the same as a lack of consensus among the very people most in need of clarity of purpose.

Policy-makers and specialists have learned and adjusted; that is, they have bent with the international storm without acquiring a clear new direction. But the business community shows little evidence of accepting institutional enmeshment, continued global income redistribution, or world economic planning; some even regard the various UN aid activities as a kind of development blackmail. Nor do we have a clear indication that congressional opinion has swung decisively behind such new objectives and methods toward foreign aid and trade as deliberate tools of social engineering.

There is as little enthusiasm on Capitol Hill as elsewhere for the trend toward autonomous UN capital aid agencies, organs that are seen as politicizing economic development activity and detracting from the sober work of the specialized agencies. Development has been perceived by Congress as part of the fight against communism. The continuation of multilateral aid under declining American control, in the face of the East-West détente, makes little sense to many legislators. A new and broader justification for such aid has yet to be widely accepted.

And why should such a sentiment arise? Americans have been assured that trade and aid will stabilize volatile nations, establish democracy, help free private enterprise abroad, teach economic planning, defeat communism, help in nation-building, and aid the American farmer, educator, and industrialist. They also see that these objectives conflict on their face and are diluted in practice by Congress and the Executive. They see further that very little of this seems actually to be realized in aid operations. They do not always understand that short-run and long-run aims may well conflict, that democracy in a generation's time can be built — perhaps — on the basis of an aid-supported military dictatorship today. But since the objectives of the UN are hardly more explicit or consistent, the rational choice of means and instruments is not made easier by the mere fact that the balance of persuasive power has shifted in favor of the UN. We must conclude therefore that the very ambiguity surrounding the objectives and successes of foreign economic policy make it more difficult for a new cohesive American consensus to arise.

New Purpose in Multilateral Foreign Economic Policy

In reality the challenge for American policy must be the recognition that the improvement of *some* living standards will make frustrations that have thus far been borne in silence break out into open rebellion, thus almost making the revolution of rising expectations the archenemy of economic aid. And one may thus have to conclude that our growing enmeshment in these institutions will lead to the attainment of none of the many objectives of foreign aid unless a far more cohesive policy toward *planned* aid and trade is adopted.

Such a plan must be calculated to achieve the basic American objectives of a prosperous world in which the individual can improve his lot with a minimum of coercion, violence, and manipulation by impersonal political and technological forces. More aid could easily be given by the United States if the OECD-endorsed target of annual contributions equal to one percent of Gross National Product is to be met. American aid has not reached that target in recent years. If the principle of the progressive income tax were used to compute national contributions to IDA, the United States could be responsible for 65 percent of the funds instead of the 43 percent actually contributed. UNIDO and the Capital Development Fund could be generously supported without making them into giant give-aways if the distribution and evaluation of aid were made the collective responsibility of the recipients and donors. Furthermore, an increase in the multilateral aid component would reduce the uneconomic practice of tying aid funds that continues to flourish. Economic aid intended to contribute to stability, prosperity, and peace in long-range terms is the shared objective of the United States and the UN. Why not increase the UN share of such aid since there is no conflict of objectives? Moreover, UN-administered aid has distinct advantages over bilateral measures: it will restore the notion of a master plan for world betterment that was lost early in UN history, and the United States will be prominently associated with this revival; countries resisting the strings of bilateral Soviet or American aid should have a multilateral program large enough to suit them if America's professions in favor of nonalignment are to be believed; economic problems could be tackled on their merits and outside the special political aims usually implied in bilateral aid and without fear of wounding sensibilities or seeming to intervene. UN intervention seems to be more legitimate and acceptable than national measures of this kind.

American aid ought to be largely multilateralized so as to avoid the need for constant — and inconsistently implemented — choices regarding who ought to receive what kind of aid and in order to stimulate recipient participation in the planning of aid measures. This ought to result in the availability of UN aid funds multiplied, perhaps, by a factor of ten over current resources; more if other donor nations follow the American lead. This will allow the mounting of more and different kinds of aid projects, permit fuller evaluation of results, and finance additional training facilities. It will also permit the devotion of larger human resources on the part of the UN to the supervision of projects. Most specifically, it will allow for the creation of large corps of career UN aid supervisors and administrators, in the form of an expanded and specially trained group of resident representatives and deputy resident representatives.

A coordinated approach implies the reduction of American support to social and economic activities in the specialized agencies which do not qualify. It also involves serious soul-searching on the part of the United States as well as all other industrialized nations as to whether their trade policies aid or hinder the economic development of the Third World. It may well turn out that the GATT approach remains relevant to trade among industrial countries while a different set of rules ought to be worked out for trade among developing nations and between them and the industrialized world. Moreover, since the trade among industrial nations accounts for so much of total world trade, special rules departing from the principles of equal, competitive, and nondiscriminatory treatment must sometimes be observed even in trade among industrial nations. This is true particularly with respect to the introduction of new products competing with the exports of Third World nations. Trade rules geared to development needs thus require some kind of planning, a periodic survey of Western trade policy in terms of its contribution to economic development elsewhere. This approach also calls for new commercial practices, such as special preferences and commodity agreements, that may actually be uneconomic from the Western viewpoint. It calls for easier credit terms and new kinds of credit to finance more uneconomic projects. It calls for a world monetary policy which respects aspirations additional to the payments and liquidity needs of the West.

These purposes call for an approach to trade and aid that is different from the hit-and-miss procedure we have favored since the mid-Fifties. Our objectives must be to advance economic modernization of the Third World *in a way that will minimize disruption of society, keep frustrations at a low*

*level, and restrain the propensity of leaders and revolution-
ary political parties to bully and manipulate their citizens.*
Our objective therefore must be redistributive, must be the
gradual reduction of the tension between North and South.
Clearly, this conception of our national interest does not deny
that the United States and the industrial world also have legitimate economic objective of their own.   The task, therefore,
is the reconciliation of the redistributive aim with the protection of living standards in the West. It can be carried out
only if aid and trade policies are considered jointly, as part
of a single package, rather than as separate and competing
strands in the web of economic interdependence.

Decolonization may very well prove to have been a cruel
hoax on the developing nations. As they became independent,
direct responsibility of the industrial nations for their welfare has declined, because independence included the right
and competence to plan and execute national economic development. But at the same time as the revolution of rising expectations triggers demand for higher production and greater consumption, technological-scientific change constantly increases efficiency of the rich nations, their trade with each
other, and their autonomy from the primary exports of the
developing nations. Far from being exploited by the rich,
the poor are simply becoming irrelevant to them.

Trade and aid policy, then, must overcome the isolation of
irrelevance, in order to satisfy rising expectations without
triggering the wholesale destruction of nonindustrial values
and institutions. This victory, however, is dependent upon the
West's acceptance of a doctrine of redistribution in which indefinite growth of productivity is unnecessary, even dysfunc-
tional. The West must be willing to forego the introduction
of synthetic materials and automated production, to decline to
make use of innovations just because they are available and
cheaper.

American and European industry, and Japan's as well,
must learn to subordinate their production and export policies
to the needs of the developing nations. American and European industry can absorb losses when Indian and Chilean

industry cannot. The first duty of the wealthy nations must be to protect and expand the prices and volume of the exports offered by the developing nations. Only thus can the poorer nations build up their own capital for industrialization. Only thus can trade take the place of aid that might well stifle indigenous adaptation and entrepreneurship. Hence, using some foreign aid funds to help adjust American producers who are adversely affected by the mass importation of textiles, shoes, and processed food from the poor nations makes more sense than investing that aid in stemming hunger or starting unproductive heavy industries.

Such an attitude, however, also calls for certain devices to protect the industrial nations from the possibility that a united Third World will blackmail developed countries.   In addition, certain Western nations may be able to derive undue advantage at the expense of others unless care is taken to avoid this. Hence concessions to the Third World and self-restraint in the West must be determined jointly: UNCTAD should become the forum for making trade rules, but OECD should be greatly upgraded to become the effective institutionalized Western caucus within UNCTAD.

The Inadequacy of Current International Planning

Most of these ideas are far from new. The novelty of the argument resides in the fact that a certain grudging and hesitant recognition is now given it in the planning of the Second Development Decade.   Some economists and scientists have suggested for some time that only some version of world economic planning can provide a unified approach to development and welfare in which trade serves the purposes of aid and in which a world monetary policy facilitates both instead of merely limping from crisis to crisis.

The preparations for the Second Development Decade illustrate the extent to which such a planning vision has become reality. In an effort to show the world how much agricultural production is needed to feed a burgeoning population a decade hence, FAO has prepared an indicative world food plan: it "indicates" who must grow what and invest how much; it cannot do more than that without appropriate national and international aid, trade and monetary policies. The UN Center for Programming and Projections has drawn up a model of world economic growth based on a limited number of variables and a series of assumptions about possible growth rates. It spells out how much trade and investment is necessary so that the rates may be realized. These projections make no provision for technological change, product substitution, changes in demand elasticities, surprises in population growth, biological breakthroughs, or political decisions to increase or curtail participation in world affairs.

This model is now being used as the focus for negotiating agreements among all UN agencies as to the proper targets for trade, aid, and investment — as well as the appropriate role for each agency in realizing the targets. The model is regularly discussed by the Secretary-General's Committee on Development Planning as to its validity and applicability in the major world regions. It is also used to determine which specialized agency will perform what role. FAO, ILO, WHO, and UNESCO are the primary participants with the task of fostering social development to make the attainment of economic targets possible.

But a great many things remain unclear. The position of UNCTAD as a negotiating forum for a unified trade-aid policy is not defined. Social development is given an instrumental task in the plan, rather than treated as a primary objective. The lending policy of the IBRD and the currency stabilization policies of the IMF remain to be coordinated with the model. Neither GATT nor OECD have been drawn into the discussions. Social, economic, and educational research done by UN research institutes is scarcely consulted in the econometrics of the indicative plan. The possibility of using the work done by UN technical and scientific agencies in the fields of climate change and satellite communications has not been considered. The work of UNAC in diffusing technological and scientific knowledge goes forward without direct link to economic development policy. In short, despite incipient planning, each sector remains autonomous. Thought remains as compartmentalized as does policy. The short run remains master over our long-term future. If no other forces in the UN are willing or able to do better, it is high time for the United States to take the initiative in doing so.

Institutions and World Planning: Science and Technology

There is nothing approaching comprehensive planning in the UN system in the field of science and technology. Separate committees, commissions, and institutes seek to isolate priority areas, to define the kind of effort that ought to be made in spurring general goals of the Development Decade. The dangers of perilously unbalanced social and economic trends, of breakthroughs in one field of endeavor checking those in another and making man more subject to manipulation by blind technological forces, are not being faced when the UN Advisory Committee on the Application of Science and Technology simply recommends such things as cheap and simple generators in villages, regional technology centers, and mass education via telecommunications satellites. How these things will affect social ties, expectations, and the structure of future elites ought to be taken into account first.

The episodic, gimmick-dependent, and uncoordinated efforts at planning suggest the need for two kinds of institutions to engage in systematic forecasting: one for economic and social aspects, another for science and technology. These organs would not "plan" in the sense of setting future goals for education, industrial production, agricultural output, and the size of cities. Such planning is beyond the scope of human ability at the moment. The forecasting bodies would not plan definitively so much as they would think out the probable consequences of innovations on social and economic structure, impartially weigh alternative paths of development, warn politicians and administrators of the implications of policies already beng planned, and advise them on the choices open to them. But this self-conscious attitude toward the possibilities and risks of innovations should be broken down into economic and social forecasting as opposed to

dealing with innovation growing out of scientific and technological change. The machinery created for planning the
Second Development Decade falls lamentably short of these
objectives. The attitudes and expectations inspiring the machinery show little evidence of being conscious of the needs
for candid forecasts. We shall return to social and economic
forecasting when we talk of institutions appropriate for trade
and aid. Here we are concerned with science and technology.

Two kinds of scientific self-awareness already are institutionalized in the web of international organizations. When
nations have recognized that control over the physical and
man-made environment can be obtained only by joint effort,
appropriate agencies have been created: the International
Civil Aviation Organization, the World Meteorological Organization, the International Telecommunication Union, and
the Intergovernmental Maritime Consultative Organization.
IAEA and UNESCO also reflect this concern. Governments
have done next to nothing in joint exploration of the physical
universe and mapping its resources; but efforts have been
made by numerous private associations of scientists united
in the International Council of Scientific Unions. They
have been carried farthest in the field of coordinated
space research under COSPAR. It is here that an international community of functional specialists has grown
most rapidly. But few links have been created between
discovery, assessment of the results of discovery, control over
the environment, and implementation of that control. The
need is for institutions now to forge such links before it is
too late.

The United States should take the initiative in creating
a UN Science Advisory Council with a mandate to examine
areas of impending scientific breakthroughs and to assess
their social implications. This Council should be composed
of eminent scientists selected by ICSU and should meet in
almost continuous session. Eventually it might be given the
power even to prohibit lines of research found to be over-
whelmingly harmful to human dignity and contentment. It
might also be given the power to license risky kinds of research for limited periods and reassess results periodically.

The United States should also take the initiative in creating a second body, a UN Conference on Environmental Control. This organ would consist of national ministerial delegates charged with responsibilities such as water and air pollution control, urban planning, rural reconstruction, and resources management. Panels of experts chosen from scientific unions associated with ICSU would be permanent advisers on trends and problems in each area of environmental control. With this advice, the conference would eventually issue instructions governing environmental control, to be implemented by the existing UN specialized agencies and any new ones needed to deal with pollution of the oceans, with weather control, and migration.

The implementing agencies would have to be reformed in order to make possible their coordinated efforts under a UN Conference, and in response to a panel of UN Wise Men. They would have to cease being sovereign agencies, each ruled by its own intergovernmental conference. The temptation to create a specialized agency for world resources management should be resisted and opposed by the United States. Further, the United States could put teeth into the policy of scientific planning and forecasting by threatening to curtail its contributions to the budgets of ITU, WMO, IMCO, and ICAO unless these agencies grow aware of the consequences of their work. Unless such pressure is brought to bear, Parkinson's Law will continue to operate, unabated, in institutional proliferation.

Institutions and World Planning: Trade and Aid

Institution-building in the economic field must accept the principle that the neocapitalistic notions on which the GATT system is based do not conform to the needs of heading off economic and social imbalances. Trading on the basis of the most-favored-nation will not help Africa develop. Investments in labor-intensive manufactures will not raise living standards unless the products find a market. Stabilizing commodity prices will not help unless the mass flight into synthetics is halted. A world currency based on a shaky dollar is not calculated to facilitate orderly economic growth.

The GATT rules—or a maximum degree of international laissez faire—are obsolete. GATT remains relevant, including its machinery for the peaceful and judicial solution of trade disputes, for the commerce among industrial nations. But since tariffs cannot be cut much more in the Atlantic area, even here the continuing negotiating function of GATT might have run its course. In short, American policy is wrong in continuing to invest in GATT as an institution or a program. GATT's role should be to prevent nations from going back on their tariff bargains. Our job, instead, is to design new institutions for coordinating a world trade and aid policy that will permit relatively painless change while we deal with the underdeveloped world's impatience. We ought to be ready to tolerate an untidy world-trading system, the growth of many new common markets and freetrade areas that derogate from GATT principles and fail to meet the stringent criteria of the optimal economic growth doctrine. We are well launched toward such a "system" anyway. Finally, the institutionalized confrontation between rich and poor— in UNCTAD and similar organs—is a fact of life. UNCTAD must therefore become the centerpiece of a coordinated and rationalized approach to aid and trade.

Placing UNCTAD in this position implies two very major institutional innovations. First, it means that the principle of majority voting must be abandoned wherever it may be permitted constitutionally. Since the first sharp splits at the 1964 conference, UNCTAD wisely makes all decisions by "consensus" and "conciliation"; that is, votes may be taken in each of the caucuses but over-all agreements are negotiated until general agreement is reached, and voting is avoided in plenary meetings. This procedure ought to be the general rule in all UN aid and trade bodies. Majoritarianism makes no sense at all when some twenty-five countries provide the aid and markets for about one hundred other countries. Second, the principle of sovereign autonomy for specialized agencies, the UN Development Program, and the

UN Industrial Development Organization must go, as must the separate status of a half-dozen planning and forecasting bodies. All these bodies must become subordinate to a centralized and coordinated approach to trade and aid, in which UNCTAD will be the centerpiece. They must give up their autonomous intergovernmental conferences and policy-making boards.

Coordination and rationalization demand the following major institutional changes: (1) in each government, creation of machinery that will be better able to make and absorb trade-aid policy and better able to participate in UN decision-making. What is to be avoided is the uncoordinated and decentralized way in which most governments participate in the General Assembly, the Economic and Social Council, the Development Program, and each of the dozen specialized agencies—especially the IBRD and the IMF. (2) For each government, a single spokesman must be able to state his nation's coordinated views. All spokesmen would sit in a re-organized ECOSOC, a UN Welfare Council with clear and sole jurisdiction over the aid-trade-money nexus. (3) The creation of a nongovernmental UN Social Planning Board merging all the present planning groups, to advise the Welfare Council and UNCTAD. (4) Elevation of UNCTAD as the central decision-making body for trade, aid, and money, accountable to the Welfare Council in principle, but powerful in ruling the totality of UN economic and social bodies. (5) Subordination of IBRD, IMF, and the Development Program to the directives of UNCTAD. (6) The subordination of ILO, FAO, WHO, UNESCO, and UNIDO to the Development Program's policies and funds. (7) Sharply increased powers of UN Resident Representatives in implementing aid policies at the national level.

Obviously, institutional tinkering is meaningful only if it provides channels of expression for existing and nascent political groupings with identifiable common interests, opposing the interests of other blocs but converging with them as well.

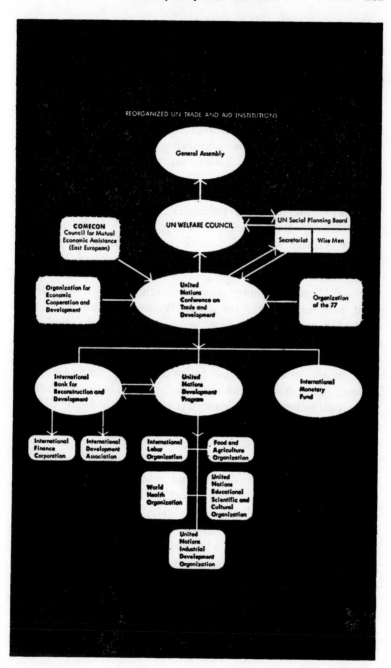

REORGANIZED UN TRADE AND AID INSTITUTIONS

Hence, just as the Third World in 1967 fashioned a standing organization to represent Third-World views in future UNCTAD negotiations, so should the West. The United States should take the initiative in converting OECD into the West's (and Japan's) spokesman and pressure group. Since we are reconciled to an untidy and overlapping economic bloc system, this would give the European Common Market its institutional expression while permitting the same to the Latin American Free-Trade Association and the East African Common Market in the Group of the 77. OECD would serve the purpose of perfecting and supervising the GATT rules that the industrial nations wish to retain for trade among themselves, including GATT's arbitral competence. OECD would also work out a common "negotiating package" for the West, to be presented to the Third World. A strengthened OECD can prevent the Third World from playing one Western country against another; it can also bring great pressure to bear on single Western nations to join in fashioning a single and sensitive approach to the trade-aid-money needs of the developing nations. Moreover, the rationalization of policy in each major camp will also have repercussions in the policies to be followed by the Inter-American, African, and Asian Development Banks. These institutions, while continuing to be financed independently from UN aid sources, will then nevertheless fit into an over-all policy pattern.

The UN Welfare Council should have a membership larger than the present ECOSOC and smaller than the General Assembly, to which it would report. The council is not conceived as a major policy-making body. Its purpose is to review, at high-level, negotiations and policies elaborated at lower levels, and thus be able to socialize governments into the habits of coordinating trade, aid, money, and development planning. The *raison d'être* of the council is the socialization function; unless governments also reorganize appropriately at the national level, it will be as marginal to UN operations as is the now familiar ECOSOC. Voting should be avoided here, as in UNCTAD.

A UN Social Planning Board is the social science counterpart to the UN Science Advisory Council. Like its counterpart, it should be made up of a number of generally respected and impartial social scientists, serving as individuals, able to weigh and judge the *interaction* of economic, social, technological, and political trends. The Wise Men should be aided by the present UN Secretariat staff scattered over the existing planning bodies, and they should maintain close links with international social science professional associatons. The board should advise and carry out studies for UNCTAD as well as for the UN Welfare Council. It might well include specialized panels drawn from international professional associations, particularly in fields such as housing, demography, and education.

The center of gravity, however, rests with an UNCTAD now made legitimate by our recognition that the world will not necessarily be shaped entirely in the American image — at least not without lots of future Vietnams. Trade, aid, and monetary policy will be *made* in UNCTAD; that is, it will be negotiated continuously. UNCTAD, where every government will be represented, ought to become the superspecialized agency with competence over the entire development nexus. The UN Development Program could then shed its present Governing Council and simply become the executing organ of the technical aid and pre-investment part of the package negotiated in UNCTAD. It should use for this purpose the major specialized agencies and UNIDO; but these bodies would have to lose their independent budgets and policy-making organs too. It therefore behooves the United States, as the major contributor, to change its policy, throw its annual bilateral and multilateral aid contribution into the UNCTAD negotiations, and go along with an UNCTAD-determined allocation for technical assistance as opposed to capital investment.

UNCTAD would also acquire control over the general policy of the IBRD, though much discretion would have to be left to the bank's staff in making specific loans. By gaining large new funds for grants and interest-free loans, IDA would be the main beneficiary of the multilateralization of American aid. Certainly, IDA's attitude toward development would have to be brought under the control of UNCTAD as well, thus implying some loss of power for the national central bank governors who now quite autonomously make IMF policy. The special role of the dollar, sterling, and gold should be curtailed further. New drawing rights of the kind now proposed for the IMF should be created and administered autonomously by the Fund's staff, in line with over-all UNCTAD directives, rather than in response to the central banks of the world's major trading nations. The rules governing the use of IMF reserves should be liberalized to permit the Fund's participation in commodity stabilization agreements, balance of payments difficulties associated with structural readjustment of economies to new production and employment patterns, and even for peacekeeping expenses. The IMF, in short, ought to become a world central bank, responsive not only to short-term balance of payments troubles associated often with national monetary mismanagement, but to the long-term liquidity needs of developing as well as industrial nations.

Eight

U.N. Protection of Human Rights After Twenty-Five Years
by
John Carey

Human Rights Obligations in the U.N. Charter

After a century of occasional use, the guarantee of the individual's rights through an international legal order reached a breakthrough in 1945 with what U Thant has called "perhaps the boldest innovation of the Charter — the unconditional and universal obligation in regard to human rights and fundamental freedoms."[1]

Human rights are mentioned a number of times in the Charter; the provisions to which the Secretary-General doubtless referred were those in Article 56 under which "all Members pledge themselves to take joint and separate action in cooperation with the Organization for the achievement of the purposes set forth in Article 55," which in turn provides that "the United Nations shall promote: . . . universal respect for, and observance of, human rights and fundamental freedoms for all without distinction as to race, sex, language, or religion."

During the three years following adoption of the Charter, the U.N. enumerated the rights therein referred to, in a Uni-

---

[1] From statement at opening of forty-fifth session of ECOSOC, Geneva, July 8, 1968. U.N. Press Release SG/SM/971-ECOSOC/2474.

versal Declaration of Human Rights. The twentieth anniversary of the Declaration's adoption in 1948 was marked as International Year for Human Rights 1968, proclaimed both by the U.N. and by the President of the United States. The final stage in elaborating an international "bill of rights" was reached in 1966, when work was completed on treaties putting in legally binding form most of the rights set forth in the Universal Declaration.

Development of U.N. Authority Concerning Human Rights

Despite the Charter power of both the U.N.'s Economic and Social Council (ECOSOC) and its Human Rights Commission to promote human rights (Articles 62, 68), it seemed for two decades to be established that U.N. activity would with rare exceptions, be confined to making general studies and drafting treaties or declarations. As the U.N.'s second decade neared its end, however, practices grew up, applicable only to colonies and to the Republic of South Africa, which took account of individuals' complaints and gave them wide notice. So extensive a set of practices was bound in the end to lap over into the broader area of human rights complaints generally.

In the first half of the decade of the 1960's the Committee on Colonialism of the UN General Assembly, followed shortly thereafter by the Committee on South African apartheid, began holding hearings for complaints and publishing their written complaints. While some felt that this process produced very little result, the mere publication of individuals' complaints, either oral or written, was a new field of activity for the UN. As a result of some of the complaints which were brought to the surface by this process in the Colonialism Committee, the General Assembly in October of 1966 in its landmark Resolution 2144 invited the Economic and Social Council and the Commission on Human Rights to give urgent consideration to ways and means of improving the capacity of the UN to put a stop to violations of human rights wherever they might occur.

The U.N. Human Rights Commission meeting in early 1967, shortly after Assembly resolution 2144 was adopted, resolved to ask the Sub-Commission on Prevention of Discrimination and Protection of Minorities to bring to the Commission's attention any situation which the Sub-Commission had reasonable cause to believe revealed a consistent pattern of violations of human rights and fundamental freedoms in any country, including policies of racial discrimination, segregation and apartheid, with particular reference to colonial and dependent territories. In addition, the Human Rights Commission asked the Sub-Commission to prepare a report containing information on violations of human rights and fundamental freedoms from all available sources.

A little later, in June 1967, ECOSOC in resolution 1235 approved these arrangements, and in addition took a step of great significance when it gave authority to both the Commission and the Sub-Commission to inspect all of the many thousands of written human rights complaints which flow year by year to the U.N. This authority was granted for the explicit purpose of complying with the duties assigned to the Commission and Sub-Commission with respect to their annual consideration of the question of violations of fundamental rights throughout the world.

Prior to June 1967, the thousands of written complaints coming to the UN each year were handled in accordance with a highly restrictive arrangement contained in ECOSOC resolution 728F under which complaints relating to any parts of the world other than colonies or South Africa were simply filed at U.N. Headquarters, and a form letter sent to the complainant advising that substantially nothing could be done. A copy was sent without the name of the author to the State complained against, for any comments which it might care to make.

The new procedure under ECOSOC resolution 1235 allowed the Commission and Sub-Commission to look at these complaints in the original form instead of in the form of mere summaries prepared by the Secretariat. The new procedure was first put into effect at the meeting of the Sub-Commission in Geneva in October 1967. The outcome was a resolution, adopted without any contrary vote, which recommended to the Human Rights Commission further investigation concerning not only those parts of Southern Africa which had become traditional targets of UN investigation, but also two countries elsewhere in the world, Greece and Haiti. When the Sub-Commission's resolution came before the Human Rights Commission in February 1968, representatives of Greece and Haiti spoke at length in defense of their policies, a novel situation in U.N. experience. The further investigation of those countries recommended by the Sub-Commission was not approved, but neither was the precedent thus set rejected, despite sharp attacks on that body.

The Sub-Commission in October 1968 discreetly said no more on Greece and Haiti, but merely drew the attention of the Commission to the further discussions it had just conducted, touching not only Greece and Haiti, but also Czechoslovakia, the Middle East, and Southern Africa. The Sub-Commission did, however, adopt by a vote of nine in favor and five abstentions, with only the Soviet and Polish members dissenting, a remarkable resolution proposing detailed procedures for handling complaints regardless of source. The carefully devised provisions, whose sponsorship included Afro-Asians as well as Westerners, adopt a tactic long employed in I.L.O. freedom of association usage, of requiring government consent for full investigation but providing for extensive preliminary scrutiny without it. This ingenious compromise between the U.N.'s human rights authority and the claims of national sovereignty recognized in Charter Article 2(7) received the full support of the U.S. Government in the next higher U.N. body, the Human Rights Commission, where it was approved in a slightly modified version and ECOSOC approval was requested.

Implementation of Human Rights Protection Under U.N. Treaties

The conventions that were written to reduce to legally binding form the Universal Declaration of Human Rights are the 1966 Covenant on Civil and Political Rights, with its Optional Protocol on handling individuals' complaints, and the Covenant on Economic, Social and Cultural Rights. These

have many signatures but few ratifications, while the 1965
U.N. Convention on the Elimination of All Forms of Racial
Discrimination became effective in January 1969.

The efficacy of treaties as a means of human rights protection is deterred by ratification problems illustrated in U.S.
experience. The submission to the Senate by President Tru-
man of the 1948 Genocide Convention (and of the less controversial I.L.O. Convention on Freedom of Association) was
followed by the Bricker Amendment struggle, whose after-
math included a State Department stance of declining any
substantial role in U.N. human rights treaty-making. No human rights treaty was sent to the Senate until President Kennedy, shortly before his death, asked for advice and consent
on the Women's Rights, Forced Labor, and Slavery treaties.
Only the last was approved, and ratification followed late in
1967. Meantime President Johnson had submitted the I.L.O.'s
Employment Policy Convention, which the U.N. classifies as
a human rights pact. Late in 1968, the Senate complied with
his request to approve a Protocol to the Refugee Convention,
another instrument concerned with human rights. The U.S.
record of human rights treaty ratification ranks near the bot-
tom among U.N. Members.

The Tools at Hand for International Protection

The use of treaties for international legislation is, without
more, one of the available tools for human rights enhancement and protection, since sometimes merely setting standards
promotes their fulfillment. Voluntary compliance is also
encouraged by the educational process which the U.N. carries on through seminars and fellowships. Where, however,
enforcement is needed, various international legal tools have
been employed, ranging in coerciveness from force of arms
to simple exposure to public view. Where naught avails, aid-
ing the victim of oppression is the international community's
last resort for righting violations.

Coercion short of force, depriving the offending government of some economic benefits, is a legal tool now in use
against Rhodesia under binding Security Council directions.

Another tool is adjudication, employed by the International Court of Justice and European Court of Human Rights and used at Nuremberg in criminal proceedings of a type now urged by some to combat South African apartheid. Non-judicial investigations by international bodies can be effective, and offer a variety of techniques for information gathering and evaluaton. Quiet negotiation to persuade officials is a tool whose effect is enhanced by the threat of exposure to world opinion through the separate tool of publicity. Such are the human rights tools developed under international law. A summary evaluation of the tools follows.

(a) Legislation and Education

International legislative measures to the number of thirty-seven are present or potential parts of world-wide or regional human rights law.[2] While not by its terms purporting to create legal rights or duties, the 1948 Universal Declaration of Human Rights is said by some authorities to have acquired the status of law. The less-than-universal but explicitly binding European Convention on Human Rights and Fundamental Freedoms is the first such legislation at the regional level. The 1948 American Declaration of the Rights of Man is being followed up by a draft Inter-American Convention on Human Rights currently under discussion by Western Hemisphere Governments.

The effectiveness of standards alone, apart from enforcement tools, can be enhanced through educational measures like the U.N.'s program of seminars and fellowships, whereby government officials and future leaders are exposed to ideas and methods employed in other lands. But where government good faith does not exist, enforcement is needed. Therefore, with U.N. adoption of the 1966 Human Rights Covenants, the drafting of standards was widely regarded as ended for the time being and attention turned to enforcement tools.

---

[2] Situation des Conventions Internationales Relatives aux Droits de l'Homme, 1 HUMAN RIGHTS J. 315 (1968).

(b) Use of Force

Scholars once believed, and some still do, that single nations could validly use their might to protect foreigners from their own governments' excesses. With the U.N. Charter, force was made illegal except in self-defense or when ordered by the Security Council. In theory the Council could, after a reasonable finding that South Africa's oppression of non-whites threatens international peace, send troops to compel apartheid's abolition. The impracticability of such an undertaking is demonstrated both by the problems of reaching U.N. consensus for far less drastic steps and by the obvious difficulties of occupying a hostile land even where the occupier is far stronger than the local forces.

(c) Coercion

The U.N. and its specialized agencies have, for human rights purposes, deprived offending states of a variety of benefits. Southern Rhodesia has been the target of three compulsory Security Council trade prohibitions, but the Smith regime remains. South African relations with other countries have been attacked in fruitless U.N. resolutions short of legal prohibition. U.N. specialized agencies like the World Bank and International Monetary Fund have been exhorted by the Assembly to withhold their favors from both South Africa and Portugal, but neither country seems to be affected. Steps by UNESCO and WHO to exclude such states from participation in their affairs have had no apparent result. Efforts in 1968 to oust South Africa from the U.N. Conference on Trade and Development failed to pass in the face of arguments questioning both their legality and their efficacy. The tool of coercion therefore offers little hope of enhancing or protecting human rights.

(d) Adjudication

Disillusionment with judicial process in human rights matters was so widespread after the 1966 South West Africa cases that the World Court was not mentioned in the Human Rights Covenants adopted later that year, despite its featured place in the 1965 Convention on Elimination of All Forms of Racial Discrimination. Numerous Race Convention Parties have made reservations against the Court's jurisdiction.

With the anti-World Court reaction and mounting anti-apartheid frustration, criminal process of the Nuremberg type became increasingly attractive in some quarters. The possibility of using the accusation phase of criminal procedure, with or without the trial stage, began to be studied. Indictment of brutal government officials by U.N. bodies was discussed as a deterrent, possibly useful even if the accused were far beyond the U.N.'s reach. While deterrence of individuals through merely *prima facie* findings of guilt is speculative, it might well do more to relieve the oppressed than protracted inter-state litigation.

(e) Investigation

For several decades the I.L.O. has shown how "supervision," its process of reviewing government reports, can produce results in human rights affairs. The U.N. too inquires of governments on many matters, these included. But governments alone are often thought not to suffice as sources of information on cases to which they are parties. Both private groups and individuals are therefore turned to for their versions of the facts.

Private groups have standing in the U.N. Charter, at least for general consultations. Some of them which have played an active role in particular human rights cases have borne the brunt of governmental wrath. Individuals have gained stature in U.N. proceedings, by being permitted to bring their complaints to the attention of a U.N. body, as described above, a possibility previously open to certain Europeans and Americans having access to regional commissions but limited at the U.N. to inhabitants of colonies or South Africa. Individuals will in some cases also have standing to complain to international bodies under the 1965 Convention on Elimination of All Forms of Racial Discrimination and, when it becomes effective, under the Optional Protocol to the 1966 Covenant on Civil and Political Rights.

Investigation has been seized on by the U.N. Human Rights Commission and ECOSOC since 1967. An *Ad Hoc* Group of Experts was assigned the task at first of looking into the treatment of prisoners and detainees in South Africa. Later the Group's mandate was expanded geographically to cover other parts of southern Africa, and substantively to include alleged violations of trade union rights. The members of the Group were asked at the Commission's 1969 session to investigate charges that the 1949 Geneva Convention on the treatment of civilians was being violated in Israeli-held Arab lands.

The effectiveness of investigation, taken by itself without appeal to world opinion, depends partly on the respondent government's good faith and partly on the skill with which the next one of the international tools for enhancement and protection of human rights is wielded.

(f) Negotiation

Quiet persuasion of governments by international agencies is of proven usefulness in relieving victims of oppression. Examples of such agencies are the U.N. High Commissioner for Refugees and the semi-official International Committee of the Red Cross. UNHCR seeks to protect and aid those who have fled their countries, including arranging for their repatriation. ICRC seeks without publicity to succor those who cannot flee. UNHCR and ICRC are allowed by governments to intercede for their citizens because of the impartiality for which both agencies are known. The proposed U.N. High Commissioner for Human Rights, to be allowed a similar role, would need the same high reputation.

(g) Publicity

Will governments which have not responded to investigation or negotiation pay heed to outside criticism which follows disclosure of their human rights transgressions? More impressive affirmative testimony could scarcely be found than that recently presented in the course of the U.N. investigation just mentioned, by former prisoners of South Africa's regime. They felt that even that regime was not oblivious to friendly

Powers' opinions. In the similar view of the Secretary-General, ". . .a purposeful and universal programme of public information is, in fact, a programme of implementation . . . ." [3]

The U.N. Human Rights Agenda

While some now feel that the drafting of substantive standards is mostly done and that more attention can be paid to measures of enforcement, the standard writing process may continue. Instruments in two fields, freedom of information and religious intolerance, remain unfinished. The threats which science and technology pose to human rights should be confronted and suitable limits drawn to protect the individual. The whole range of human rights could be embodied, as some have urged, in a collection patterned after I.L.O.'s International Labor Code.

Intenser interest has been shown in standards which relate to fields of hot contention. Charges of oppression against inhabitants of Vietnam, Biafra and Israeli-held Arab territories have brought a call for revision and up-dating of the 1949 Geneva Conventions on treatment of certain persons in wartime. Frustration at their inability to combat racial policies in militarily powerful South Africa and Rhodesia have led to substitution of oppressive individuals for whole governments as the objects of international legislation, and criminal standards have been set, not only in the 1968 U.N. Convention on Non-Applicability of Statutory Limitation to War Crimes and Crimes Against Humanity but also in sundry enactments of the General Assembly having in theory no binding effect. Interest in branding racial wrongs as crimes may tend to flag, unless quite soon some hijacked airplane yields a practitioner of apartheid, who then would find little solace in his government's assertion that its racial policies are solely of domestic concern.

The U.N. human rights agenda for enforcement includes much that is urgent. The Sub-Commission's proposals for con-

---

[3] U.N. Doc. A/6301/Add. 1 at 5 (1966).

sidering complaints outside the colonial and South African areas were sent on with little change by the Human Rights Commission and will have been acted on by ECOSOC in June 1969. If adopted without serious deletion, they will open a new day in U.N. human rights affairs. If truncated or defeated, they may deter the General Assembly's 1966 demand for U.N. action to "put a stop" to violations wherever they may occur.

The next most immediate item on the enforcement agenda is the organization of the Committee on Racial Discrimination provided for in the 1965 Convention. The Committee will have been chosen in 1969, and will doubtless reflect in its makeup the paucity of western members among the States Parties.

The two 1966 Covenants, on Civil and Political Rights and on Economic, Social and Cultural Rights, with the former's Optional Protocol allowing individuals' complaints, are far short of sufficient States Parties for effectiveness. Thus results the importance of the Sub-Commission rules, to fill the gaps in human rights enforcement left by tardiness or straight refusal of nations to join. Even when both Covenants, and the Protocol, have the Parties for effectiveness, these rules will still be needed so that all men everywhere may have some chance of being heard when their governments oppress them.

Rules are needed also on the details of procedure. Samples for the use of the Racial Discrimination Committee have been privately prepared and promulgated,[4] but further work is needed for use by other tribunals, such as the Human Rights Committee visualized by the two 1966 Covenants. The Human Rights Commission's *Ad Hoc* Group of Experts, after floundering for two years without adopting even the simplest basic rules, approached thus unprepared the turgid subject of alleged Israeli oppression in occupied Arab lands. Without rules to buttress its impartiality, the Group could have little hope of influencing disinterested observers of its work.

---

[4] Rules of Procedure for the New Tribunal: A Proposed Draft, 56 CAL. L. REV. 1569 (1968).

Even more essential will be rules to guide the criminal process in human rights matters. "The possibility of establishing a grand jury of legal experts for Namibia for the protection of life, personal safety and rights of the inhabitants of that territory," [5] is one of several current proposals for international criminal process requiring the greatest care in their development. The pains taken at Nuremberg earned the respect of mankind. Without similar pains, the gathering of evidence and *prima facie* findings of criminal guilt will naught avail. Drastic charges without restraint would only dissipate the sympathy that might be earned by tight   procedures guardedly applied.

Structural changes are on the agenda for international organizations both regional and global. The draft Inter-American Convention on Human Rights currently under discussion provides for "organs of protection," a commission and a court.[6] The Arab League projects regional human rights institutions whose shape has not yet become apparent. Regional machinery where none exists was considered by an *Ad Hoc* Study Group of the U.N. Commission, a clear consensus holding that consent of the governments concerned would be prerequisite. Coordination problems may arise as regional measures evolve and tend to compete with U.N. procedures.

New U.N. machinery has been urged, including a U.N. Organization for the Promotion of Human Rights (UNOPHR) with status like UNCTAD and UNIDO, gathering in all the now scattered functions and with a Human Rights Council as its main organ.[7]

Most pressing at the global level is the question of the proposed U.N. High Commissioner for Human Rights. After slowly clearing the lower bodies, the matter came to rest in the General Assembly, where its proponents are reluctant to

---

[5] From document prepared by a special rapporteur for the UN Human Rights Commission. E/CN.4/979/Add.3 (1969).

[6] OEA/Ser.G/V (1968).

[7] Sohn, *United Nations Machinery for Implementing Human Rights*, 62 AM. J. INT'L L. 909 (1968).

force it to the test in an atmosphere of Soviet hostility and Afro-Asian coolness born of various apprehensions. The type of informational and negotiating function sought might better be achieved at this time by grafting further powers on the role of an existing and generally trusted official, the High Commissioner for Refugees. The tragedy of his statutory inability to aid those suffering in Biafra because officially they have not fled their country shows where the first graft is needed, to permit UNHCR to enter countries where his protection is required and permitted.

The U.N.'s nearly unique institution of private consultative status must be strengthened in the human rights field. The 1969 review of non-governmental organizations with this status has afforded their opponents the chance to urge a principle whose acceptance would hamstring this important aspect of international human rights protection. The notion that an NGO may not criticize a government in whose territory the NGO has no members, while imbedded in I.L.O. usage,[8] has a technical ring to it like some of the more ancient rules of evidence not applied in modern administrative investigation. If the U.N. would borrow the I.L.O.'s more imaginative procedures for human rights protection, the absorption of I.L.O.'s few less productive rules could be sustained. The I.L.O. on its fiftieth anniversary in 1969 was more than twice as far along in these matters as the U.N. on its twenty-fifth, but the gap is narrowing, a process likely to be facilitated by closer coordination.

It is often said that the basic need for human rights protection is not at the international level but in each state, where government oppression must be curbed. Ambassador Richardson of Jamaica has expressed the belief that "the coercive powers we are attempting to give to international institu-

---

[8] See for example 52 I.L.O. OFF. BULL., No. 1, Supp. at 19 (1969).

tions will be of little effectiveness for a very long time to come."[9] This view accepts that truly adamant regimes cannot be moved by the world community, and leads inevitably to revolution as the only remedy. Where neighbors are aroused, such revolution threatens the peace. But even accepting this counsel of despair, the U.N. is not without its means. Education, not revolution, is its final expedient. The Italian proposal adopted by the General Assembly in 1968 took this line, asking for "regular study of the United Nations and the specialized agencies and of the principles proclaimed in the Universal Declaration of Human Rights and in other declarations on human rights, in the training of teaching staff for primary and secondary schools."[10] Today's restless youth, impatient with injustice, will soon have the power to bring their goals into being. As the Assembly added, "all means of education should be employed so that youth may grow up and develop in a spirit of respect for human dignity and equal rights of man without distinction as to race, colour, language, sex or faith."[11]

---

[9] Report on Annual Conference of the Non-Governmental Organizations in Co-operation with the United Nations Office of Public Information, Annex III at 7 (1967).

[10] Assembly resolution 2445 (XXIII).

[11] Resolution 2447 (XXIII) (1968).

Nine

Making the United Nations Work Better: Organizational and Procedural Reform by Roger Fisher and Peter D. Trooboff

Since its establishment in 1945, the United Nations has grown into a vast, complex and expensive organization. In 1945, the United Nations had 51 member states. Today, there are 126. Over 1,000 representatives and advisers acting either as members of national delegations or as observers from specialized agencies came to New York from September to December, 1969 for the General Assembly's 24th annual session. These participants studied and debated over 1,200 documents containing thousands of pages of reports on the work of the United Nations. The delegates appropriated a budget of 164 million dollars for fiscal 1970. This budget includes provisions for a Secretariat staff which now includes over 9,000 people of more than 100 different nationalities.

Increased size, both of membership and operations, is not the only difference between the United Nations now and the organization created twenty-five years ago. Today, more problems confront the United Nations; and more member states means more points of view. Expressing these diverse views results in longer agenda and debates, and a growing backlog of unfinished business. These internal pressures prevent the orderly conduct of business which is at best difficult. At the same time, rapid advances in science and technology and the growing demands of developing countries have thrust upon the United Nations considerably more complex issues to resolve during each session of the General Assembly. Delegations have to face and attempt to resolve problems ranging from water pollution to decolonization and from sonic boom to primary goods prices. Responsibility for considering such problems is frequently spread among a number of committees, councils, commissions and specialized agencies. On some occasions, delegates have not had the expert advice and comprehensive evaluations necessary to reach wise decisions concerning these issues. The existing machinery for determining United Nations action has fallen behind in coping with today's global concerns. The present United Nations organization and procedures are often working against fulfillment of the very purposes which they were designed to serve.

This chapter suggests some ideas on how the United Nations might proceed in trying to cope with the difficulties presented by its size and by the complexity of the issues before it. These ideas are not presented as *the* solution to the problems of the United Nations. Many of the organization's current difficulties transcend the structural and procedural reform recommended here. Some of these ideas require refinement; others may prove impractical. The purpose is not to lay out the single path which the United Nations should follow to come out of its current difficulties. Rather, it is to suggest ways in which this twenty-five-year old institution can better equip itself to face the next twenty-five years.

Let us suggest four organizational and procedural reforms:

I. Create standing, working sub-committees within each Main Committee;

II. Consolidate existing procedural rules and interpretations and adopt procedural reforms heretofore recommended;

III. Establish a United Nations Resolution Consulting Service;

IV. Appoint a special commission of experts to study and recommend changes in the organization of and allocation of responsibilities among committees, councils, commissions and specialized agencies of the United Nations.

Each of these proposed reforms can be evaluated separately.

I. Create Standing, Working Sub-Committees Within Each Main Committee

Previous United Nations-sponsored reviews of the procedures of the General Assembly have proposed establishing sub-committees or working groups in the Main Committees. Member States and the General Assembly have not adequately followed up these proposals. This inaction resulted, in part, from a failure in prior reviews to specify how such proposals should be implemented and also, perhaps, from misunderstanding as to what these sub-committees could accomplish.

During the first session of the General Assembly, Main Committees used sub-committees to study agenda items in detail and to prepare draft texts and reports for plenary meetings. For example, the Fourth Committee (Trusteeship and Information from Non-Self-Governing Territories) set up two sub-committees — one to work out trusteeship agreements and the other to consider treatment of information submitted under Article 73 (e) of the Charter as well as the summoning of a conference of non-self-governing peoples.[1] In a 1947 report titled "Procedures and Organization of the General Assembly," the specially created Committee on Procedures and Organization urged the Main Committees to "consider carefully at an early stage in their work how their programmes might be expedited by the establishment of sub-committees."[2] Despite this report and similar recommendations from individual delegates to subsequent sessions of the General Assembly, the Main Committees have not made extensive use of sub-committees during their meetings. Sixteen years

---

[1] 1 (2) U. N. GAOR, Fourth Comm. 116 (1946).
[2] U. N. Doc. A/388 at 5 (1947).

after this initial report, the *Ad Hoc* Committee on the Improvement of the Methods of Work of the General Assembly said that it was

> of the opinion that in many cases the examination of agenda items by the committee would be greatly facil- itated if, as soon as possible and especially when the main points of view have been expressed, the com- mittee decided, on the initiative of its Chairman or one or more of its members, to set up a sub-committee or working groups . . ..[3]

Like the 1947 report, the 1963 report has not led during the past six years to a significant increase in the use of sub- committees by the Main Committees.

As the passage from the 1963 report suggests, the prior studies of the procedures of the General Assembly have recommended the use of sub-committees or working groups for a limited and primarily technical purpose. Thus, the Committee on Procedures and Organization said in 1947 that "[t]echnical questions on which there is no substantial disagreement should be referred to subcommittees as quickly as possible."[4] With a similar purpose in mind, the *Ad Hoc* Committee in its 1963 report stated that a procedure of using sub-committees "might be particularly helpful when there is general agreement on the question under discussion but dis- agreement on points of detail."[5] Neither the 1947 nor 1963 studies recommended a radical departure in the normal de- bating procedure in the Main Committees—a long general debate, followed by proposal of resolutions which occasion more general debate, and finally a debate on specific resolu- tions, although even this last stage includes many assertions made during the two prior general debates. The sub-com- mittees or working groups recommended in the two earlier reports would have had a place at the end of this long process.

---

[3] U. N. Doc. A/5423 at 15 (1963),

[4] U. N. Doc. A/388, *supra* note 2, at 5.

[5] U. N. Doc. A/5423, *supra* note 3, at 15.

Their purpose would have been to take some of the discussion of details at the end of a debate out of the Main Committee. Under both of the earlier proposals, the basic progression of business in the Main Committees would remain unaltered.

It can be argued that the way in which business progresses through the Main Committee should not be altered, and that any sub-committee work should take place after full debates in the Main Committees. This procedure assures all member states of the opportunity to express their points of view on every agenda item before the Main Committees. For smaller nations, which frequently have difficulty finding an audience for their views in other forums, this right to be heard within the United Nations is most important. The current Main Committee procedure, by including all members, preserves the important principle of "sovereign equality" among all states belonging to the United Nations.

Despite these arguments, the General Assembly should consider undertaking reorganization of the procedures of the Main Committees so that before being debated in a Main Committee all or most agenda items are referred to a standing, working sub-committee. These working sub-committees, whose size would be limited to perhaps 25 members, would do the major work on the issues presented by each agenda item. By the time a question reached a Main Committee, it would usually be in the form of a specific proposal for action—a draft resolution. Questions might also appear in reports for the consideration of a Main Committee. A working sub-committee would include representatives from member states having particular interest or competence in the subjects with which that sub-committee was concerned. The fact that major powers would presumably sit on more sub-committees than would small members would provide benefits comparable to those which might be obtained through weighted voting without, however, raising all the political difficulties which such proposals involve.

The establishment of standing, working sub-committees would not, it should be emphasized, bar the expression of any point of view. Recommendations from the working sub-committees would be subject to debate in the Main Committees. Even though all delegations would not be included on each working sub-committee, each delegation would sit on at least one sub-committee and all would have an opportunity to be heard in the Main Committee debate on recommendations by working sub-committees. This debate would be on specific recommendations for action by the Main Committees. Whatever remarks delegations wished to make could be made during such debate. However, this procedure would, it is hoped, serve to focus these remarks on the specific possibilities for Main Committee action which are being debated. The success of each working sub-committee would depend on its ability to take account of various points of view in working out draft resolutions and reports acceptable to a majority of a Main Committee's members.

The proposed new procedure for conducting business in each of the Main Committees could be implemented in two stages by resolutions of the General Assembly. In the first resolution, the Assembly would ask the General Committee to:

(a) suggest the general terms of reference for each of several standing sub-committees for each of the Main Committees;

(b) suggest for the coming year which members should sit on which sub-committees, taking into account the interest of the members and their ability to handle a number of sub-committee assignments;

(c) propose the sub-committee to which each item on the agenda should be referred.

The General Assembly, at the following session, would receive the General Committee's report and would proceed to consider a second resolution implementing the General Committee's recommendations. In this second resolution, the General Assembly would decide that each of the Main Committees would establish a certain number of specified standing, working sub-committees organized by subject matter to consider agenda items in those areas prior to Main Committee debate on these items. The General Assembly would name the members to serve on these new bodies in the second resolution. This resolution would make clear that the power of these bodies—to discuss, to narrow issues, to prepare draft resolutions and reports—in no way limited the competence of the Main Committees to deal with each agenda item assigned to them as they saw fit.

A few examples illustrate how this procedure could operate and some of its potential benefits. At present, the Committee of Twenty-Four (The Special Committee on the Situation with regard to the Implementation of the Declaration on the Granting of Independence to Colonial Countries and Peoples) operates as a sub-committee of the Fourth Committee. The Committee of Twenty-Four itself has four sub-committees whose jurisdictions are divided on a geographical basis. These sub-committees and the Committee of Twenty-Four do a great deal of work and do relieve the Fourth Committee of much of the burden of hearing petitioners and considering the details of individual situations. In a procedural way, they serve the kind of role here being suggested. As a substantive matter, however, the role played by the Committee of Twenty-Four and its sub-committees is quite different from that visualized. By and large, the Committee of Twenty-Four has seen itself as having been given a mandate to bring about a given result—independence—in every case that comes before it. The working sub-committees for the Main Committees here proposed would, it is contemplated, be more representative of the full range of views on any given question and more "neutral" as to what the appropriate result might be with respect to agenda items referred to them.

Under the new procedure, the First (Political and Security Questions) Committee might have a working sub-committee examine the facts underlying allegations from various member states concerning the perennial Korean Question. By narrowing the issues and focusing on what real disagreement exists at the time of the debate, the working sub-committee would enable the Main Committee to avoid the endless polemical exchanges which accompany the annual discussion of this agenda item. In studying the work of the Eighteen Nation

Committee on Disarmament, the First Committee would benefit from working sub-committee reports indicating what action could be taken to influence the Eighteen-Nation body on particular aspects of its negotiations. A separate sub-committee might concentrate on a given field, such as nuclear weapons, chemical and biological weapons, and conventional arms. Similar examples of how working sub-committees would operate in the other Main Committees should be apparent. The basic idea is to focus Main Committee debate by working through preliminary matters and making specific proposals in sub-committees. This reform should, if adopted, promote the work of the Main Committees by providing high quality proposals for debate by all member states and by permitting these committees for the first time to consider all the agenda items referred to them by the General Assembly with the same amount of care.

The Committee on Procedures and Organization recommended to the General Assembly in its 1947 report that

> [i]f a debate in full committee showed that there was general agreement on the question under discussion but disagreement on points of detail, it would clearly be desirable to set up a small, drafting committee to prepare a resolution for submission to the Main Committee.[6]

Creating standing, working sub-committees should help to fill the gap which the 1947 report recognized. However, even with these new sub-committees, it might still be desirable to make greater use of drafting committees, both within the Main Committees and in the new sub-committees themselves.

In international organizations and negotiations, the use of *ad hoc* drafting committees is now a well-recognized practice. Large numbers of persons have considerable difficulty in working out detailed language for an agreement or a resolution. This procedure is particularly effective when, as the 1947 report mentioned, there is substantial agreement on the issue before a larger body and only points of detail remain to be

---

6 U.N. Doc. A/388, *supra* note 2, at 5.

decided. An *ad hoc* drafting committee may also be useful when disagreement centers on only a few countries. By including these countries, along with a few others, in a drafting committee, agreements can often be worked out more efficiently than in a larger body. Finally, the drafting committee is sometimes an effective instrument even when there is no agreement among parties. In the drafting committee, the parties to a dispute can, at least, understand what it is about which they disagree. At this point they may decide to report alternative drafts or—perhaps more likely—to avoid the question.

II. Consolidate and Implement Procedural Rules

The General Assembly has encountered considerable resistance to amending its procedural rules or even to modifying its procedural practices. Despite the recommendations contained in four special reports on General Assembly procedures, only minor changes have been made in the rules adopted at the first session in 1946. The special committees which prepared these reports did recommend a number of procedural reforms which would not necessarily require amendment of the rules. Unfortunately, a number of the new rules which were adopted and many of the recommended reforms in General Assembly practice have not been fully utilized or implemented. These earlier reports and their recommendations deserve more attention.

The previous reports on procedures identify a number of difficulties which still hinder the work of the General Assembly. The first study concentrated on the problems involved in setting up a new organization.[7] However, even at that early date, the Committee on Procedures and Organization was concerned with the problem of limiting debate,[8] and making the procedural rulings of various committees available.[9] The second study, completed in 1949 by the Special Committee on Methods and Procedures, resulted in a number of

---

[7] U. N. Doc. A/388 (1947).

[8] *Id.* at 5.

[9] *Id.* at 5.

important amendments to the Rules of Procedure.[10] Yet, the member states have failed to utilize some of the new amendments which were adopted after this second study, *e.g.*, Rule 74 limiting the number of times a delegate may speak. Reluctance to use Rule 74 and others designed to prevent unproductive debates and even delaying tactics has meant that a number of the problems identified in the 1949 study continue to hinder the General Assembly's work.

The two other studies were extensive investigations of a wide range of procedural problems which appeared to be causing delay in completing the business of the General Assembly. The reports of those studies covered many issues, but they caused little reform in the rules and practices of the General Assembly. During the 7th session of the General Assembly, the agenda included an item on "Measures to Limit the Duration of Regular Sessions of the General Assembly." The Secretary-General submitted a memorandum containing his ideas on how the business of the General Assembly could be expedited.[11] The General Assembly then established a Special Committee on Measures to Limit the Duration of Regular Sessions of the General Assembly. Despite the large number of problems considered by this committee, it made only a few recommendations for changes in the rules of procedure.[12] Probably its most significant proposal—to curtail debate on a procedural motion limiting the time allowed for a speaker or fixing the number of times a delegate may speak—failed to gain approval in the Sixth Committee. Without this amendment Rule 74 and Rule 115 on limiting debate remain nearly dead letters as the long and often inconclusive debates of the General Assembly and the Committees demonstrate. The extensive 1953 study led to only two minor procedural changes.[13]

---

[10] U. N. Doc. A/937 (1949); *e.g.*, fixing of a closing date for each session of the General Assembly at the beginning of the session (Rule 2) and permitting one third of the members of a Main Committee to constitute a quorum for discussion of agenda items (Rule 110).

[11] U. N. Doc. A/2206 (1952).

[12] U. N. Doc. A/2402 (1953).

[13] U. N. Doc. A/2512 (1953) and G. A. Res. 791, 8 U. N. GAOR Supp. 17, at 49, U. N. Doc. A/2630 (1953).

The most recent study of United Nations procedures occurred as a result of a carefully prepared memorandum by the President of the 16th session of the General Assembly, Mongi Slim.[14] The General Assembly appointed an *Ad Hoc* Committee on the Improvement of the Methods of Work of the General Assembly to consider the issues raised by the former Assembly President. The committee produced a long report on General Assembly procedures,[15] and this report generated a useful debate on procedure in the plenary meetings of the General Assembly.[16] The Assembly passed a resolution urging greater compliance with procedural rules and recommending steps which member states could take to facilitate the completion of work by the Main Committees.[17] Yet, the only tangible product of this latest examination of the organization's procedures was adoption of a resolution authorizing purchase of mechanical voting equipment for the General Assembly.[18] This equipment is now installed and used regularly by the Assembly and by some of the Main Committees when the Assembly is not in session. Despite this installation and the time saving which the equipment permits, the basic procedural problems identified in the 1963 report, as well as in the three that preceded it, continue to trouble the General Assembly and its committees.

Some may conclude that further procedural reform in the United Nations is unnecessary. Small nations, for example, are concerned that additional changes could unfairly curtail their right to make their views known. Other member states insist that consideration of agenda items in a democratic fashion is possible only if unlimited discussion is allowed for the presentation of all points of view. Experienced observers of the United Nations have often explained that many agenda items

---

[14] U. N. Doc. A/5123 (1962).

[15] U. N. Doc. A/5423 (1963).

[16] 18 U. N. GAOR 1256th meeting 27, 1278th meeting 1.

[17] G. A. Res. 1898, 18 U. N. GAOR Supp. 15 at 4, U. N. Doc. A/5515 (1963).

[18] G. A. Res. 1957, 18 U. N. GAOR Supp. 15 at 9, U. N. Doc. A/5515 (1963).

are extremely complicated. To settle the issues raised by these complex agenda items, considerable time for debate, study and drafting is necessary. An outsider seeing or reading the debates may regard them as excessively discursive or insufficiently conclusive. However, something is served by having time in which every delegate can unburden himself of whatever is on his mind regarding a highly controversial international problem. Finally, there can be no doubt that some member states view lengthy debates and innumerable procedural objections as a safeguard against precipitous United Nations action. To these states, procedural reform often appears as an indirect method for removing obstacles to action which they do not want the United Nations to undertake. These states would point out that on a number of occasions the General Assembly has taken decisive action, but only after giving careful consideration to all views.

Despite these arguments, the General Assembly should consider some techniques for encouraging greater use of existing procedural rules and experimentation with new procedural practices. To overcome the fears and objections noted above, it would be desirable to demonstrate that specific procedural changes would not have the adverse effect which many anticipate. One possible approach to gaining gradual approval for procedural reform would be to institute various changes on a selective basis. For example, it might be worthwhile to carry on some specified debates under a rule limiting the length of each delegate's speech or the number of times each delegate could speak. To make such experimental use of limitations on speaking rights acceptable, delegates could be given an opportunity to vote at the end of the restricted debate on whether they wished to follow their discussions by further, and this time unrestricted, debate. Main Committees should be encouraged to attempt such experiments when dealing with relatively non-controversial reports. Member states may find that limitations on the length of speeches and on the number of times delegates may speak do not encroach on their desire to give adequate consideration to the merits of each agenda item. On the contrary, such limitations should sharpen speeches made during debates. If this is their experience, they may eventually be willing to attempt imposing similar limitations on more controversial debates. A motion to limit speeches made during a debate will frequently appear to be directed against the delegations which would be most affected by the particular limitation at the time when it is imposed. To overcome this problem, Main Committees may want to include an item on their agenda titled "debate rules". This item would be discussed before conducting debate on any substantive matter. The Main Committees would decide in advance what restrictions, if any, they wished to apply to debate on each agenda item. In that way, the restrictions would not be directed against any particular delegation and would affect all sides equally.

The example above on implementing rules allowing restrictions on debate could serve as a model for the carrying out of other procedural reforms. The 1963 report urged the chairmen of Main Committees to exercise more of the authority given to them by the rules of procedure.[19] Chairmen may want to begin exercising their powers more extensively on a selective basis—choosing only debates in which such use of the chairmen's powers will not cause undue controversy. If working sub-committees are used more extensively,[20] Main Committee chairmen may wish to focus debate on the specific proposals emerging from these new groups. The General Committee could also use this technique of gaining gradual acceptance of reform. For example, the 1963 report recommended that the General Committee should bear in mind the possibility of grouping related agenda items in preparing a provisional agenda for the General Assembly.[21] By attempting such grouping of agenda items for a few subjects each session, the General Committee might be able to demonstrate the value of this method for curtailing multiple debates on the same issues. Eventually, the Main Committees themselves

---

[19] U. N. Doc. A/5423, *supra* note 15, at 18.
[20] See p. 221 *supra*.
[21] U. N. Doc. A/5423, *supra* note 15, at 14.

would, it is hoped, make similar attempts to group agenda items, as the 1963 report also recommended.

For the time being, it does not appear necessary for the General Assembly to undertake an effort to revise its rules of procedure. The 1963 report and the comments of delegates during the General Assembly debate on that report indicated that the existing rules "provide an adequate framework for the Assembly's work . . .."[22] However, the new situation which might arise by virtue of making greater use of standing, working sub-committees may eventually necessitate another study of the procedural rules. Similarly, difficulties in implementing the existing rules may suggest ways in which those rules could be modified in order to facilitate their use.

One important procedural reform which is being undertaken is the preparation of a Repertory of the Rules of Procedure of the General Assembly. The Secretariat is currently preparing a paragraph by paragraph, sentence by sentence, explanation of the Rules, consisting of descriptions of procedural incidents and cases which have occurred in plenary meetings of the General Assembly and in meetings of the Main Committees and General Committee. It is now intended that the Repertory will cover experience through the twenty-third (1968) session of the General Assembly. The Secretariat hopes to be able to keep the Repertory up-to-date. It is certainly desirable that means be devised for doing so.

III. Create a United Nations Resolution Consulting Service

The General Assembly should consider establishing a Resolution Consulting Service composed of experts on the work of the United Nations and international law. The resolutions introduced in the General Assembly and its Main Committees sometimes fail to take account of the organization's extensive experience in working with resolutions. Delegations, particularly ones with a small staff, are often unable to give adequate attention to choosing the best mechanism for

---

[22] *Id.* at 8.

resolving a particular dispute, getting the most useful report on a special problem or causing a member state to follow a particular course of conduct.   Similarly, resolutions have on occasion reflected a need for devoting greater attention to action previously taken by the General Assembly.

This Resolution Consulting Service would be an independent advisory service for drafting and redrafting proposed United Nations resolutions.   Although the Secretary-General could supervise its establishment, this service should probably operate independently of the regular Secretariat.   Some members of the service might work at the United Nations for only a limited period—for example, two years.   By making such periods of service short and appointment to this advisory body an honor, the United Nations should be able to attract from member states experts on the organization and on international law.   A procedure of having a limited period of service for some members would assure a constant renewal of people with fresh ideas.   Others might be career people who would become increasingly familiar with precedents.   Since the service would be primarily professional rather than political, selection procedures should not be too difficult to arrange. The service should not be too large, perhaps no more than half a dozen experts should be included at the outset.

A proposal to establish such a Resolution Consulting Service might generate considerable opposition.   Some member states will be afraid of the power or influence of an independent body of experts.   Others will question whether such a service is really necessary.   They would maintain that the Secretariat already provides, on an informal and unofficial basis, ample assistance to delegations in the preparation of resolutions.   Some observers of United Nations activities might conclude that the way to improve resolutions is not through an advisory service, but by upgrading the personnel on the staff of individual delegations.   Yet, it is difficult to see how the United Nations could play a role in achieving this upgrading and even a suggestion to this effect is likely to be highly offensive.   Delegations are likely to be concerned about the representativeness of the proposed Resolution Consulting Service. While the service would nominally fulfill only a professional function, there can be little doubt that differences in political and legal outlook would result in varying approaches to problems presented to the service. Experienced diplomats will emphasize that the working out of language for a resolution is an important part of the political process and cannot be regarded as simply a technical exercise.

Some of the expected objections to a Resolution Consulting Service and the anticipated fears about its power and functions can be allayed in the course of defining the group's authority. At the beginning, the service would confine its activities to receiving draft resolutions from member states for comments and for suggestions of possible revision. The experts in the service would give advice on how draft resolutions could be made more effective, more precise or more appropriate for carrying out the proposed objective. The service would obviously not have any authority to impose its views on any particular delegation. Instead, the experts would gain respect for their advice by virtue of its cogency and its appropriateness to the circumstances for which the particular resolution was proposed. It would be useless to create a service representing only one point of view with respect to the United Nations and international law. If that were done, some delegations would simply refuse to submit their resolutions to the service for comments or advice. The function of the service might be compared with that of first class law firms, specializing in public international law matters, made available on a retainer basis. It would be as though the United Nations had retained such a group. Each adviser would be available without charge to individual delegations who would like expert assistance on the formulation or drafting of United Nations resolutions. By drawing upon the over twenty years of United Nations practice and eventually on its own experience, the members of this new service should measurably improve the quality of resolutions and, as a result, the effectiveness of the organization.

As time passed and the service gained the confidence of member states, it might be possible to expand its functions.

It might, for example, begin to prepare resolutions for delegations based on a description of what the proposing member wanted the General Assembly or a particular Committee to do. The service's function, however, would remain essentially professional rather than political. If qualified experts are selected for this group, they should understand, on the basis of their previous national experience, how to perform an essentially professional role, not a political one. Although the line between these two functions becomes blurred at times, the final authority would always rest with the individual delegation. Since the service's work would be confidential, member states would not be obliged either to accept the advice received from the experts or to explain their reasons for rejecting proposed resolutions. Similarly, the credit for introducing new ideas in well-drafted resolutions would go to the individual delegation, not to the Service.

IV.   Establish a Commission to Review Organization and Procedures

The current organization of the world body grew over the years as new concerns appeared and new committees were created to deal with them. As a result, the United Nations now consists of an enormously complex structure of committees, councils, commissions and specialized agencies trying to cope with a variety of problems. Some groups created by the General Assembly to study a particular problem are no doubt well-conceived and are treating their agenda as efficiently as possible. But others are too small or have inadequate powers or duplicate work done elsewhere.

Secretary-General U Thant discussed the problem of overlapping responsibilities in the introduction to his annual report to the 18th session of the General Assembly. He noted that this difficulty appears in the political as well as the economic field. The Secretary-General cited the example of the issue of non-self-governing territories where

> some four committees and special committees are dealing with matters that might usefully be combined, thus relieving the concerned delegations of otherwise added

burdens and at the same time reducing costs and staff requirements.[23]

Similar overlapping may well occur when the same problems are being treated by geographical and functional groups. In some cases, problems now being treated on a geographical basis should perhaps be consolidated and studied functionally; in other situations, functional analysis now in progress should be divided among smaller geographically organized bodies.

The United Nations should consider undertaking a major project designed to examine, and where appropriate, to restructure the existing internal organization. This proposed study is necessary in order to identify problems in organization such as the one noted by Secretary-General U Thant and others which are apparent to observers of the United Nations current operations. This analysis of the present organizational structure is essential if the United Nations is going to be equipped to cope as well as possible with the complex problems created by recent scientific and technological developments. To carry out this project, the General Assembly should appoint a special commission of experts on the allocation of responsibilities and the internal organization of the United Nations and its specialized agencies. After this commission of experts has completed a comprehensive review of the existing organization of the United Nations, it should recommend appropriate reallocation of existing responsibilities and propose how various committees, councils, commissions and specialized agencies might be restructured to improve their operation.

A number of member states might respond to a proposal for this type of comprehensive review by pointing out that there already exists machinery within the United Nations to coordinate activities and programs undertaken by various groups. In the economic field, for example, the General Assembly has called upon the Economic and Social Council to establish an Enlarged Committee for Programme and Coordination which would

---

[23] 18 U. N. GAOR Supp. 1A at 4-5, U. N. Doc. A/5201/Add. 1 (1967).

undertake, as a matter of priority and in the light of continuing work of other United Nations bodies in the field of co-ordination, planning and evaluation, a review which would provide:

(a) A clear and comprehensive picture of the existing operational and research activities of the United Nations family of organizations in the field of economic and social development and an assessment thereof; [and]

(b) . . . recommendations on modifications in existing activities, procedures and administrative arrangements . . ..[24]

The Enlarged Committee has set out a program for accomplishing the work assigned to it by the General Assembly. It has begun meeting to consider reports prepared for it.[25] In a similar effort, an *Ad Hoc* Committee of Experts has recently submitted a lengthy report with recommendations designed to coordinate the financial procedures of the United Nations and the specialized agencies.[26] Finally, the Administrative Committee on Coordination has taken steps to promote cooperation among its members. These include all the specialized agencies, a number of United Nations programs such as the Children's Fund and the Institute for Training and Research and such groups as the General Agreement on Tariffs and Trade.[27] With all these efforts to coordinate various United Nations activities, one may well ask why a comprehensive review of the organization of the world body is necessary.

The projects mentioned above and other similar projects to promote coordination of activities among various United Nations bodies are certainly useful. But they do not represent the kind of comprehensive structural examination and reform which is being recommended here. No United Nations body

---

[24] G. A. Res. 2188, 21 U. N. GAOR Supp. 16 at 37, U. N. Doc. A/6316 (1966).

[25] U. N. Doc. E/4435 (1967) and E/4599 (1968).

[26] U. N. Doc. A/6343 (1966); see A/6465 (1966) (note by the Secretary-General on the *Ad Hoc* Committee's second report).

[27] For a review of the Committee's activities see its 23rd Annual Report, U. N. Doc. E/4337 (1967).

has ever, in fact, attempted such a task.[28] After nearly twenty-five years and after the creation of thousands of different committees, councils, commissions and specialized agencies, such an undertaking is now in order.

A commission concerned with organization is particularly desirable in view of growing concern with the cost of some United Nations operations. For example, the United States, the United Kingdom and France were recently reported to have sent Secretary-General U Thant identical notes recommending that the United Nations budget be frozen at its present level for the next two years, except for small adjustments that are inevitable because of past commitments.[29] These notes apparently showed dissatisfaction with the high rate at which the United Nations budget has grown during the past few years. The three-power initiative was viewed as a "warning to the small countries that they cannot vote for unlimited spending just on the basis of a numerical majority in the [G]eneral [A]ssembly."[30] One objective of the notes was to prevent any further budget increases for employment until a committee of experts completes a manpower utilization study recommended by the Advisory Committee on Administrative and Budgetary Questions and set up by

---

[28] There was one recent proposal to undertake a comprehensive review "of the programmes and activities of the United Nations, the specialized agencies, the IAEA, the UNICEF and all other institutions and agencies related to the United Nations system in the economic, social technical cooperation and related fields . . .." U. N. Doc. A/6201 (1965).

The committee which would have been appointed to conduct this study would have been asked to make recommendations for improving existing programs where it found duplication or other problems. It would also have identified new programs for the United Nations to undertake and new methods for increasing the effectiveness of United Nations work in the fields studied. To date, the General Assembly has not passed a resolution establishing a committee to make such a study. The proposed review would not, of course, have included consideration of the way in which the United Nations deals with political questions, nor would it necessarily have dealt with problems of organization.

[29] N. Y. Times, April 19, 1969, at 7, col. 1.

[30] Id.

the General Assembly in December, 1968.[31]   In another in-
cident reflecting this same concern for United Nations costs,
the United States decided not to participate in the 1969 trip
to Africa by the United Nations Committee on Colonialism.[32]
The United Kingdom took similar action several years ago.
The recent American decision meant that the United States
did not take part in a four-week trip that cost the United
Nations over $142,000. The purpose of this journey
to Africa by 21 delegates and a staff of 48, including a camera
crew, was to hear testimony from African leaders of liberation
movements in the Portuguese colonies, Southern Rhodesia and
Namibia. The United States appears to have concluded that
much of the testimony which would be obtained in Africa could
be received by bringing the African rebel leaders to the United
Nations headquarters in New York. In fact, in previous years,
many of these leaders have testified before the Committee on
Colonialism in Africa and have then appeared again in New
York for the annual session of the General Assembly. De-
fenders of the trip have pointed out, however, that the presence
of a United Nations committee on African soil has been an encouragement to leaders of liberation movements and that previous investigations had given the committee "more direct knowl-

---

[31] Advisory Committee on Administrative and Budgetary Questions
Report, U. N. Doc. A/7207 at paras. 47-50 (1908) (recommending
"that the Secretary General should undertake on an urgent basis a
careful and detailed survey, preferably desk by desk, of existing personnel available to him, their deployment and utilization."); Committee
on the Reorganization of the Secretariat, Report, A/7359 at paras. 60-
65 (1968) (confirming the findings of the Advisory Committee, supporting the recommended survey and suggesting establishment of a
single management review service for the Secretariat); Fifth Committee Report, *Budget Estimates for the Financial Year* 1969, A/7476
at para. 65 (1968) (approving the Advisory Committee recommendation for a survey and expressing its confidence that the Secretary General would implement "opportunities for a reorganization of work or
a redeployment of staff . . ." found during the survey); Secretary General, *Information Circular to the Staff*, ST/ADM/SER. A/1336
(June, 1969) (explaining the purpose and procedures for the survey
and creating a new administrative management service).

[32] N. Y. Times, April 6, 1969, at 15, col. 1.

edge than before of conditions in the territories and deeper understanding of the wishes of their peoples." [33]

To illustrate how this proposed study of organization would proceed in the United Nations, it will be helpful to refer to an analogous effort which took place in a domestic setting—the two Hoover Commissions in the United States. The first Commission on Organization of the Executive Branch of Government (called the "Hoover Commission" after its chairman, former President Herbert Hoover) undertook a thorough examination of the entire operation of the Executive Branch of the United States. The Commission set up 25 special research projects for study by task forces composed of experts on each subject of a project. The full Commission received the task force reports and then issued a report making 273 recommendations. By adopting 196 of these recommendations, the federal government is estimated to have saved about $7 billion. The Second Hoover Commission, set up in 1953, made 314 recommendations on 19 areas of government after working for nearly two years. [34]

The United Nations could not, of course, adopt the Hoover Commission model without making significant modifications. But the member states could adopt the basic idea—a complete review of existing organizational structure for the purpose of recommending how responsibilities should be allocated and where programs should be located. The United Nations might also adopt the principle of division of responsibility which governed the work of the Hoover Commission. In a statement on Armistice Day, 1948, former President Hoover, describing the task of his Commission, said:

> Our job is to make every government activity that now exists work efficiently. I take it that major functions of

---

[33] Id. (Mahmoud Mestiri of Tunisia, committee chairman).
[34] For discussion of the First Hoover Commission see Symposium, The Hoover Commission, 43 Am. Pol. Sci. Rev. 933 (1949); for the Second Commission see Fesler, Administrative Literature and the Second Hoover Commission Reports, 51 Am. Pol. Sci. Rev. 135 (1957) and N. MacNeil and H. Metz, The Hoover Report: 1953-1955 (1956).

the government are determinable as needed by the Congress. It is not our function to say whether it should exist or not, but it is our function to see if we cannot make it work better.[35]

The General Assembly is responsible for determining what functions the United Nations performs so long as they are within the scope of the Charter. The task of the special commission of experts recommended here would be to determine how those functions could be performed more efficiently and effectively than under existing organizational arrangements. This commission of experts would look at the way in which existing bodies within the United Nations carry out their functions. The commission's primary function would be to describe what these bodies should do next about allocating responsibilities and reorganizing the present structure. In addition to suggesting a better division of responsibilities among existing institutions, the commission should look at the means which each institution uses to accomplish its task and see if better means should be employed. Organizations tend to get set in their ways. They do not often re-examine their own procedures to see if they could be improved. They do not often consider whether techniques being applied by some other institution with great success might be adapted and used by them. One of the tasks of the commission would be to make any suggestions it might have for procedural improvements in the international agencies it was studying.

Details of establishing the proposed commission would have to be worked out in a resolution for the General Assembly. The personnel of the proposed commission should include persons having considerable experience with the actual operation of the United Nations, such as past Presidents of the General Assembly who are still members of their national delegations. For political reasons, each of the five permanent members of the Security Council should probably be permitted to name one experienced individual to the group of experts. The four-

---

[35] Aikin and Koenig, *Introduction: The Hoover Commission: A Symposium*, 43 Am. Pol. Sci. Rev. 933, 935 (1949).

teen intergovernmental agencies, including the specialized agencies, which have a relationship with the United Nations based on various agreements should perhaps each be included either directly or indirectly in the commission's membership. The commission should not be too large, so that its members can develop a smooth working relationship. For this reason, additional members of the commission might be limited to ten or fifteen individuals chosen with due regard to their experience with the United Nations and also to both geographical and political distribution. The General Assembly might want to direct the commission to consider at the outset establishing special task forces to prepare advisory reports on the various subsidiary subjects which must be considered in conducting its review of the organization of the United Nations.

The Assembly could agree, for example, to hear as a matter of priority any request from the commission for a special allocation of funds to support the work of such task forces. Finally, the General Assembly might, to demonstrate its interest in the commission's progress, ask that for the next Assembly session the group prepare an interim report on its activities and include any preliminary recommendations which are ready to be discussed. Similar interim reports could be provided at each annual Assembly session until the commission of experts completed its work and issued a comprehensive statement of its findings and recommendations. The General Assembly would then proceed to examine the commission's report and to implement its recommendations to the extent that member states found such action advisable.

Unlike the Hoover Commission in the United States, the special commission of experts should perhaps not be dissolved upon the completion of its initial study. The General Assembly might conclude that although the commission could be reduced in size, there would still be a need for a continuing commission on organizational problems. This continuing group would concern itself with the proper allocation of responsibilities when new problems come before the General Assembly. It could also continue to study the various techniques of organization which have facilitated the administration of programs in various United Nations bodies. The techniques for carrying out programs change rapidly. United Nations bodies might benefit from a coordinated effort to share experience gained in implementing various programs established by the General Assembly. Eventually, such a commission would perhaps become a clearing house for information on the latest and most successful administrative procedures and organizational practices of United Nations bodies. It might even find it worthwhile to work towards publication of a handbook on these techniques. For the time being, however, it would no doubt be adequate, if such a commission of experts is appointed, to indicate that it should consider, among other matters, what continuing role the commission itself might play in the United Nations organizational structure.

Ten

Financing the United Nations
by
Howard J. Taubenfeld
Rita F. Taubenfeld

From the earliest days of its existence, the question of financing the United Nations has occupied statesmen and scholars. Broadly speaking, the financial issue has arisen with respect to three broad categories: general and regular expenditures, "peacekeeping" expenditures, and the financing of development around the world. While the so-called "financial crisis" of the UN arose over the peacekeeping aspect of expenditures, some statesmen and many scholarly reports, including some made by the Commission to Study the Organization of Peace, have urged some independent revenue for the UN for one, or another, or all of these purposes.

The Present Budgetary System

It is useful to recall that the UN's overall expenditures remain quite modest, at least by the standards of developed countries. Under the terms of the Charter, all Members contribute to the regular budget of the Organization with both the budget itself and the apportionment among Members being determined by the General Assembly. Contributions to this budget are compulsory for Members. The developed states contribute the overwhelming bulk of the budget; the United States, for example, pays about a third of the total costs. Under the system of apportionment in use, the approach to incidence thus involves a form of rough progressiveness, with ability to pay a major criterion. All Members, however, are "equally" sovereign in the United Nations, and *all* are expected to participate, at least to a minimal degree, as equal sovereigns, in its financial support and thus share in the support of its normal international activities. This is quite reasonable since the total fiscal burdens of UN membership are modest for most states, when compared with the overall expenses of any government. It is consistent with the conception of the UN as a creature of and servant of all the "equal" sovereigns, not just the strong and rich, that universal participation, even at a modest level, be a basic principle of UN fiscal operations.

Since its creation, this system of financing "normal," traditional international organizational activities has proven adequate for the UN's ordinary needs. While the UN system has not been treated especially liberally as to financial needs by the members, financing the regular budget has not given rise to major difficulties. On the other hand, attempts to use the same budgetary system for peacekeeping and proposals that it be used for redistributionary income transfers and international welfare support have been bitterly opposed by those who would be called on to pay. Despite the complaints, the bitterness and the demands of the poor states for development support, and despite the actual facts of widespread poverty and dearth, the rich have refused to be levied on for compulsory transfers on group standards for the benefit of the poor. At the same time, the "poor" have been unwilling to accept "interference" or the imposition of group standards for their internal economic, political and social development policies. As a result, unlike the regular budget, to which Members are obliged to contribute under the terms of the Charter, contributions to peacekeeping and the maintenance of world order in general, and for development, are normally handled by voluntary contributions from members both inside and outside the UN. The crisis of the 19th General Assembly was formally caused by the insistence of some states, particularly the United States, that peacekeeping assessment by the Assembly could be considered compulsory leading to a loss of vote in the Assembly for extended non-payment. Russia and France, among others, refused to pay and, after a year, the United States reluctantly accepted this fact of life and the UN began to function again more normally. This all points the fact that in this present decentralized, horizontal system of world order, in which each state's main reliance for survival rests ultimately on its own strength, the states have to date been quite unwilling to trust the UN with power or wealth, for wealth implies power.

It is also apparent that peacekeeping, the maintenance of order in general, and the imposition of redistributionary aid for the development of the poor and the unfortunate are activities which are quasi-governmental in type. They are costly activities. To be supported reliably by some enforced, compulsory system of revenue raising and disbursement, they imply the existence of an integrated community based on the existence of a community spirit strong enough to form the basis of support for political institutions which can effectively decide all such important political and peacekeeping issues on the basis of *group standards,* or at least on the basis of authoritative decisions by the legitimate group decision-making organs with "final say" and *effective enforcement powers.* The reliability of financial and material support of these enforcement powers becomes, indeed, the central issue, a key to the effectiveness of the central political institutions. Once this exists, the power of the institution possessing them to impose its will on its members is great. It should be obvious therefore why obligatory international enforcement of the peace has been kept on a voluntary basis, in the ultimate control of the contributing state or states.

The UN as a Transitional Political Organization

At present, the UN is in fact more a servant of peacekeeping alliances than the master of any conflict ridden political or peacekeeping situation. It is far more like a traditional international conference of states than like an all powerful central government with "final say," and legitimate, authoritative institutions of final choice, and enforcement powers. Yet at times it has mounted forces responsive to the purpose of the power and parliamentary majority within it. Thus, one must be wary of taking too static a viewpoint. The UN can be viewed as an evolutionary, growing political institution. At the same time, it must be clearly remembered that the present UN is not yet the prototype of a democratic-type decision-making body. The governments of the world each have one vote; the people of the world do not. There is no responsible legislature in the usual sense; there is no responsible executive. It represents a politically primitive if perhaps unavoidable transitional form if we accept the model of a democratic-type government as a goal. Of course, in a dynamic institution, evolution of institutional form and of effective capacity to decide and to govern are both possible either simultaneously or discontinuously as a response each to the other. A UN which received some reliable source of revenue substantially independent of the will of individual Members would have taken an important step in this dynamic route.

How should the UN raise such revenues? A perfectly integrated, democratic world government would choose a national taxation and revenue disbursement program suited to the material desires and ethical norms of the society. When the UN became such a government, it could "rationally" maximize the social welfare resulting from its fiscal program as well as other governments now do. Then the fiscal program could be evaluated for the progressiveness [1] of the overall burden of taxation and for the achievement of other commonly cited fiscal goals, such as widespread participation of the Members and the achievement of society's macro-economic goals such as full employment, minimal material welfare for all, a fair price level, etc. For the foreseeable future however, we cannot apply such standards with the same rigor to alternative sources of potential

---

[1] In one commonly accepted standard of equity, a tax is assumed to be well designed if all groups in a community are called upon to contribute, that is, to participate in the costs of their common endeavors, up to their ability, on a concept of equality of sacrifice. This means that if a tax is "progressive," as the term is generally used, the poor pay proportionately less.

UN revenue. Presumably it will prove useful for the transitional UN to advance its financial capacities to cope with world problems in whatever are the most promising directions available to it.

Independent Revenue for Peacekeeping and Development

The very real difficulties in obtaining adequate, dependable, broadly derived financing for United Nations activities from the traditional sources, particularly in the crucial peacekeeping field, and especially in the last decade, have led many observers to search for sources of independent revenue for the Organization on a far larger scale than that modest independent income already derived from sale of postage stamps, tours and the like. These revenues are currently used to help defray the general budgetary expenses of the Organization.

To lay the basis for a UN independent income, several studies have examined areas opened up by new technology in which the UN could potentially make a genuine political contribution by providing a legal regime to facilitate peaceful development and exploitation of new resources. It is hoped thereby that UN interposition would prevent or contain a possible colonial-type set of international conflicts and, at the same time, it is hoped that facilitating the exploitation of these new frontiers will yield a revenue resulting from this politically vital, economically fruitful UN role. The importance of a UN role to permit the peaceful exploration and exploitation of newly available areas, as well as visions of potentially great wealth, partially captured for international purposes, has led observers to concentrate on the Antarctic, outer space and the seas and seabeds. Clearly, giving the UN direct control of a real resource base (even if presently "remote"—under the seas or in outer space) would be a path-breaking innovation in the history of international organizations. It is likely to be done only with extravagant safeguards against a great UN power base or a great tax base inadverently growing therefrom. We will examine some aspects of these suggested revenue sources briefly. We must note that the UN has already in fact been by-passed in the initial regimes for outer space, for the Antarctic and for the seas.

For our purposes, and admitting that recent decades have proven how risky it can be to predict the rate of technological advance in regions of long-run economic potential, we will here focus primarily on the oceans which seem at present to promise to be potentially the most fruitful and therefore politically the most pregnant with conflict. We will also include some brief comments on some of the more sanguine possibilities from outer space activities. The Antarctic does not seem to offer imminent promise of income to anyone.

The Oceans and the Seabeds

If the United Nations is to be granted rights to license, regulate and tax the exploitation of ocean resources, it seems wisest to assume, as do most recent studies, that areas and resources in which national states now assert strong interests will not be offered to the international organization. These unavailable resources and areas would include primarily one type of resource, fish and crustaceans, and two types of area, continental shelves and strips along national coasts, whatever the geological formation.

The exclusions from potential UN control or taxation seem preempted by already established or claimed interests. While the fish of the high seas do not "belong" to any nation, special national rights in fish "farming" and conservation purposes have already been recognized in several treaties. Furthermore, a limited number of states are inordinately dependent on using their traditional "rights" for food and for sale to other nations. The incidence of an international tax burden on these activities would be discriminatory, falling primarily on such nations and at least initially on one group of entrepreneurs and workers, the fishermen, of all nations. Enforcement of such an inequitable burden would be virtually impossible if nations were ill-disposed to the levy since the only practical way to collect it would appear to be through substantially voluntary cooperation, probably involving use of national authorities on shore when the catch arrived. Similar problems of incidence, equity and enforceability arise with most excise taxes proposed in favor of the UN such as a tax on international trade and therefore, as we shall see, with most suggested taxes on the produce of the high seas.

Aside from fishing, the harvesting and processing of plankton or the extraction of minerals from sea water itself have both been discussed as possible sources of UN income. Plankton is not now desired as a food resource and would presumably be of interest principally to the poor. Development and popularization of this resource would require significant investment and then thereafter taxing the food of the poor would appear an ill-suited, regressive source of UN income which would be difficult to collect in view of the probable ease of entry of the ships of all nations to the industry.

Extraction of certain minerals from sea water is feasible and such operations are already in existence in many countries. Costs are too high for most minerals to make this a procedure of widespread use however. Perhaps with the development of fusion power, these almost limitless supplies will take on new significance. These are nevertheless *land based* operations today and are already within the control of the states. Floating extraction factories may of course some day become practical; then a UN profit seeking enterprise might become feasible. All the problems conjured up by the UN competing in the market place with existent mineral suppliers would be relevant to any such UN operations. Alternatively a UN licensing or taxing regime would again face serious problems of enforcement. Entrepreneurs in this narrow range of high seas activities could be expected to resent being saddled with any special burdens in favor of the UN. Logic and history (see, for example, the eventual by-passing in the 1930's of the British stations for the regulation and taxing of whaling in the South Atlantic) suggest that unless the nations of the world were united in support of and ready to police the enforcement of such a tax, it would be regularly evaded.

Turning from the high seas to the prospects of UN income from the seabeds, we note that all nations now claim sovereignty in waters and ocean beds adjacent to their coasts ranging in distance from three to two hundred miles. The reasons range from national defense to economic requirements and the

Geneva Conferences on the Law of the Sea of 1958 and 1960 demonstrated how strongly states insist on their claims. Furthermore, all states now follow the lead of the United States in claiming exclusive rights in the "continental shelf," the extension of the continents out under the seas.

The term "continental shelf" is defined in Article 1 of the 1958 Convention on the Continental Shelf as:

> The seabed and subsoil of the submarine areas adjacent to the coast but outside the area of the territorial sea, to a depth of 200 metres, or beyond that limit, to where the depth of the superjacent waters admits of the exploitation of the natural resources of the said areas.

Article 2 goes on to recognize the "sovereign rights" of the coastal state in the shelf for the purpose of "exploring and exploiting its natural resources." Thus much of the presently and even prospectively most desirable and accessible regions of the seabed are by definition already recognized as being under national jurisdiction, if not sovereignty. A British arbitrator has already suggested that there is no reason why the subsoil at any distance, unlike the surface of the seas, should not be the exclusive property of one nation since ownership would not interfere with navigation or fishing rights. In general, since Article 1 in defining the extent of the shelf itself is geared to changes in technology, as has been widely recognized, the sooner nations attempt to limit their own claims in favor of an international arrangement, the more likely it is that agreement could be reached and the development of a new region of power rivalry forestalled. If techniques for underseas exploitation are developed first, we may eventually see all or most of the seabed acquire the status of nationally "owned" continental shelf, though not without overlapping claims and bitter disputes. Indeed "mid-ocean" lines have already been suggested by some political leaders and the U. S. Congress has been urged to refuse support to any vesting of "title" in an international regime thus risking losing the resource for "future generations".

Restricting the shelf to present dimensions or to those the states might be willing to agree to,[1] what prospects for UN income remain? We face the problem that deep subsurface mining is probably technologically too difficult and expensive to contemplate for the near future. Yet there is considerable present experimentation with creating small colonies of humans living on the ocean floor for extended periods. In recent years it has also been observed that nodules of ores can be found lying on the ocean floor in various locations. It seems possible that developments in technology may make the nodules available through dragging, scraping and lifting operations in the near future. The licensing of exploration and exploitation with royalty payments to the UN might therefore be technically relatively easy in this type of situation but some international patrol system and the assistance of nations in preventing illicit operations would be necessary. Alternatively, the regime of the seas could remain unchanged and the UN could go into the business, along with other competitors, as is true of all sea-oriented economic operations, using its profits to support its work.

The possibility of exploiting petroleum fields under the high seas also is receiving scientific study. While areas of the continental shelf again offer the greatest potential, exploration and exploitation are already taking place at substantial distances from shore, as in the Gulf of Mexico and in the Middle East, and experts state that deep-sea drilling is a short-run possibility. In fact the possibility of an extensive oil field in the Gulf of Mexico at substantial distance from shore was reported in the summer of 1962. Oil companies have reputedly been reluctant to explore this type of possibility due to the clouded nature of national rights in the seabed at these distances, leading at least one U. S. Congressman to suggest that the UN provide a "satisfactory legal framework for commercial exploitation of this oil field and auction the drilling privileges."

---

[1] The American Branch of the International Law Association has already proposed that national claims be extended to a depth of 2,500 meters (over 8200 feet).

Thus if it regulated access to the seabed, the UN would serve its prime purpose of obviating national conflicts; obtaining revenue, if any, would be an important bonus. There is also an extensive sulphur mining operation already in existence in the Gulf of Mexico with the above-surface facility "well out to sea" and some "four or five blocks" in length.

Offshore petroleum resources are now made available in a country like the United States by offering mineral leases to would-be exploiters generally on a competitive bid basis which assures the government of an initial payment plus royalties or lease payments based on production. These have run to millions of dollars. Similar lease arrangements could be made under the UN for exploration and exploitation of petroleum and mineral resources. Again, rationing of the leases among aspirant companies or aspirant states might present political problems. Cooperation would be necessary from the nations to prevent unauthorized drilling. The analogies of the fur seal and fishing conventions and, indeed, of traditional treatment of pirates as *hostis humani generis* are at hand. The right of arrest and punishment in all nations, combined with a firm refusal by all to admit ores or oils improperly taken from the high seas, could serve as a sufficient deterrent if all nations participated. The licensing authority could also be charged with preventing operations from unduly interfering with transit on the surface or with fishing and other maritime pursuits.

In sum, exploitation of presently unexploited sea and undersea resources appears to be a potentially feasible source of revenue for the UN. Certain special barriers remain in addition to the overall political difficulties implicit in any independent source of UN income. First, Article 1 of the Continental Shelf Convention extends the national shelf to where "the depth of the superjacent waters admits of the exploitation of the natural resources of the said areas," thus arguably extending the "shelf" to mid-ocean or beyond as technology advances. Second, there is a traditional right cherished by all and valuable as an income source to large sections of many national populations, of free use of the seas by all for peaceful purposes. Third, for at least some sea resources, there would be an unwillingness of nations to place any "unfair" tax burdens on a long-established and often vital industry, such as fishing. On the other hand, new industries also develop vested interests and the "fairness" and enforcibility of burdening any partial economic sector, new or old, for the benefit of the UN can legitimately be questioned. Fourth, there is a host of economic considerations involved in any such commercial venture as, for example, oil production. Most important, there is the politically sensitive question of allocating the licensing of operations among the states and companies. Then there is the economically sensitive issue of the effect of new production on the petroleum market and on the value of other existing oil assets. In the United States today, production by national wells is limited and foreign oil faces restrictions. Would "UN oil" face tariffs or quota barriers in many areas? Would the UN cooperate to maintain oil prices above their competitive price level? Should it? In sum, the potential effect of UN or UN-licensed exploitation on the oil and gas market and industry raises economically and politically sensitive problems which affect both the political feasibility of the proposal for a UN role and the possible adequacy of the yield for UN purposes. And beyond the economic problems there is the ever present shadow of national insistence on reserving the seabeds for strategic uses.

There are, at the same time, factors favorable to a UN interest in the seabeds and in other sources of the seas. Primary among them is the positive value to the world of an overall regime which would avoid national conflicts of interest. In addition, true deep sea mining and drilling operations and plankton harvesting are still for the future and their true economic potentials are as yet unknown, so current interest on the part of the nations is not as high as it may become. Moreover, the deep seabed has not traditionally been thought of as under the jurisdiction of any state and the seas in general are thought of as both free and international. Action already under way at the UN proposes the internationalizing of the seabed through General Assembly resolution and formal treaty and the nations, through an *ad hoc* committee of the Assembly, seem to have recognized that there is some area of the seabed and the ocean floor which is beyond the limits of national jurisdiction. Then too international programs for control and conservation of aquatic resources—seals, whales, fish—already exist to a limited extent. In addition no nation is being asked to give up a resource which it now has in hand. Of course once the potential of such UN operations becomes more obvious, much of this relatively favorable political climate will not doubt disappear.[1] It will also disappear if the nations develop military postures involving the seabeds. Thus action in the UN and outside it to credibly prevent such a development seems urgent now. Internationalization of the region could be one such action. In sum, since there are already real qualms about the present inchoate regime for the seabed, a UN organized regime, if not a UN regime, would probably give real political value for its money and would facilitate the use of this region.

A Note on the Possibilities of UN Revenue from Outer Space

The question of the peaceful development of outer space resources has thus far been so closely connected with defense and prestige problems that there has been little role for the UN to play in operations. Nevertheless, if only modest revenues are sought, it seems likely that the UN could perform

---

[1] In theory it would seem easier for a nation to give up a potential source of wealth before anyone knows it is in fact valuable. How much practical political logic is there to this *in re* the seas? The UN will not be working with secret data on resource potential. If a resource is known to be conceivably valuable to the UN, it will be known to be potentially valuable to others. As we know, even though it is of little present economic use, the Antarctic Treaty of 1959 was reached outside the UN and the regime accepted for space activities to date, while reached largely under UN auspices, has also denied the UN any substantial role.

As a source of immediate help for the UN, the non-national new resource frontiers have two obvious drawbacks. First, they are not likely to produce adequate amounts of revenue in the short run or they would not be available now. Second, they could conceivably prove dangerously, indigestably valuable to the UN from the nations' point of view in the long run.

international regulatory services connected with space systems, especially communications systems, and quite legitimately charge for the services rendered. This could include the politically challenging services of allocating the limited areas of space for the placing of stationary satellites for best coverage, avoiding overlap of services, providing administrative services for any celestial body operations, establishing safety and traffic rules for operations which used both air space and outer space, and the like. In making it easier for national and joint systems to be accommodated and become profitable earlier, the UN's position as payee for services rendered would be easier to accept.

The remote possibility that man will seek to exploit the mineral resources of the celestial bodies for the direct benefit of earth should also be noted. The present regime for the celestial bodies bars national appropriation. In this sense, a natural role for the UN arises for extraction operations since, in the absence of national sovereignty, a control organization to make and administer rules is, in time, essential, especially if a population is present. Different forms of UN participation are again possible. We can assume that the actual activities will be carried out by states, perhaps under UN license. Other alternatives are possible but this seems the most realistic. Even after the first decades of stupendous outlays by national states, the United Nations would face problems with the Moon, for example, similar to those faced more currently in Antarctica. Exploitable finds of great value, value sufficient to warrant the cost of processing and shipment to earth, would have to be made and access to them made available before a rental or tax on production or a "profit" from UN enterprise would be feasible. Since scientists expect the composition of the close-in bodies to be much like earth itself the likelihood of financially sound major mining activities seems remote for the present. If valuable finds were made, the allocation by the UN of rights to their exploitation would certainly be pregnant with international political problems. The resolution of such potential conflicts under UN auspices would be a major contribution to the peace.

The Acceptable Uses of an Independent Revenue

If what we seek for the UN is only a small independent income, small profits from a venture would be enough. Though we have not discussed these in detail it is possible that there might be found enough commodities and activities which people would agree to see taxed by the UN—luxuries like seal skins, harmful commodities similar to opium and the like—so that a modest, regular income from feasible taxation might result. This would raise problems of fair incidence and of enforcement. All "taxes" must, of course, be diverted from some one and have some incidence, whether on the new or the old. Who "gains?" Who can afford to pay? What activities need to be promoted or discouraged? If the UN were to establish a tax program, it would have to face these political issues. Furthermore taxes must be collected, at some cost, and enforced with the help of a police and court system. Clearly UN taxation, whether of an excise or income tax variety, would require the willing cooperation of the states whose citizens were actually to pay the imposts. Alternatively we have seen that very important international political services might be performed by the UN in the seas and outer space and that UN activities in these regions might yield an independent revenue to the UN. These possibilities induce us to ask again how much independent income is enough for the UN? And how much financial independence is likely to be tolerable at present to the world's governments? This in turn depends in part on the uses to which the new funds are to be applied. This in turn leads to such questions as to whether an independent UN income should be "tied" in advance to specific uses and which bodies should make decisions on its allocation. In a democratic society, the legislature of course decides on both the acquisition and disposition of revenues. Assuming an independent revenue is achieved, what procedures for its use would promise to make the greatest contribution to the growth of the present UN as an institution capable of reliably supervising the maintenance of a just, peaceful international system?

One obvious possible use of a new fund would be to follow UN tradition and apply it to reducing the burden of the traditional regular budget on the Members. On normal fiscal standards for international organizations, this might prove highly deleterious to the morale of the organization. It is recognized as clearly desirable that all states participate financially and otherwise in the traditional, regular UN activities so that they maintain their interest in, their perspective on and their shared control over the Organization. All sovereigns can afford to meet these relatively modest assessments, despite the many complaints. The broadest participation in all UN activities and in their financial support is also politically desirable if a democratic-type institution is to be preserved and the sense of common action, mutual sacrifice and community is to grow.

A second possible use of independent revenues is to increase the welfare role of the UN, its capacity to distribute emergency aid and to assist economic and political development on internationally defined standards without levying financially directly on the rich. These latter will nevertheless remain the major sources of real international developmental capital and can be expected to insist on retaining a large say concerning access to their resources.

The third use, in accordance with our earlier analysis, is as a major source of funds for enforcement and peacekeeping. It is here that the most vigorous objections must be expected; increasing the freedom of the UN to by-pass the Security Council and even the General Assembly in this role is now neither practical nor, indeed, safe. Note again that the real resources, arms and men in this case, must come from states with major resource bases. Money income only represents an important way of buying into such a resource base *if the sovereign is willing.* UN dependence on sovereign states will thus remain very important even with an independent revenue until the real capacities of the Organization grow. Even if it becomes possible, as many predict, for small colonies of men to live under the seas in "UN areas" and even if the material wealth in resources of the seas proves very large, modern arms production requires a major industrial establishment which the seabeds could probably not support alone. Even this possibility, however, once perceived, would keep the states from allowing the UN a major operational role in developing the seabeds.

Moreover, the UN is not yet a well-wrought governmental system and the problem of the choice of tyrannies is inherent even in more highly perfected democratic constitutional systems. The "tyranny" of the present UN majority would be undesirable on reasonable political and ethical (i.e., constitutional) grounds, as would also the "tyranny" of an independent, rich Secretary-General. Of course, a great growth of genuine enforcement power might finally force the issue of UN constitutional reform. Yet states cannot be expected to choose deliberately to hasten such a UN constitutional crisis.

It seems politically likely that, if the independent UN revenues are not at least partially tied, they will be used as the modest amounts already available have been, to reduce normal assessments and neither for peacekeeping nor welfare and development. Not only would such an outcome undermine the fiscal participation of the members in the Organization, it would make the most minimal contribution to the development of the UN as an institution and to the financial problems implicit in such growth. It seems clear that the best outcome for those desiring the development of a more powerful, more effective, growing UN would be to assure that a large part of the revenue did go to the now financially undernourished roles of the Organization. How could this be accomplished safely from the members' point of view so that it would have some chance of political acceptability?

One possible method is to rely principally on the traditional agreed methods of determining the utilization of UN funds, that is, to follow current UN "legislative" practice and let the members, acting in the General Assembly, decide on the allocation of new funds, with the sole proviso that these new funds should *not* be used to cover the "normal", traditional activities of the Organization which have been regularly supported by the assessment system. Such an approach would

be facilitated by the segregation of new independent sources
of UN revenues into a "Special Emergency and Development
Fund" (SED) to be administered separately from the regular
budget but subject to normal General Assembly guidance and
control. This would tend to require that the funds be used
to expand the capacity and usefulness of the Organization in
ways to which the members can decide to give priority. This
would permit both development and peacekeeping activities
to be supported. It raises the interesting possibility that the
Security Council could attempt to use the new revenue resources for peacekeeping activities when the Council, using its
normal voting rules, including the veto, could agree to do so,
provided, perhaps, that the General Assembly agreed to such
a use of these revenues. (It is quite possible that the Assembly
would prefer other uses such as development.) It would permit the Assembly and the Security Council to decide to allow
the Secretary-General access to an increased, modest emergency fund available both for emergency and for short term
support of observation and peacekeeping activities. In all, the
Assembly would thus be enabled to establish and review regularly the achievement of the relevant general norms and criteria
for the expenditure of the new funds by itself, by the Security
Council, or by one or another aid and development agencies
set up by it to utilize the new funds for the purposes it deems
desirable. The important point then, is to assure that the new
revenues are utilized not to reduce present state contributions
to and participation in regular UN activities but for the further
development of the UN system and its capacity to serve its
members and the cause of international peace in ways that
would be acceptable to the members since they would remain
in ultimate control of them.

There is, of course, always the possibility that some organ
could "misappropriate" funds, at least from the point of view
of governments not in sympathy with some UN activity. Thus
the General Assembly might set up a force under something
similar to a Uniting For Peace Resolution and utilize any large
accumulated independent revenue for financing peacekeeping
operations.

This suggests that governments will feel under pressure not to allow funds from UN independent revenue to grow to a major scale or to accumulate over time until they become substantial. Security is offered to the states by the fact that for the foreseeable future net revenues from the "new" resources in question promise to be modest. In order to further assure the states that such resources will not accumulate dangerously, provision could be made requiring that all Special Emergency and Development Funds, above some modest General Assembly-established minimum, be committed for the UN-specified appropriate purposes within perhaps three years of its accumulation. Failing this, uncommitted accumulations could then be applied to the regular budget. In a world of great social need, there would seem to be no good reason not to expend UN income relatively rapidly. Indeed deflationary and balance of payments pressures for the nations might result from major UN hoardings.

If, as seems clear, it is desirable for the peace of the world that the UN should grow in its financial capacities to perform governmental type services, it is important that ways be found to do this which can be viewed as safe and acceptable by the member states. Perhaps then the best strategy for achieving genuine institutional and constitutional growth for the UN would seem to be to encourage the achievement of a UN independent revenue *now* to be used principally for the material benefit of mankind in general, not for the reduction of regular contributions from members for regular UN activities. This would reinforce the capacity of the UN to perform a welfare state role and to assist gradually in the development of common, centrally (internationally) defined and achieved common standards of welfare which are themselves often thought to be a necessary prerequisite to integration. It would increase the UN's real political and economic powers and prestige. Yet while as we have suggested, some funds might be made available for the use of the Secretary-General for short emergency uses, any direct attempt to establish a major, independent, independently supported UN enforcement force, which would inherently be regarded by members as a threat to their military security, would be neither feasible (because the UN would need to acquire reliable sources of men and material) nor acceptable to the states. The members need to be reassured on this *or the UN will not be given any independent revenue at all.*

Finally we must stress that revenues derived by the UN from the seas, the seabeds and outer space would indeed be *earned* by a UN which genuinely facilitates the peaceful, competitive exploration and exploitation of these potentially conflict-ridden areas. Failure of the UN to provide a peaceful regime for activities in these areas would itself be a major default on the part of the UN, revealing its incapacity to deal with serious potential dangers to the peace. For the benefit of all nations, it is essential that the UN be given a constructive role here; without it, as Wolfgang Friedmann has written, "the prospects are truly alarming." A new colonial-type struggle for control of the best prospects seems likely. It is therefore important that the interesting possibility that the UN could also achieve some independent revenues thereby not be allowed to prevent it from fulfilling a politically necessary role in the "new" areas.